THE HAND
OF THE ANCIENT ONE

THE HAND
OF THE ANCIENT ONE

Juanita P. Fike

P. O. Box 336010
Greeley, CO 80633

Cover design by Deborah Friend, P. O. Box 1058, Thoreau, NM 87323.

© 2003 by UIM International, PO Box 336010, Greeley, CO 80633

Publisher's Cataloging-in-Publication
(Provided by Quality Books, Inc.)

Fike, Juanita P.
   The hand of the ancient one / Juanita P. Fike.
   p. cm.
   Includes bibliographical references.
   ISBN 0-9725213-0-5

   1. Norris, Art. 2. Norris, Emalou. 3. Missionaries
   --Biography. 4. Indians--Missions. 5. Navajo Indians.
   I. Title.

E59.M65F55 2003   266'.0092
                         QBI33-1054

Printed by Central Plains Book Mfg., Winfield, KS 67156, United States of America

TO

- All whom God used in bringing Art and Emalou to faith in Christ and in influencing their spiritual growth and service,
- All volunteers and career missionaries who served with them,
- All who prayed and gave sacrificially over the years so that the Norrises could focus on the ministries at hand, and
- Our gracious and merciful God who chose them, led them, provided for them, encouraged them, and enabled them to be useful vessels in His sovereign hand.

"Before the mountains were born, or Thou didst give birth to the earth and the world, even from everlasting to everlasting, Thou art God."

— Psalm 90:2

CONTENTS

FOREWORD

My earliest childhood memories include Art and Emalou Norris, their family, and their ministry with the Navajos. They visited our home and local church many times, and it was through them I first became aware that God was prompting me to become involved in ministry with Native Americans.

In practical ways Art and Emalou showed their belief that God was completely trustworthy and faithful. They perceived nothing as impossible. They fully believed that God could and would change anyone who came to Him on His terms through Jesus Christ. They witnessed to anyone who would listen. These faithful servants clearly understood the process of making disciples of Jesus Christ, and as people came to Him, they trained them with the goal of making them into witnesses and trainers of other new Christians. Their life-long passion was to see God raise up faithful Native American Christians who would pursue God's purposes.

Art and Emalou trusted their brothers and sisters in Christ among the Navajos and partnered with them in every aspect of life and ministry. Many of the witnesses and disciples whom they trained have become strong leaders of indigenous churches and of missionary teams. The Norrises have encouraged these Christians to pursue God in every aspect of life no matter the cost.

As you read their life story, you will once again be reminded that "with God, all things are possible"! You will also see the need to pray the Lord of the Harvest to send forth more laborers who will partner with Native American Christians in making disciples of Jesus Christ throughout North America and around the world.

Warren F. Cheek
General Director
UIM International

PREFACE

UIM International's director, Rev. Warren F. Cheek, and I were talking one day in my office about the impact of missionary biographies on our lives. "We need some biographies of modern-day missionaries," Reverend Cheek alleged.

"That would be good," I replied. "Art and Emalou Norrises' story would be a great one." We agreed and returned to our respective duties.

A few days later I looked up from my desk to see Art Norris entering my office. In the nearly twelve years that I had served in Flagstaff, Arizona, as secretary to the director, I did not remember having seen the Norrises at what was then UIM's headquarters.

"Good morning, Art," I greeted him. We chatted a moment, then I ventured, "Art, Reverend Cheek and I were talking just a few days ago about the need for modern-day missionary biographies. One of you and Emalou could certainly challenge people toward mission involvement. Would you be interested?"

"Well," Art drawled, somewhat breathless from the 7000-foot altitude, "we'd have to think and pray about that."

He sat down in the waiting area near my desk to rest. After a few minutes he spoke again. "You know, if we could wait a few years until Emalou and I have more time . . ."

Wait? I thought to myself. This couple is past eighty, and he's dealing with heart trouble and prostate cancer!

Art returned home later that day, and I heard nothing further for several months. Finally, I wrote to see if the two of them had considered the possibility of a biography. "If God can be honored, we're willing," came the reply.

I shared their message with Reverend Cheek. "Good!" he replied. "I want you to concentrate on that project."

I knew at that moment that my assignment was a God-sized one, but it has been a joy to learn to know Art and Emalou as well as many of their family, friends, and former co-workers.

The spiritual impact of some lives emanates not from dramatic experiences but from steady perseverance and faithfulness to the Lord through the day-by-day, week-by-week grind. Such is true in the case of Art and Emalou Norris. Their goal was the salvation and spiritual training of Native Americans, for whom God had given them intense love. No task was too menial if it furthered that goal, even if it seemed repetitious or unrelated. On numerous occasions the Norrises' comments have echoed that of the Apostle Paul, "I will not presume to speak of anything except what Christ has accomplished through me . . ." (Rom. 15:18a).

My own life has been enriched and challenged by the Norrises' commitment to serve Him until their dying breath. I trust that the Holy Spirit will use what follows to challenge others to increased involvement in going, giving, praying–and persevering–that the world may know the hope of eternal life through Jesus Christ, our Lord.

ACKNOWLEDGMENTS

As Art and Emalou Norris considered the possibility of a biography, Art thoughtfully wrote, "We'd like to write a book about remembrances of friends that helped. The teachers would be amongst those who gave the greatest help. And we can't help but thank God for sending our way devoted Navajo missionaries who served so well in getting out the Gospel. So many gave, helped, encouraged, and prayed." On and on he wrote, mentioning his brother, volunteers, the Gideons who gave Bibles and New Testaments, the mission board, and many others. He told how each assisted and how much he and Emalou thanked God for the dedicated team members who had helped them to accomplish the work He had entrusted to them.

Just as numerous people were involved in the work with Art and Emalou, so also many have contributed to the writing of their story. Without information gathered through personal interviews, correspondence, and telephone conversations with nearly 250 of their family, friends, and co-workers, this book would not have become reality. Because of the large volume of data received, only highlights and representative anecdotes have been presented. Many of the non-footnoted quotations were taken from mission publications, the Norrises' reports and newsletters, and conversations. Since memories have faded and some written materials lacked dates, I have taken the liberty to arrange and reconstruct some events. However, the material presented is based on fact. Great effort has been made to be accurate; I apologize for errors that may have slipped through. I am grateful to have been given the Norrises' approval of the book's contents prior to Art's homegoing.

My deep gratitude goes to UIM missionary Sandra Friend, who transcribed pages upon pages of taped interviews; to Muriel Chambers, Kathy Dane, Lois Faram, Martha Gushee, Martha Menne, Ruth Mortenson, Frances Von Helms, and Rosemary Watson, who provided editorial assistance; to Warren Davis, Betsy Newman, and Lois Martin for helping with the spelling of Navajo terms; to Alpha Pfeifer for formatting the book; to David Stiller for his computer assistance; to Deborah Friend for designing the cover; to Tom Wilson for preparing the maps; to Esther Spieth for proofreading; and to the many who stood with me in prayer and encouragement. Most of all, I thank God for His enabling. The longing to honor Him and challenge His people motivated me to persist when at times the task seemed insurmountable. May He use the resultant story to spur us on "to love and good deeds."

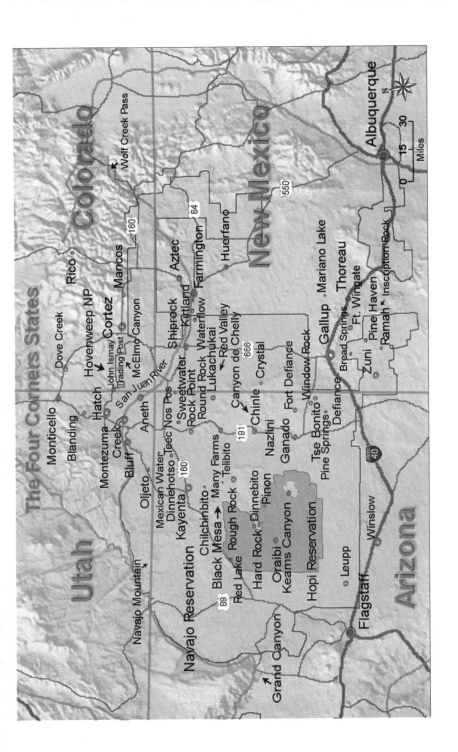

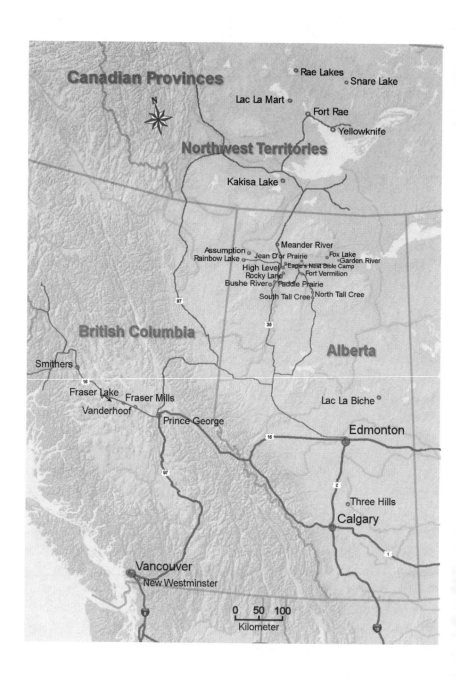

1
Prodded by a Discovery

"For I am not ashamed of the gospel, for it is the power of God
for salvation to everyone who believes . . ."
— Romans 1:16

Art's work-roughened hands clutched the steering wheel. Perspiration trickled down his neck. As he maneuvered the green Volkswagen bus around holes and wind-worn rocks, dust billowed into the air and blanketed the parched terrain. Rugged sandstone outcroppings lined the dirt trail in southeastern Utah. Sagebrush clung to the rocky hillsides. Art Norris stole a glance at ancient Indian toeholds marking a nearby cliff as he pondered the best way to encourage Navajo Christians to share the Good News of Christ. Navajo Bible Institute (NBI) in Cortez, Colorado, was a good start. Taking students from hogan[1] to hogan as he was doing now provided choice training opportunities. Surely the Lord would reveal other ways to spread the Good News among Navajos . . . perhaps even among other North American tribal people.

The slender, Canadian-born missionary and his two students, Henry and James, bounced and swayed as they negotiated the dusty hills and curves. Art sensed the students' struggle to share Christ with their fellow tribesmen. Sharing the Gospel, especially with relatives steeped in animism,[2] was intimidating. But both students loved the Savior, both respected their seasoned mentor, and both were eager to learn.

"About time for lunch, eh, fellows?" Art asked as he pulled off the rough road near Hovenweep National Monument. James reached for his lunch sack. Art scarcely noticed the lack of verbal response; after thirty years on the reservation, he had adapted to these people of few words. James' action was sufficient.

Art pointed in Navajo style with his lips. "Let's eat over by the oil well." The chug of the gasoline engine drew him like a magnet. The three tromped across the dusty ground, tufts of dry grass brushing their pant legs. Sitting on boulders, they ate in silence. Three pairs of eyes scanned the stark, sun-drenched earth. Little more than clumps of dull green grass dotted the landscape. The dust-coated orange of globe mallow blossoms accented the desert vista. Deep blue sky nuzzled the earth, the skyline unbroken by tree or shrub. Nearby the engine hummed incessantly, the pump arm in constant motion.

Looking to the left, Art puckered his lips and lifted his chin. "There's a mound." The students' eyes followed his. Art's casual demeanor belied the intensity of his interest. Hundreds of years earlier the Four Corners area had been heavily populated by Indians living in cliff houses and caves. Had the men come across a home site of some of the Anasazi, the Ancient Ones? Brushing the crumbs from their mouths, the trio stuffed lunch sacks into their pockets and sauntered toward the mound.

"Pottery," James observed, kicking aimlessly with his scuffed cowboy boots.

Art bent over to inspect the black, white, and red shards, some with designs etched by fingernails. Surveying the surroundings, he noted a circular depression about fifteen feet across tapering toward the center. In the middle lay a flat rock about two feet in diameter. "That rock must have been put there on purpose," he commented.

Again the students followed Art's gaze. "To keep lambs from falling into a hole," James explained, tipping his cowboy hat to shield his eyes from the glaring sun.

"We always protect lambs," Henry added, standing spread-legged, his thumbs hooked into his jeans pockets. He saw nothing out of the ordinary.

If a hole existed, Art *had* to look. With the students' help he moved the rock, then knelt and peered in. A kiva[3]? A storage area? His adrenalin surged. "Seven or eight feet deep," he commented. The call of the mysterious hole was too great. He dangled his feet through the opening, eased his tall frame into the cool darkness, and dropped to the dirt floor. He could see nothing. Slowly he groped his way around the perimeter of the small, rock-walled room. Plastered with mud, he noted. The muted pum, pum, pum of the oil well's one-cylinder motor droned in the distance. If only I'd brought a flashlight, he thought. A shirt-pocket search produced one paper match. As the tip ignited, Art scanned the wall. There at eye level, well preserved in the mud mortar, was a medium-sized handprint, the impressions of the thumb and fingers distinctly discernable. Carefully, with awe, he placed his large hand over it.

That hand belonged to someone smaller than I, smaller even than James or Henry, Art mused. He recalled the late 1930s when size nine shoes were nowhere to be found on the Navajo Reservation. More recent information indicated that the physical stature of Navajos was increasing. That has to be the handprint of an Anasazi, he reasoned. He gently lifted his hand and gazed at the imprint, hardly breathing. Had these people heard the Gospel? That a whole generation might never have heard of Jesus gnawed at him. The match flickered out. In the ebony darkness Art sensed God's presence and His bidding. "Lord," he responded, "I can't do anything about those people, but as long as You give me life, I'll do everything I can to make sure the present generation of Indians knows about Jesus." It was a solemn pledge, a never-to-be-forgotten interlude in an otherwise ordinary day.

Slowly Art retraced his steps toward the opening. "Could you two give me a hand?" he called. He knew the Navajo mind as well as any white man ever would. Unquestionably, the students were wondering why anyone would want to look into a hole. In many ways Art had become like one of them, but the white man's constant and abundant curiosity was a mystery beyond their comprehension. James and Henry, who had lingered nearby, clutched his upstretched hands.

"Part of an ancient kiva, I think," Art commented casually, brushing the dirt off his pants as he readjusted to the sunlight. "I found a handprint in the mud, fingerprints as distinct as any inked on today's Navajo Police records. Must have been there at least 800 years."

They replaced the rock and strode to the VW. During the afternoon as Art transported the students to a number of hogans to share the Good News, he pondered the fate of the Ancient Ones. "Lord, help me to find ways to keep another generation from entering eternity without ever hearing of the Savior," he prayed silently.

That evening Art deposited James and Henry at the Bible school campus and swung the bus into his driveway. Family responsibilities often kept Emalou, his wife, from accompanying him on ministry trips, but she always looked forward to hearing about them. He greeted her, then washed his hands while she put supper on the table. As he gave thanks for the food and God's grace in their lives, his voice broke. Emalou waited. Tenderheartedness and sensitivity before the Lord were nothing new for her husband, but verbalization did not come easily for him. No doubt something had touched him deeply.

As they ate, the story unfolded. "Dear, during lunch break today the students and I found what I'm sure was an ancient kiva or perhaps a cache. Pitch black in there! Fortunately, I had a match. Saw a distinct handprint in the mud plaster. It *had* to have belonged to an Anasazi. It was a lot smaller than most Navajos' hands."

The two ate in silence for a moment. Then, setting his glass of milk on the table, Art continued, his voice breaking. "Those people probably never heard of the Savior. That has haunted me all afternoon. God help us! I know I can't do anything about *them,* but I will do everything I can to tell today's native people. Not one of them should ever be able to say he never heard of Jesus!"

2
God's Steadying Hand

"Bless our God . . . who keeps us in life, and
does not allow our feet to slip."
– Psalm 66:8a-9

Although Art had sunk his roots deep into Navajo country, he was Canadian born and of English descent. Three years before his birth, his father, Edward John, known as "Ted," trotted the horses into the courtyard of England's Torquay Baptist Church. It was Sunday morning, April 21, 1912. Climbing down from the

Art's parents,
Ted and Keren Norris

buggy, Mr. Norris assisted his wife, Keren-happuch, to the ground, then reached for his two sons. Nodding to other parishioners, they entered the church and seated themselves.

As the pastor led the congregation in prayer, Mrs. Norris kept a watchful eye on three-year-old Cyril (Cy) and two-year-old Edward. She could never be sure what her active sons might do. Concentration was difficult. ". . . and Lord, we pray for all who are mourning loved ones lost at sea."

Lost at sea? Alarmed, Mrs. Norris stole a glance at her husband. His expression was impenetrable. The rest of the prayer and the sermon that ensued fell on unhearing ears. The Norrises' departure for Canada was only two weeks away. They were ticketed on the *Olympic*, sister ship and second only in size to the magnificent *Titanic*.

Mrs. Norris scrutinized her husband. His eyes were fastened rigidly on the pastor, too rigidly perhaps. Fears stormed her mind. What if the ship . . . ? Surely it has lifeboats. But . . . the boys . . . so active.

The service over, Mrs. Norris directed Cyril and young Edward out of the pew and toward the door, politely greeting acquaintances. Mr. Norris helped his family into the buggy and picked up the reins.

"Ted," Mrs. Norris began, fingering her gloves nervously. "What was the pastor praying about? You haven't said anything about a tragedy at sea."

Mr. Norris slapped the reins and spoke to the horses. "I didn't want to alarm you, Keren. The *Titanic* sank last Monday. Hit an iceberg."

Mrs. Norris sat stunned, her heart beating wildly. Then, straightening her shoulders, she spoke with a weak but determined voice, "Ted, I don't want to make that voyage to Canada!"

"That's why I didn't tell you about the *Titanic*, Keren. We already have our tickets and all arrangements are made. My brother and his family made it fine. They're expecting us, and I can find work easier there. Don't worry, Keren; God will care for us."

But Mrs. Norris did worry. Two weeks later she reluctantly accompanied the family to the seaport. In her mind, boarding what was now the world's largest steamship was akin to suicide. As they entered their cabin the first night, the man in the adjoining cabin proclaimed loudly, "I'm going to sleep whether this boat sinks or swims!" Hardly the lullaby Mrs. Norris needed.

Hailed as the "World's Wonder Ship" on its maiden voyage ten months prior to the *Titanic*'s, the *Olympic* steamed out of Southampton's harbor and headed to open sea. The stately four-funneled vessel forged steadily westward through the same cold waters traversed a mere three weeks earlier by the ill-fated *Titanic*. Rich passengers mingled with poor emigrants, all eager for new opportunities in Canada and the United States. The ship's open promenade deck provided a spectacular view; it also added to the fears of an already concerned mother. That the ship boasted sixteen watertight compartments was of little consolation.[1]

To Mrs. Norris' profound relief, the *Olympic* arrived safely in Halifax, Nova Scotia, three weeks later, and they boarded the train to travel the tiring 4800 kilometers to Vancouver, British Columbia. The coal-burning locomotive labored noisily. Ash and cinders spewed into the air and through loose-fitting, single-pane windows, coating everything with grit and grime. In the absence of a dining car, the women prepared meals on a stove provided for them, their food supplies replenished en route by Salvation Army personnel.

With great gratitude the Norrises safely reached British Columbia (BC). They reveled in the beauty of gentle hills; tall, dark green firs; alder and birch trees still in winter nakedness. The settlement of Sapperton, established in the mid-1850s by British soldiers known as "Sappers," nestled on the banks of the Fraser River. Later renamed "New Westminster" by Queen Victoria, it became the Norris family's new home. Near the post office, farmers watered their horses at a large concrete trough and tethered them to a hitching post. Fish, vegetables, fruit–even Devonshire cream, for which Mrs. Norris had developed a fondness during her childhood in Devonshire, England–were sold in small stalls nearby.

The Norrises resided with Ted's brother for a time, then rented a house on Hospital Street. A year after their arrival in New Westminster, three-year-old Edward succumbed to spinal meningitis. Two years later on April 1, 1915, Arthur Stanley's birth brought new joy to their home.

Purchasing a lot at the top of Hospital Street, the Norrises finally built their own house overlooking the Fraser River Valley. At the bottom of the street sprawled the hospital. Between it and the Norris home stood Sapperton Baptist Church (SBC), a mission outreach of Olivet Baptist. The Norrises were delighted to live near a young fellowship that was already pushing beyond its own walls with the Gospel. Employed as a mail carrier, Mr. Norris also invested much time and energy as Sunday school superintendent and general helper at the church. Mrs. Norris taught Sunday school and the mission band, an auxiliary of the Sunday school which provided a special mission emphasis for the children. Sometimes she coached the girls in Bible memory competition and diligently visited homes in the nearby "bush country" with another deaconess.

Art's memories of those early years, though scanty, were nostalgic: his head nestled on his mother's soft shoulder, a pet guinea pig, a wagon his father had given him and Cy. He also remembered riding in the buggy with his father to deliver Christmas packages. Then there was the incident with his swollen salivary gland. His mother had fetched eclectic oil and called, "I'll heat this up to put on your neck in a minute, son."

"The minute's up!" young Art had sassed, and the resulting pressure his father had applied to his backside had reminded him that his mother was to be respected.

The love and influence of Art's father had an eternal impact on his sons and on many in Sapperton Baptist Church. One Saturday evening while he was laying carpet at the church, Mrs. Norris decided to walk to the store to purchase meat for Sunday dinner. "I'm going to stop by the church and walk home with Papa," she told five-year-old Art and eleven-year-old Cy.

After their mother left, the boys engaged in a lively game of soccer in the kitchen with a sock ball. Suddenly Cy exclaimed, "Look, Art! It's dark outside. The street light's on!" Perching on their knees before the window, they peered into the dusk, waiting.

"Why don't Mama and Papa come?" Art whimpered.

Finally, a lady from the church walked up the street and turned into their house. Cy opened the door. "Your father is very sick," the lady explained quietly, gathering the boys tenderly in her arms. "I'll stay here until your mother comes."

Mrs. Norris eventually came. She drew her sons close and tearfully stroked their heads. "Sons, Papa's heart stopped working. He's with Jesus now and won't ever have pain or be sick again. Someday we can go to be with him. Until then, God will be our Helper." When Mr. Norris' body was brought to the house and laid on the couch, curtained from the rest of the room, she called, "Come here, sons." Pulling back the curtain, she stood with an arm around each of them, crying. Helplessly Art clung to her, determining to take care of her when he grew up.

The black arm band Mrs. Norris wore, like all widows, reminded others to guard their words around the grieving. The family's lives seemed to have taken a sudden "detour," but that is a term foreign to God's vocabulary. Fervently Mrs. Norris leaned on Him, confident that whatever He permitted, He would use for their good. She reminded Art and Cy that God "is a father of the fatherless." She tried not to worry about finances, but the government subsidy of $16 per month for each child under age sixteen, plus income from housecleaning jobs, hardly sufficed for a family of three. Her house was small. The boys' attic bedroom was accessed by a ladder from the kitchen. Using her husband's $1000 life insurance benefit, she had a bedroom, a bathroom, and a living area added to make room for boarders—nurses, schoolteachers, laborers, preachers, or missionaries. Faithfully God supplied every material need.

In addition to their physical needs, Mrs. Norris was concerned about her sons' spiritual needs. Having only a third-grade education did not hinder her from deeply imprinting their lives. She loved God, fed on His Word, and taught godly living by word and example, spending much time on her knees in their behalf. Her prayers were often translated into action, like the day at the dinner table when seven-year-old Art's manner indicated a gnawing conscience. After the meal, he walked out the door and down the steps. She saw him pull something out of his pocket and stuff it into his mouth. "Come here, Art," she summoned. Hurriedly he swallowed and turned to face her.

"What were you eating, son?"

"A chocolate-coated teddy bear."

"Where did you get it?"

"At the store."

She knew that he had no money. "Son," she demanded, "you march right over there with this penny and pay for that candy. Tell the clerk you're sorry." Obediently Art complied.

When it came to helping their widowed mother, Art and Cy were a team. For heating and cooking fuel, they gathered coal tailings which fell from railroad cars. On special occasions they spent their meager savings for presents for their mother, discovering years later that she had exchanged them for grocery money. When her interests were not at stake, however, their relationship was less than congenial. They seldom spoke to each other; when they did, their words were not complimentary. Teasing sometimes bordered on violence. The pair of scissors Art threw at Cy inadvertently struck his mother, leaving her with a scarred wrist. Prayerfully and persistently she sought to tame their rebellious natures.

From an early age Art loved music. He enjoyed singing with the junior choir at church and playing records on the hand-wound gramophone with a large horn speaker. However, free piano lessons from his cousin were definitely unappreciated. "Art," his mother would say repeatedly with the threat of a raspberry switch, "fifteen minutes of practice, then you can go outside."

On the other hand, anything scientific or mechanical captivated Art. Rolling his Christmas gift watch down the sidewalk was fun, but taking it apart and investigating how it worked was even more fascinating. A lid jiggling on a teakettle of boiling water mesmerized him. Eventually he learned how to harness such power to turn the wheels of a toy steam engine. Then came his first exposure to radio in the 1920s. His preteen mind could not comprehend hearing intelligible sounds from air waves simply by turning a dial on his friend's Atwater-Kent radio. He experimented with a thin crystal, bending and running electricity through it, changing its color and, in some instances, creating noise. He also wrapped insulated wire around an empty oatmeal box and connected the wire to a crystal and a pair of earphones. He was ecstatic when his primitive "radio" brought in a program not only from a nearby station but from Station KOMO in Seattle, 150 miles across the Canadian/U. S. border! Next he created a battery from pieces of lead, a Mason fruit jar, and some acidic water and stored it under his bed. His creativity was unappreciated when his unsuspecting mother knocked the battery over with a dust mop and spilled the acid on the varnished floor.

As early as age ten, Art's enthusiasm for adventure surfaced. What a thrill to fly down Hospital Street on a bicycle without brakes and become airborne on a self-constructed bicycle jump! Since thirteen-year-old children of widows were permitted to drive, Art, unknown to his brother, took Cy's car for an occasional spin. On one of those occasions, he accidentally backed into a telephone pole. Fortunately, the rear spare tire absorbed the shock and prevented serious damage.

Winter months provided adventures of a different kind. Plummeting temperatures transformed the Fraser River into a great place for Art and his friends to ride bicycles and play ice hockey. One day a policeman yelled from the bank, "Get off that ice! It's too thin!" Confident that the overweight officer would not pursue them, the boys ignored the command. Fortunately, they suffered no tragic consequences.

The one-cylinder, two-stroke Cleveland motorcycle Art bought for $5 at age fourteen functioned well on the level and downhill. Uphill it nearly died. Riding it was exhilarating, as was speeding down the sidewalk on a bobsled, that is, until a friend died in a bobsledding accident. The loss was a traumatic one for Art.

That same year Cy bought a 1926 Model T Ford. "I'd sooner do carpentry than mechanics. Would you put a rear end in it for me?" he asked Art.

Art enjoyed such challenges. He wanted to learn electronics, welding, soldering, and carpentry, but his mother was set against his attending technical school. "Boys who go to technical school are rough. You might get into bad company," she asserted. She did not understand how stormy Art's teen years were internally. Nobody understands me, he agonized. People pay attention to Cyril but not to me. At times the tumult became so intense that he thought he was losing his sanity. Quiet and often alone, he kept his paranoia so private that neither his mother nor his brother was aware of his inner turmoil.

In his late teens Art eyed his neighbor's Willis Overland with desire. As he began to earn two dollars a day, his dream grew. No matter that the car was rusted, the tires were flat, and all the window glass was broken. Who cared that it wouldn't start? Walking past it every night for several weeks, he found the pull irresistible. Trembling, he knocked on Mr. Renny's door. Yes, eight dollars was an agreeable price, payable at two dollars each week.

A spark of camaraderie began to develop between the brothers as Cy helped Art tow the rusted gem to the top of the hill. Art spent hours working on it, and Cy installed ordinary window glass. Finally, the magical day arrived, but the crank was missing. They could push it downhill in gear and let out the clutch. However, if that failed, the car would sit at the bottom of the hill until someone towed it up again. To spare themselves the embarrassment and delay, they jacked up a back wheel, put a block under the axle, removed a lug bolt that held the rim to the wheel, and inserted an 18-inch steel rod. Then, with the car in high gear, they rotated the back wheel as fast as they could. In spite of adjusting the spark, priming the carburetor, and pouring gasoline into each of the cylinders, the Overland refused to start. A day or so later, Art tried again, this time without his brother's help. He put the car in high gear, pulled the throttle wide open, and again rotated the back wheel. The engine started and the steel rod whirled, knocking him to the ground. Stunned, his pant leg ripped, blood dripping from a gash on his leg, he was nonetheless thrilled at his achievement.

Though Art lacked the stabilizing effect of an earthly father, God had His hand on young Art's life. Not all of his activities were the adventurous kind. As a child, he was fascinated by missionary stories and lantern slides about China. In the children's missionary group he and his friends strung beads for the Chinese, although what they would do with them was a mystery to him. Nevertheless, these exposures engraved on his heart both the Gospel and the need to share it. What if God called *him* as a missionary? Schoolwork was hard for him, and he was sure he would never be able to learn enough for such a task.

As he entered the preteen years, he became more aware of spiritual realities. Sapperton Baptist's pastor, F. W. Auvache, a former missionary to India, yearned for God to move some of his flock into worldwide ministries. He faithfully preached the Word, but it made no sense to Art. "Do you understand him?" he asked his brother.

"Sure," Cy answered.

By the time the next pastor came, Art understood the Scriptures only too well. Arthur Boutel was a joyful man who made the Gospel painfully clear. He knew the Savior personally, a relationship Art did not enjoy. Hiding from Pastor Boutel's gaze behind vertical slats in the backs of chairs was difficult, but Art tried. Nevertheless, the Holy Spirit convicted him of his need, and he confessed Christ as his Savior.

"Do you want to be baptized?" Pastor Boutel asked after explaining the meaning of baptism.

"No, I'm not ready yet, " Art replied. He continued growing under the teaching of Pastor Boutel and Charley Hone, the youth leader, and requested baptism sometime later. However, he remained uncertain about his salvation. Every time the Lord's coming was mentioned, fear gripped his heart. Returning from his paper route one day, he found his mother absent. She usually left a note in such circumstances, but he found none. Had the Rapture occurred? He rushed to the telephone and dialed the pastor's home, certain the pastor and his wife would be among those meeting the Lord in the air. Seconds became millennia. Finally, Mrs. Boutel answered, and he quietly hung up, greatly relieved that the Rapture had not yet occurred. God used his church's street meetings to eliminate his fear. As he stood on a street corner in front of a pool hall one evening and openly declared himself to be a Christian, his concern about his salvation vanished. The Holy Spirit used scriptural truth and public confession to bring comforting assurance.

Since early childhood Art and Cyril had heard God's Word and observed their parents' involvement in outreach to the lost. Members of Sapperton Baptist Church lived out the Book of Acts–praying, giving, and witnessing. The Norris boys could not have escaped the fact that the people of the world were without Christ, nor could they have failed to know the need for missionaries. Parents, pastors, youth leaders, and missionary visitors left an indelible impression on Art's life.

A mission opportunity existed nearby. The town of Fraser Mills had been colonized by immigrant Greeks, Chinese, Japanese, East Indian Hindus, and many Scandinavians who came to work in the lumber industry. The town, however, had no churches and became a spiritual wilderness. Concerned, SBC members began a Sunday school in the community hall above the general store. Art's mother was among those who worked tirelessly to increase attendance and meet spiritual needs. Undeterred by fog or occasional flooding from melting snow and spring rains which coincided with high ocean tides, she and a friend rode the Interurban, a tall, swaying electric train, every week to Fraser Mills, the end of the line. Hour after hour the ladies tramped along plank sidewalks built over a swamp as they went from one clapboard-sided house to another, inviting children to Sunday school.

Mrs. Norris' example was not lost on Art. While he was still in his mid-teens, he drove his mother and other teachers to Fraser Mills every Sunday in Cyril's Model T. During services there, Mrs. Boutel played the pump organ; at times Art served as pianist. He eventually taught a Bible class. In wintertime the group sat on backless wooden benches around a potbellied stove, moving farther back as the stovepipe began to glow red.

In his late teens, Art attended a farewell party on a ship for a young missionary couple leaving for China. Ribbons and streamers lined the gangplank. A roasted pig graced the first-class dining room table. The celebration, the prayer, the dedication–all stirred him. As he contemplated the couple's dedication and the potential life-and-death realities they faced, his own sense of inadequacy resurfaced. He was more certain than ever that he lacked both aptitude and training for such a challenge. He had successfully completed his final physics and chemistry exams for graduation from Grade 12, but he had failed French grammar, literature, English grammar, and history.

About that time Leslie Smith and his wife from California came to pastor Sapperton Baptist Church. "Art, you and Cy ought to go to Bible school," Mrs. Smith advised. "Biola (Bible Institute of Los Angeles) would be a good place. It costs eight dollars a day, but you could earn that in our termite business there."

Art and Cy attempted to discern God's will concerning Bible school using the method Mr. Hone, their youth leader, used. "I just open my Bible and read a verse," Mr. Hone had told the youth group on numerous occasions. For a time the two of them thought that Biola *was* God's choice, but peace eluded them. Perhaps there were other ways to discern God's will. After gathering information about Prairie Bible Institute (PBI), they learned that it was closer to home and in a rural setting, which made it preferable by far to the wicked city of Los Angeles. The total cost for tuition, room, board, hair cuts, and laundry was $100 per year. As they prayed, peace came to their hearts. God seemed to be leading them to PBI.

3
His Revealed Way

"And your ears will hear a word behind you,
'This is the way, walk in it' . . ."
— Isaiah 30:21a

Dried beans and canned produce kept hunger from the doors of many homes in 1934, and cardboard soles extended the usefulness of worn-out shoes. Nineteen-year-old Art and twenty-five-year-old Cy wondered how they could afford an education at Prairie Bible Institute in Three Hills, Alberta, but both were convinced of God's leading. Their mother's care was their greatest concern. Cy purchased a used reversing-barrel washing machine and gave her some cash, but he and Art ached at the thought of leaving her. Friends at Sapperton Baptist rallied around them and their mother, and a man in the area offered to haul in her wood, shovel snow, and do whatever was needed. As Art and Cy towed Art's Willis Overland to the city dump and toppled it over the edge, they acknowledged the end of an era. Eternal priorities would be their focus from now on.

Thus, early in October 1934 the Norris brothers and their friend Orville Carlson clambered into a 1928 Chrysler sedan. Reminiscent of the widow giving her two mites, sixty-one-year-old Mrs. Norris waved with broom in hand as her two sons headed to PBI. "Keep up your Ebenezer,[1] boys!" she called.

Art, Cy, Mother Norris

15

Art needed that reminder in Three Hills. The Canadian plains were a sharp contrast to the lovely western coast, and he felt exposed. There were no bushes to hide behind, nothing to stop the wind. But, there were benefits of being where the Lord had led. As Art and Cy shared the same bed, the same desk, the same wardrobe, and the same classes, God began a work in their hearts. "Please forgive me for the way I've treated you in the past," Art requested of Cy one day. Cy graciously forgave, and the Lord began to bond them together in a lasting friendship.

The brothers soon adjusted to life at PBI. Plumbing in the dormitory was a nonexistent luxury, the outhouse less than cozy in the dead of winter. Water buckets and basins sufficed for bathing. When school guests came, male students relinquished their beds and slept in classrooms on straw mattresses. From the time Art awoke at six in the morning, he moved methodically through the day: devotional time and breakfast, general assembly, classes, a required work project, then a well-earned rest period. Refreshed, he tackled the books again, dutifully observing lights out at 10 p.m. Except for mandatory floor scrubbing, Saturdays were less regimented.

Rules abounded at PBI. Men and women were segregated in classes, chapel, and dining room. For exercise, females walked south and males north on any given day, switching directions the next. On one of Art's two required nights as night watchman, he obediently refrained from conversing with girls. He did, however, slip one of them a note, and she responded in like manner.

PBI's work assignments to help defray expenses were devised to cultivate in students a willingness to do anything for Christ's sake. They did farm work, baked bread, and mopped floors. Art carried vegetables from the root cellar to the young ladies who prepared the food. "Weighed 1564 pounds of potatoes for next week's use. Hauled snow," one of his diary entries read. Students hauled water by horse and wagon from a distant spring or well. In winter they filled the cisterns with snow, fetched coal from a mine, and fired furnaces for steam heat. All the assigned tasks prepared them for the primitive living conditions they would doubtless encounter on the mission fields of the world.

Art's studies were extremely demanding, but the spiritual atmosphere and presentation of God's Word energized and enlightened him. "Don't use commentaries and Scofield Bibles with study notes. Just pray about assigned passages, utilize research questions, and compare Scripture with Scripture. The Holy Spirit will be your Teacher," the professors assured the students. During classroom recitation Art was as amazed as the others to find that nearly every student had arrived at similar conclusions about the passages studied.

The discipline of memorizing Scripture for witnessing assignments impacted both Art and Cy. Art experienced spiritual growth that he had previously felt was lacking. Fellowship with 350 like-minded young people was an encouragement, as were testimony meetings and the singing of powerful Christ- and mission-centered hymns. He benefited from participation in the male chorus and singing classes and bought and learned to play an accordion.

The godly life and preaching of PBI's president, Leslie Maxwell, also greatly influenced Art. President Maxwell's spiritual strength and example resulted from time spent in God's Word and on his knees in prayer. He and Mrs. Maxwell held street meetings in the tiny town of Three Hills and involved themselves in other mission outreach. They practiced what they proclaimed. In fact, the entire faculty modeled a joyful daily reliance on God, sharing equally in the meager financial gifts that were given to the school.

Chapel times were special. Mr. Maxwell could "move from the hilarious to the serious in one sentence,"[2] and Art's heart was searched. Often he and the other students left the chapel in silence, pondering what they had heard. Dying to self was Mr. Maxwell's central theme, and he believed the cross to be the key to all Scripture. Quoting Galatians 2:20, he exhorted the students, "The secret of possessing life is to have no master but Christ." He instilled in the students the truths that the heathen are lost even if they never hear the Gospel and that their only hope of hearing is through Christians giving themselves unreservedly to world evangelization.[3]

The message was clear: missionaries were urgently needed around the world and God used anyone willing to live a life of self-surrender. Art was stretched. "Lord," he prayed repeatedly, "help me to die to self, regardless of the cost!"

Representatives from many mission organizations visited the campus and appealed for help in India, Africa, the West Indies, South America, China, and countless other locations. Mission agencies were accepting large numbers of PBI graduates. Art contemplated China until he remembered what Miss Taylor, a missionary to China who had boarded with his mother, had said: "It gets exceptionally cold there. Chinese homes have no fires or thermometers. They describe temperatures as 'one coat cold,' 'two coats cold,' or 'three coats cold.'" Art was not fond of frigid temperatures and surmised that China was not the place for him! Later, convicted of his unwillingness to consider China, he prayed, "Lord, if that's where You want me, I'm willing." Immediate peace replaced his inner struggle, and he sought out the next China Inland Mission representative. The representative sensed that, though Art was willing, he likely was not called to China and suggested that he pray about it some more and see how the Lord led.

Art also considered the West Indies Mission in Haiti. Perhaps the Lord wanted him there even though his eight years of studying French had resulted in negligible academic success. If men were willing to give their lives for their country, should he not sacrifice for his Lord?

As his first year at PBI drew to a close in the spring of 1935, Art was convicted through prayer to return to his home province to serve with BC's Sunday School Mission. Earlier in the year a visiting missionary had reported on that work. Art and three friends had been praying regularly for the salvation of those living in Hazelton, Smithers, Prince George, Burns Lake, and Fraser Lake. Funds for his trip home were nonexistent, but he knew from having observed his mother that when God directs, He also provides the required resources.

Soon he learned of a meat-packing company that was seeking helpers for a cattle train en route to Vancouver. Provincial law required that cattle transported for more than thirty-five hours be unloaded, fed, and watered. Art volunteered to work for passage, boarding the caboose with a foul-mouthed crew. As the train wound through a six-mile tunnel, a knuckle joint broke, and the train coasted down a long incline in the darkness, coming to a standstill just outside the tunnel. With the new part quickly installed, they were on their way again. On Sunday morning near Vancouver, Art learned that the cattle would not need to be moved. As the train slowed through New Westminster, he jumped off. Who but his Sunday school teacher drove by at that moment and offered him a ride!

Charley Hone had a job waiting for Art at his shingle mill. Art was grateful, but as soon as the $100 for the fall semester was in hand, he quit. "Quit?" Mr. Hone questioned, understandably upset. "But I saved this job for you for the whole summer!"

Art's burden for the lost had developed into focused action. "How can I waste time earning unnecessary money when people need to hear the Gospel?" he reasoned. Together with a small group of other students, he headed north under the direction of BC's Sunday School Mission. From Prince George they moved to Vanderhoof and Fraser Lake, then went as far west as Smithers, where the road ended. Art and his friends covered many miles holding vacation Bible schools and teaching adult Bible studies in the evenings. Many came to the Savior. Through farmers, God provided food in exchange for work. He protected the students when their car smashed through an ill-marked barricade at a partially

Art in VBS ministry

washed-out bridge. He also preserved them and kept their work unhindered in the face of several threats. One evening after the men had pitched their tent, God exposed Art to some of Canada's First Nations people. Art sauntered over to a nearby campsite and watched with fascination as the natives cooked fish and moose over an open fire; tanned hides; and made beautiful moccasins, gloves, and leather jackets.

With the summer ministry over, Art returned home to help Cyril ready the car he had purchased for transportation to PBI for their second year. Six students packed themselves in and drove to Three Hills through dust, chilling rain, and mud. Front seat passengers warmed themselves with heated stones and blankets; those in the back snuggled under a horsehide robe. Their suitcases, which were secured on the running boards against the side windows, helped to protect them from flying mud. They traveled 300 miles on three cylinders and sustained a bent tie rod and axle near midnight–mishaps allowed by God as He prepared them for the responsibilities ahead.

By his April 1937 graduation, Art was still uncertain of God's will for his future. "Be thou faithful unto death" (Rev. 2:10, KJV) became his all-consuming desire. While waiting on the Lord, he served another summer with the Sunday School Mission, then superintended the Fraser Mills Sunday school. One day it seemed that Joshua 1:9 stood out in large print surrounded by light: "Have not I commanded thee? Be strong and of good courage; be not afraid, neither be thou dismayed: for the LORD thy God is with thee whithersoever thou goest."

Soon thereafter he approached his mother. "Mother, I believe God is leading me into full-time missionary work, but it's so hard to think of leaving you alone. I'm torn about what I should do."

"Son," Mrs. Norris replied, "if the Lord has laid His hand on you for missionary service, you must obey. Nothing could give me greater joy. I gave you to Him before you were born. Follow His leading. He'll care for my needs."

That fall a letter arrived from Berlyn Stokely, director of the Navajo Indian Evangelization Movement in Oraibi, Arizona. "We need you here in the work among the Navajos," Art read.

Was this God's leading? After more prayer, he answered with both joy and trepidation, "I'll be there by February of next year." What lay ahead, only God knew.

4
Following with Confidence

"I delight to do Thy will, O my God . . ."
– Psalm 40:8a

S tay home, Art. Take care of things here," a church member had advised. "If God wants the Navajos saved, let *Him* get them saved." Twenty-two-year-old Art winced as he recalled the conversation. Taking care of things at home *had* been a serious consideration, but God's call had been heavy on him. It was 1938, and the lanky six-foot Canadian sat erect in the Northern Pacific Railroad car as the train rumbled southward from Bellingham, Washington. Art ran his fingers through his thick mass of straw-colored hair and stared out the window, his blue eyes framed by heavy black eyebrows. Snow-covered 14,000-foot Mount Rainier, piercing through billowy clouds into the rare blue of a February sky, captured his attention

Art Norris

only momentarily. Thoughts of leaving his aging mother had long been painful, the parting in Bellingham even more difficult. He swallowed, his throat tightening.

Pastor Leslie Smith had driven him and his mother to the Bellingham depot that morning where she had stood on the platform bravely waving her white handkerchief. She had encouraged him to follow the Lord's leading and rejoiced that he was entering missionary work. She had even named him Arthur *Stanley* after Sir Henry M. Stanley, the British journalist and explorer who searched for David Livingstone in Africa and later became a missionary. But could her joy dissolve the ache in her heart as the train bore him away to the Navajo Reservation? Was it right to leave her? Was ministering to the Navajos more important than helping Cy to care for her? Should he have heeded the church member's advice?

Thoughts coursed through Art's mind like flood waters through a canyon. His mother had sacrificed so much for him and Cy. Her frugality and firm faith had eased many difficult situations. "The Lord can answer prayer at the eleventh hour," she often declared, and indeed God's provisions had often come at the exact moment of need. Art now recognized the Lord's hand behind those lessons.

Suddenly his reverie was broken. Was he imagining it, or was the man across the aisle really watching him? Art fingered his coat pocket, satisfied that his wallet, pastor's letter of reference, and immigration papers were still there. Traveling long distance was not a familiar experience, traveling alone even less so. He did not know what to expect or whom to trust, but he would not be caught off guard.

Relaxing, he reviewed evidences of God's faithfulness and pondered His guiding hand through mysterious ways. Mr. Stokely had arranged the trip details and obtained the railroad pass, free to missionaries. That he was a missionary at all was God's doing. It had seemed such a remote possibility; now here he was headed to the United States. Wasn't the United States a Christian nation? Africa or India or Haiti, even China needed missionaries, but the U. S.? Art reveled in God's leading. He thought of the SBC mission conference at which his pastor's wife's cousin, Mrs. Berlyn Stokely, had spoken. She had come with Miss Beulah Hartwick to represent Navajo Indian Evangelization Movement in Arizona. The ladies had stayed in the Norris home and told many fascinating things about the Navajos in the southwestern part of the United States. He still remembered "Dooda," the Navajo word meaning "no," which Mrs. Stokely had taught him. All of these things were, no doubt, tiny pieces of God's mysterious ways.

The train crossed the Columbia River and passed through Portland, Oregon. Art noticed angry-looking clouds brooding over Mount Hood and surveyed the forested foothills of the Cascades. Those hills brought back memories, memories of Mr. Hone's fun-loving spirit, Bible teaching, and godly example. He remembered the youth classes, singspirations, and scavenger hunts in the wilderness along the banks of the Fraser River. He recalled the youth trip to Vancouver in the back of a two-ton firewood truck. Mr. Hone had never tried to persuade any of them to become missionaries, but he had always challenged them to follow the Master and had involved them in ministry to troubled youth in the Boys Industrial School.

Art thought of the trips to Bellingham in the back of a Model T truck for weekend spiritual retreats at The Firs conference grounds. He and his friends had ridden the fifty miles sitting on straw under a canvas top. His thoughts lingered on the teaching of the great Bible preachers: Drs. John Mitchell and Willard Aldrich, Sterling Keys and Max Stowe, Grant and Otis Whipple, Chester Rutledge and others. How grateful he was for godly men who clearly proclaimed God's Word!

He thought too of Sapperton Baptist's sanctuary and the large wooden map of the world. Emblazoned above it were the words, "Go Ye, Preach, Teach All Nations." A tiny flashlight bulb shone in Africa where one of their group had already gone. Art was the second to represent the church. Soon a bulb would shine for him in Arizona. In time, more than twenty other Sapperton youth would follow God's call in about as many years. Bulbs would light up in Africa, India, the Philippines, North America, South America, Jamaica, Haiti, and Europe.

Art became aware of drizzly rain finding circuitous pathways down the train windows. Near Grants Pass, Oregon, the drizzle turned to downpour. He watched tiny stones tumble down the dirt bank beside the track, gathering mud as they rolled. Rain pounded the coach car. The locomotive slowed and coasted to a halt. Minutes passed. Passengers peered through windows, straining to see the cause of the unscheduled stop. Some murmured about the unexplained delay. Art was more curious than perturbed. Finally, a conductor entered the coach. "Ladies and gentlemen, there's a mudslide ahead. Could take quite a while to clear it. Make yourselves as comfortable as possible. I regret that the dining car is closed."

The closing of the dining car was of little concern to Art. His budget did not allow dining car service; he had brought some food with him. Ten hours later the track was clear. Eventually, the train chugged into San Francisco and Art got off, eager to head eastward across California toward his new Arizona ministry. People bustled in all directions. He had never seen so many people or so many ethnic groups in one place. He sat down to watch and wait.

Minutes ticked by. The eastbound train was long overdue. Art's thoughts wandered. Was God preparing a wife for him in Arizona? At PBI he had not been interested in girls nor considered marriage. Talking with the opposite sex had been against the rules–good reason for the dining hall to be known as the "Red Sea." The girls had sat on one side, which the boys duly named "Egypt," and the boys on the other, referred to as "The Promised Land" by the girls. Following God's call to a certain place of service was acknowledged by his teachers to be of prime importance. Art concurred with their belief that if God desired a companion for someone, He would burden the heart of the right one for the same field of service.

The public address system crackled to life. "East-bound trains have been delayed by heavy rains. Passengers holding tickets to Barstow and points east, please check at the ticket window about five this afternoon. For anyone desiring to take in the World's Fair, known here as the Golden Gate Exposition, the bus stops directly in front of the depot."

The Golden Gate Exposition! Art was glad he had checked his few belongings–a sleeping bag, two Hudson Bay blankets the church had given him, a pair of high-topped leather shoes, and a few personal items. He hurried out the door and climbed aboard the bus. He couldn't see everything at once, but he tried. At the exposition he was astounded by television and other dazzling exhibits. At Moody Bible Institute's science exhibition he saw Dr. Irwin Moon standing on a generator holding a piece of wood. Hundreds of people watched as volts of electricity crackled through his body, igniting the wood in his hand.[1] How did that happen? Art wondered. After the demonstration, Dr. Moon invited everyone to the meeting room. No doubt he'll use that demonstration as a lead-in to the Gospel, Art thought approvingly.

Back at the depot, Art finally boarded the train. Mile after weary mile it sped eastward, its rhythmic clatter lulling its passengers into oblivion. At Barstow, California, he learned that floods had washed out the main tracks to Winslow, Arizona, where Mr. Stokely was to meet him. I must call the Stokelys and stop them from making the 200-mile round trip to meet me, he thought as he headed for the waiting room. His attempts were futile; the phone lines were out. His food supply was nearly depleted. Hungry, fatigued, and adjusting to warmer temperatures, he slumped down on a hard, straight-backed bench.

Eleven hours passed. Finally, a loudspeaker announcement! "Ladies and gentlemen, thank you for your patience. All our usual Santa Fe Railroad engines are in use or stranded. We're making up a rump train from some of our older equipment; it will run on older tracks. You should be boarding before long."

Activity outside the depot increased. Old coaches and an antiquated coal-burning steam engine emerged from storage sheds and were coupled together. Once boarded, passengers jostled and jolted as the train rattled across the desert. Smoke and soot blew into the loose-fitting windows; dust and dirt settled over everything and everyone. Up onto the Colorado Plateau and through the Kaibab National Forest the train chugged, snaking through ponderosa pines at the base of the San Francisco Peaks and coming to a halt in Flagstaff, Arizona. Quickly Art jumped off and ran in search of inexpensive food. The stop was so brief that he almost missed the train. It rumbled past volcanic cinder hills and down through the pinyons bordering the large Navajo Reservation.

It was early morning when the sleepy town of Winslow came into view. Compared with San Francisco or Barstow, it could hardly be called a town. Art stepped off the train. A few people sauntered back and forth, the Stokelys not among them. Finding a telephone, Art deposited 65 cents and dialed. Mr. Stokely answered.

"Deposit your money, please," an operator interrupted.

"I did," Art replied. Coming from a family that carefully managed every cent, he would not willingly pay twice. He had no cash to spare. Two churches had pledged a monthly total of $20; his mother's widowed friends hoped to send a dollar occasionally with his mother's letters. Many had sacrificed for him to be among the Navajos, and 65 cents was 65 cents! With persistence he was permitted to speak with Mr. Stokely.

"Hello, Mr. Stokely? This is Art Norris. I'm in Winslow. Can you come to get me?"

"Just got back from there. We waited hours. Why didn't you call? I've just driven 200 miles through nothing but an enormous mud puddle, more mud than puddle! Wore out my tire chains."

"I'm terribly sorry," Art said humbly as he tried to explain. That his delay had caused great inconvenience was evident, but he could not change that. He retrieved his luggage, put it at his feet, and sat down on the hard wooden bench to await Mr. Stokely's arrival. Leaning back, he sighed a deep, weary sigh. Homesickness mingled with doubt. Wonder what Mother and Cy are doing, he thought. Wonder what the reservation's like. Suppose I'll ever learn Navajo? Hope Pastor Smith won't wish he'd never written that reference letter for me to the U. S. consul.

Seven hours later Mr. Stokely appeared with Bruce Yazzie, a Navajo mission worker. They led Art to the Stokelys' new, mud-plastered pickup. "We'll have to buy another set of chains before heading back," Mr. Stokely announced. "You're in for a real initiation. Snow, rain, mud–facts of life here. In dry months we battle dust, grit, and ruts."

They drove westward on pavement for ten miles, then stopped to put on the new tire chains before turning north onto a mud road. The truck was off the road to the right, off the road to the left, in the ditch, out of the ditch, across the road, sideways, spinning here and there. It was evening when the men arrived in Oraibi, a village on the Hopi Reservation, which was surrounded by the Navajo Reservation. By that time the new chains were banging against the fenders, no longer new, no longer useable. The pickup looked like a chocolate-coated hump rolling into the mission compound, even more conspicuous as it passed shiny new cars belonging to other missionaries. Finding new cars at a mission station was hardly what Art had expected.

Mr. Stokely emerged wearily from the pickup. "Come on in. Mrs. Stokely has supper ready. We'll get you set up in your own place after we eat."

Mrs. Stokely greeted him warmly. "Welcome! We're glad you're here, Art. We certainly need your help."

"We've fixed up a woodshed for you," Mr. Stokely informed Art. "It's small but should be a cozy place to call your own." Later Art learned that the shed was the birthplace of noted evangelist Theodore Epp during the time his parents were missionaries to the Hopi Indians.

After supper Art was taken to the remodeled shed. The outside was covered with native stone, the inside plastered with ordinary mud over which had been spread an extraordinary mixture of water and colored sand from the Painted Desert. At last he was "home," four long, weary days from all that was familiar. With a gas heater and a kerosene lamp, his little haven would be quite comfortable. Uncertainties were countless, potential difficulties already obvious. But, God would direct each step of the pilgrimage ahead. His hand could be detected in every segment of Art's nearly twenty-three years. With that knowledge and the faithful prayers of supporters, Art knew he would not walk the path alone or without adequate provision.

5
Making His Way Known

"That Thy way may be known on the earth,
Thy salvation among all nations."
— Psalm 67:2

A pril snow covered the ground. In his tiny room Art sat near the gas heater, reading and reminiscing by the light of a candle and a kerosene lamp. Wonder if the Lord has a wife for me, he pondered, his mind flitting briefly to a letter he had received from a girl in British Columbia. The print in his book seemed to grow dim. He nodded, then roused. The lamp flame burned low. Out of kerosene? No, nor did the wick need to be trimmed or turned higher. Then the candle flickered. Alerted, Art quickly opened a window. At once the flames danced higher. "Thank You, Father," he breathed. "I didn't know this room was so airtight!"

A never-ending stream of Navajos came to the mission for help. Meeting their physical needs was time-consuming. Reliance on medicine men and suspicion of Anglo ways contributed to their inadequate medical care. Travel was limited to horse and wagon. That, coupled with unpaved roads, prevented the people from easily reaching the reservation's two Public Health hospitals. Missionaries treated many minor illnesses, using aspirin and cough syrup supplied by the U. S. Government. They also transported patients to a hospital as necessary.

People's physical needs were important, but Art yearned to meet the spiritual ones. Large areas of the reservation remained unclaimed for Christ, and the few believers needed encouragement. Day after day he learned countless cultural ways and heard more Navajo words than it seemed possible to learn. His store of knowledge continually increased as he observed his co-workers' interactions with the people. Bruce Yazzie, Albert Tsosie, and Edgar Clark were invaluable Navajo ministry partners, witnessing to their own people and serving as interpreters for the missionaries. "Let's go witness on the reservation today," Mr. Stokely would suggest. Time after time the men climbed into the pickup and bounced over rocks and rutted roads, going from hogan to hogan.

Navajo Indian Evangelization Movement (NIEM), often referred to as "Stokleys' Mission," was headquartered in Oraibi in buildings rented from the Mennonite Mission. Navajos came to exchange wool, rugs, and firewood for food, clothing, and quilts. NIEM's guest hogan frequently housed overnight visitors. At Christmastime as many as 200-300 Navajos came to receive gifts provided by friends of the mission. Each heard the Christmas story. The continual flow of people afforded great opportunities for witness, but the missionaries longed for permanent mission headquarters closer to the Navajos' homes.

Obtaining permission for a land lease on the reservation was a lengthy process. After submitting a formal request to the Department of the Interior, Mr. Stokely made several 100-mile journeys to Window Rock, Arizona. Art accompanied him on one such trip. The road was a one-lane quagmire, with ill-fated cars stranded on both sides. With a generous dose of divine help, the men crossed the pass between Ganado and Window Rock, sometimes spinning, sometimes sliding. Ponderosa pines gradually gave way to pinyon, juniper, and sagebrush as they inched their way down the other side of the pass. A red sandstone ridge loomed in the distance. "See that window in the red rocks, Art?" Mr. Stokely pointed toward the ridge. "That's the rock from which the little town of Window Rock gets its name. It's right behind tribal headquarters."

At the lengthy Navajo Tribal Council sessions Art listened intently to the dialogue, hearing everything in Navajo, then in English for the benefit of Anglo government officials. His Navajo vocabulary increased considerably that day. For one who had failed French and English grammar, he was always aware that the ability to learn this complicated language was God-given.

Art was thrust into the mainstream of daily Navajo life in May 1938 when he and interpreter John Bizadi moved into a one-room dirt hogan at Diné Bito'. Numerous children lived in the area, so the men began Sunday school in one of the hogans and sought other opportunities to witness to God's love and justice.

On a hot July day Art and Albert Tsosie, a Navajo missionary, started out on a trek, trudging through loose, sandy soil and rugged, rocky stretches under the desert sun. When they arrived at a Navajo camp, a group of hogans occupied by members of an extended family, they were refreshed by the coolness of a hogan as well as by the warm welcome and fellowship of believers. Over the next four hours they taught a chorus, a memory verse, and scriptural principles. "The entrance of God's Word brings light," Art commented joyfully as they returned home. The next day they found nothing but four empty hogans within the first five miles. Plodding on, they discovered a hogan that was occupied, but the owner saw them coming and sauntered off to his corn field. Disappointed, Art reminded himself of I Samuel 8:7b: ". . . they have not rejected you, but they have rejected Me. . . ."

Late that afternoon the two men came upon an old woman, her long hair tied in the traditional tsiiyééł hairstyle, an oblong roll of hair wrapped with homespun yarn at the nape of the neck. "Have you ever heard about the Savior?" they asked.

"No."

"May we tell you?"

The woman nodded but soon interrupted, "I can't understand. I don't want it. We Navajos have our own story." Sadly, the men returned home.

Every day brought unique opportunities, like the day Art and Albert visited a home where a family member had been killed by lightning several days earlier. Because of Navajo taboos about touching the dead, the deceased person had not yet been buried. By the time Art and Albert arrived, the decomposition process was well underway.

"Bury him," the family requested. A new concept of missionary work, Art thought, but perhaps being an impromptu undertaker is a way to build relationships so I can share the Gospel.

After digging a hole, the men wired the body to a pole and carried it to the burial site. "Death doesn't have to be the end," Albert told the family. "When you trust Jesus, He gives everlasting life." How the men longed for the bereaved to comprehend the Truth they shared!

Learning a culture permeated with animistic beliefs was a lengthy and complicated process. One day Art accompanied Miss Hartwick, the mission nurse, to the home of a young boy who had an infected tooth.

Ducking his tall frame through the door of the windowless hut, Art followed Miss Hartwick. In the dim light they saw the boy lying on a sheepskin, spitting blood. Beside him on the dirt floor knelt a medicine man, his long black hair tied in a knot.

"A healing ceremony," Miss Hartwick whispered to Art. They stood quietly, observing.

"Blue medicine, white medicine, red medicine," the native practitioner chanted. "Blue medicine, white medicine, red medicine."

The words and the drone of the man's chant captivated Art. When the medicine man stopped, he ventured respectfully, "Who are you singing to?"

"Anybody that will help. Just anybody," the old man mumbled, pulling the drawstring closed on his corn pollen bag. He stood to his feet, gathered his paraphernalia, and left.

Miss Hartwick knelt to check the boy's pulse. "He needs to be in the hospital," she urged his parents. "We'd be happy to take him there." The offer was refused, and the lad slowly bled to death.

Witnessing so many tragic deaths, Art's sense of urgency and determination grew. Knowing the ways and language of the people was vital to sharing the Gospel with them, but there was so much to see, to learn, to do. He worked at it ceaselessly, wishing the process did not take so much time. "We're going to talk only Navajo with you," his Navajo co-workers teased. Art was undaunted. Though not easy or comfortable, that would doubtless be the quickest route to effectively learning the language. He had learned to read Navajo; he prayed for understanding and ability to speak it. Few white men had ever conquered the language sufficiently to converse fluently, to joke, or even to preach. Art wanted to learn it well enough to share heart to heart with the people. He welcomed the increased opportunities to learn the language and culture that came as a result of not living at the mission headquarters and sought to develop relationships with those around him.

For many a Navajo in the late 1930s, meeting Art Norris was a puzzling experience. Disillusioned and bitter about The Long Walk of 1864, they had become accustomed to white men who acted as though they had all the answers, administered programs from their own cultural perspective, and expected everyone to speak English. Art treated them with respect and asked questions concerning their ways. He persisted in learning their language and sought to understand their thought processes. They knew no other such white man. He seemed to care deeply about them. Education and material possessions seemed of little consequence to him. This white man even kept his promises, reportedly a rarity among white government agents. The building of the railroad across New Mexico and Arizona in the 1880s had brought intoxicants, disease, and other undesirable elements of white society. Art showed concern for those dealing with alcoholism and illness. He exhibited no desire to exploit them, no sign of deceit or trickery. He was neither power hungry nor unfriendly. On the contrary, his friendliness netted him acceptance among these people whom other white men had deemed backward. In short, Art Norris was an anomaly, bearing little resemblance to the white men older Navajos had known and about whom younger ones had heard much.

Art enjoyed ministering with Navajo Christians who were burdened for the spiritual welfare of their people. Navajo children, parents, grandparents, aunts, and uncles–all lived together in a camp. Arriving at a hogan, Art and his co-workers visited with the adults while barefooted children pattered from hogan to hogan within the camp or from the sheep corral to the weaving loom under a nearby tree. Dogs lay inside the door, racing out intermittently to bark at real or imagined intruders. Occasionally, an older woman in velveteen blouse and pleated satin skirt tended freshly butchered mutton over an open fire.

At one home Art and a fellow worker found a couple sitting in their chaha'oh, a pole-framed shade house covered with tree branches. The husband professed to be a Christian, but some who knew him said that he still held strongly to traditional, non-Christian practices. As the four conversed, cries of distress reached their ears. They looked up to see a young girl leading an old man down a knoll. The pair inched forward, stopping repeatedly to rest. When they arrived in front of the chaha'oh, the observers looked questioningly at the girl. "He's 105 years old and can't see or hear," she explained. "He moans and mumbles all the time. Maybe his spirit is troubled." She walked several feet away, apparently relishing brief freedom from her charge.

The elderly man, his clothing ragged and soiled, squatted to keep his balance. He groped around him, crying out piteously. Ephesians 2:12

Sheep under chaha'oh

flitted into Art's mind: "Having no hope and without God in the world." Older Navajos had often told him, "You come too late. My ears are too heavy. I'm too old to start on a new road." But this man could not even hear about the true Way. Art's heart ached. Even recent joy over a terminally ill medicine man who had cried to God for mercy could not diminish the intensity of his grief over this poor man.

At times Art and a Navajo helper rode horseback over the windswept terrain seeking those who had not yet heard of the awesome love of God. That undertaking often involved unexpected adventure. As the men rode near a wash one day, they spied a gathering in the distance and rode in that direction, hoping for a chance to witness. Suddenly they realized that the group ahead consisted of several naked women emerging from a sweat bath. Embarrassed, they turned abruptly but not before the women saw them. "Mą'ii bikéyahgóó dínááh!" (Go to coyote land!), the women screamed. Kicking their horses, the men speedily left the area.

In spite of extensive missionary travel and visitation, the late 1930s and early 1940s were spiritually lean years on the reservation. Navajos, immersed in animism, perceived the white man as ana'i (the enemy). Hearing the Gospel through interpreters, they did not easily accept Christianity. "The white man has his religion; we have ours," they declared repeatedly, a logical conclusion for someone not understanding the eternal difference. Navajo religion, tightly intertwined with activities of daily living, seemed impenetrable to God's Truth.

Meeting a leader of a large foreign mission organization one day, Art decided to seek counsel. "Progress among the Navajos is extremely slow," he stated.

"Do they have a written language?" the man asked.

"No," Art replied.

"Do they run their own trading posts?"

"No. The government attempted to establish indigenous trading posts, but that failed. Customers were family and clan members who made purchases on credit. Culturally, it's nearly impossible for a Navajo trader to refuse credit to or to extract payment from his own relatives."

"Then you have a hard field! No wonder visible results are few if the people don't have God's Word in their own language and are not accountable to their indigenous leaders," the mission leader declared.

But, God's way was being accepted by some Navajos. Edgar Clark was one who bore the imprint of His hand. When he requested baptism, Art wondered where one could baptize in high desert terrain with few lakes and rivers and little rainfall.

"Let's dig a hole and line it with a canvas," Mr. Stokely suggested. As Art helped to dig the grave-like hole, he pondered its significance. What an appropriate illustration of dying to sin and rising to new life in Christ! Art thought.

By August 1938 NIEM was granted permission to establish headquarters near Hard Rock, and the missionaries enthusiastically set to work to build before winter. Art chafed at having to leave his evangelistic work at Diné Bito to assist in the construction, but he worked diligently and without complaint. Most of the construction and the digging of the well would be done by hand. As soon as they encountered solid rock at the well site, a drilling rig would be brought in. Excavation for the 34- by 50-foot stone chapel began, using horses, plows, and wagons. Harnesses broke frequently, but the Navajo workers adeptly repaired them with shoes, trousers, flour sacks, diapers, or bailing wire. The men blasted the final two feet of the foundation with dynamite. Afterwards, they hauled building rock from a nearby quarry.

In addition to the chapel and other facilities at Hard Rock, Art learned that vacation cabins also were to be built for some of his co-workers at Southwest Bible and Missionary Conference grounds in Flagstaff. Inwardly, he was disturbed at the thought of having to devote precious time to such projects. People needed the Savior! About 85 percent of the Navajos could not speak English, and he longed for more time to study the Navajo language. His Navajo friends had begun to correct his errors, but proper accents and tones still eluded him. However, construction was his current assignment. Except for two weeks of work missed due to an appendectomy necessitated by his having eaten pinyon nuts, shells and all, he stayed with it.

Whenever Mr. Stokely was unable to direct the construction, Art and co-worker C. B. Matheny, with whom Art now lived, eagerly turned their attention to preaching. They savored every opportunity to proclaim Christ and to teach those who had trusted Him. Due to gasoline rationing, the two tramped long distances across mesas, along dry stream beds, through sagebrush and scrubby desert vegetation. On one trek when an unsaved man was their interpreter, Mr. Matheny declared, "You have to believe on the Son and trust Him as your Savior."

"You have to believe in the sun and trust him as your savior," came the interpretation. Although Art's ability in Navajo was still in its infancy, he recognized the error and quickly corrected it.

Art had heard glowing reports about the fellowship among missionaries and Indian Christians and about spiritual feasts around God's Word at the yearly Southwest Bible and Missionary Conference retreats. He decided to attend late that summer and was not disappointed. The uplifting fellowship, songs, and messages brought spiritual refreshment and, while working in the kitchen to pay his way, he even had opportunity to observe a nice young missionary lady who served tables. He returned to Hard Rock with renewed passion to tell more Navajos about Jesus.

6
Light on an Unknown Path

"And I will lead the blind by a way they do not know, in paths they do not know I will guide them. I will make darkness into light before them . . ."   – Isaiah 42:16a

It would be a great help if you had your own car, Art," Mr. Stokely suggested in the spring of 1939. To finance a vehicle Art worked in Pastor Smith's termite business in California for a time. Crawling under houses, cleaning out junk, and spraying for termites was dirty work, but it provided $95 for a 1931 Oldsmobile. While in California, he was able to speak in a church, gaining additional financial support.

Roads on the Navajo Reservation did not always exist where Art needed to go. After returning from California, he continued to walk many miles seeking opportunities to become better acquainted with the people to whom God had called him. While observing a ceremony in which a handshaker had been hired to diagnose an eye problem, he realized that the unwritten religious beliefs of traditional Navajos varied widely. All were based on fear. For thirty minutes the handshaker moved her hands over the patient, pointing a finger first here, then there. All the while she chanted, invoking a spirit. Suddenly she stopped.

"What did he say?" the patient inquired, referring to the spirit being entreated.

"Not good, not good," the handshaker replied. "You'll have to have the Hóchxǫǫ'jí (Evil Way) Ceremony."

Specialized shamans were hired to perform specific ceremonies. Even if a physical cure were not realized, patients seemed to benefit somewhat from hearing others say, "You look much better." Most ceremonies lasted five to seven days and doubled as social events. Everyone contributed food, including a freshly butchered sheep for mutton stew, blood sausage, and roasted intestines.

In June, during a break from construction work, Art and C. B. Matheny set out on foot for another evangelistic trip. After tramping miles and passing several deserted hogans, they almost despaired of finding anyone. Finally they spied a small child in the distance caring for a flock of sheep. Weary and footsore, they trudged toward her. Approaching the little sheepherder, they asked, "Where do you live?" The young girl tilted her chin and pointed with her lips in the direction of some juniper trees.

Behind the trees the men found a hogan where a small boy was coughing, breathing rapidly, and groaning with pain. For three days a medicine man had been chanting and rattling a gourd in an attempt to expel an alleged evil spirit. In his hair was a turquoise bead believed to have power to stop the boy's cough. Repeatedly the native practitioner offered the boy sips of an herbal drink. Art turned to the boy's father. "May we read you the creation story?" he asked in his best Navajo. He could not assess how much was understood, but the father grunted his pleasure. The men visited a while and gave the family dried peaches as tokens of love. As the afternoon sun neared the horizon, they left.

For several days they trekked across the reservation visiting as many Navajos as they could. One day they spotted another hogan tucked away in a grove of junipers. Shy, young sheepherders were returning home with their flocks. Their mother's broad smile assured the men of a warm welcome. Losing their shyness, the youngsters took the two white men into the trees to show them lambs that had succumbed to the previous night's cold temperatures. One of them returned with a dead lamb in his arms and tossed it into his mother's lap. "Go throw it under the trees!" she commanded, shoving it back into his arms. Then she rinsed her hands in a skillet of water, made fry bread, and invited the men to a meal of bread and coffee. Sitting cross-legged beside a canvas spread on the ground, they ate heartily, trying to forget that the hand-washing and the frying of the bread had occurred in the same skillet.

In that home the men found three daughters and one son who were Christians. After supper everyone gathered around the fire to sing hymns and listen to a message from God's Word. At bedtime, Art and C. B. retired beneath a large juniper tree and drifted to sleep thinking about the nearly 300 Navajos they had contacted on the trip. The next day they went home and picked up their construction tools to work on the stone chapel once again.

The following month Art boarded the train in Winslow and began the long journey to British Columbia for his first vacation. His mother had kept him abreast of family and church news, and he was eager to see her and Cy. Also, for some time he had been searching his heart regarding a nameless uneasiness, and he needed time to prayerfully examine these vague stirrings. His missionary colleagues had high moral standards and their desire for the salvation of the Navajos was as burning as his, but the gap in living standards between the Navajos and the missionaries deeply disturbed him.

It was indeed good to be home. He helped his mother with a number of maintenance jobs, and they spent hours talking about his experiences. People at church were also interested in hearing about the Navajos, their colossal spiritual needs, and how God was working among them.

Almost before Art knew it, July was over, and he headed back to Arizona, believing that God was leading him to another location. He dreaded facing his co-workers, but he felt he must follow the Holy Spirit's leading. Since he planned to resign, he did not want to ask anyone at the mission to meet his train. "Would you please let me off near the Leupp Trading Post?" he asked the conductor. That was a bit closer to the mission in Oraibi than the depot in Winslow was. He began walking in the sweltering, midday sun, hoping for a ride, but none came. His neck became increasingly sore. There was not so much as a culvert under which to seek shade. Finally he spied a thin strip of shade beside a fence post and stopped for a brief rest. Plodding on, he eventually reached the trading post and found a ride to Oraibi, where he went straight to the Stokelys and announced his resignation.

Soon all his co-workers knew of his impending departure. "I'm sure it's not the Holy Spirit that's leading you to leave," one of them declared. "You're losing some of the best friends you'll ever have."

Art felt dreadfully alone. He was a foreigner in the U. S. with no rights. Mr. Stokely had signed the initial papers guaranteeing him a job. Now he had no job and his immigration papers were no longer valid. He would have to inform the immigration officials. Will they require me to return to Canada? he wondered. Wishing for a confidant, he packed his meager belongings into his five-passenger, trunkless Olds and headed to Flagstaff for another Bible conference. His only consolation was knowing that, though circumstances change, God never does.

Arriving late in the evening, he drove into the conference grounds nestled in tall ponderosa pines at the base of Mt. Elden. All was dark; no one stirred. The day had been long and tiring. Plunking his sleeping bag down on a smooth place under the ponderosas, he slept soundly. As dawn began to permeate the canopy of dense-needled pines, he was startled awake by laughter and the chatter of female voices and saw several young ladies coming toward him. He was on the path to the outhouse! He pulled his clothes on inside his sleeping bag and vacated the path just in time.

The singing and Bible messages were reminiscent of PBI days. To Art, it was like a hearty meal after a lengthy fast. Along with the fellowship, the conference gave him a spiritual transfusion as he faced the uncertainties ahead. He was again assigned to kitchen work in exchange for room and board. Again he noticed Emalou Anderson, the same young missionary who had waited tables the year before.

During the conference Rev. Howard Clark, founder and general director of Navajo Bible School and Mission (NBSM) in Window Rock, learned about Art's situation. "We're in the process of starting a Bible training school. Why don't you come minister with us?" he suggested. "Native leadership is beginning to develop, and we intend to combine academic training with practical field assignments as God provides the necessary personnel. You could accompany teams of Navajo evangelists into unreached areas."

NBSM's goal paralleled Art's own–to preach the Gospel and to train native Christian leaders to do the same among their own people. For more than forty years missionaries had preached among the Navajos, yet few of the natives knew Christ. Many had not even heard of Him. The United States Government was seeking to develop initiative and leadership among American Indians, and Art felt that the Christian church should lead the way. He was eager to minister alongside Navajos, hoping to gain greater language fluency in the process. Mr. Clark's invitation seemed God-directed, and he looked forward to the plans God had for him in the days ahead. That Emalou Anderson was associated with Mr. Clark's mission was also a pleasant thought.

40

7
By a Mighty Hand

"'And you shall remember that you were a slave in the land of Egypt, and the LORD your God brought you out of there by a mighty hand and by an outstretched arm . . .'"   – Deuteronomy 5:15a

Young Emalou Anderson awoke, startled. Moonbeams filtered through cottonwood leaves, leaving lacy patterns on the bedroom floor. The eerie beat of drums assaulted the still fall night. Drums and chants were not unfamiliar. Emalou lived with her family at the edge of the Navajo Reservation in New Mexico. Pulling the covers over her head, she could not shut her blue eyes tightly enough to erase memories of the hideous Yé'ii Bicheii[1] masks on the dancers who had recently come to their home requesting food for a ceremony. This time her father had donated a goat. The handwoven rug on the living room floor was a token of the Navajos' gratitude for a previous donation of flour and sugar.

Born December 20, 1915, Emalou was the fifth of twelve in the Levi and Jessie Anderson family. Many of her English, Norwegian, and Swedish ancestors had immigrated to the United States in the 1800s under the auspices of the Mormon Church. Grandpa Norton was her only grandparent with American citizenship. Though born in Mississippi, he had declared himself a Yankee and fought with the North in the Civil War before moving his family to Eagar, Arizona.

Emalou's parents, Levi and Jesse Anderson

Emalou's mother found minimal time for giving individual attention to each of her children. Doing the laundry was in itself a time-consuming task: hauling water in barrels from the San Juan River, heating it on a wood stove, then scrubbing clothes on a washboard. During rainy seasons the mud had to settle out before the water was useable. Frequently her back-breaking labor was interrupted to nurse or diaper a baby or to care for one of the other little ones. Assisting Grandma and Grandpa Norton was an additional responsibility.

"Jessie," Grandpa called one evening, "bring the milk pails to the corral!"

Mrs. Anderson knew by her father's voice that he wanted the pails immediately, but she could not leave her newborn. "Hurry, Emalou! Take these pails to Grandpa," she urged.

Four-year-old Emalou sped down the path. Near the barn she tripped, and her head collided with one of the milk pails. When her grandfather found her, she was unconscious, a large lump adorning her forehead. The next morning she awoke, her eyes swollen shut, but more serious complications did not materialize.

When a favorite uncle came to visit, Emalou reveled in being hugged, tossed into the air, and bounced on his knee. On his subsequent visit, however, her five-year-old heart was broken, for he paid little attention to her. Am I no longer special? she wondered.

By age seven Emalou was herding the family's sheep and goats. She loved roaming the fields, watching them nibble grass. One spring day she and her sister herded the flock near the dam which diverted the river around their farm. "Let's go wading!" Emalou suggested. Stripping to their underclothes, they plunged in, talking and laughing. Soon they were floating downstream under a deep blue sky. The water was higher than normal, the current stronger. By the time they stopped, they were farther from the dam than intended. Wading upstream was arduous.

"Girls, where are you?" they heard their dad calling in the distance. They saw him standing near the dam, his hands shielding his eyes from the sun as he scanned the surroundings.

"He probably found our clothes," Emalou commented. "We're down here," she hollered.

"Get out right now and come here!" he ordered. Sand burrs in bare feet was a costly price for such a leisurely excursion.

In the summer, the family moved their flocks and cattle close to the mountain and camped nearby. Here, as at their winter home, evening stillness was often broken by chanting at nearby squaw dances, dances held as part of healing ceremonies. Countless times Emalou watched a hogan burn after a death and pondered the ways of the Navajos.

Secretly, Emalou feared losing her father. That fear escalated the day his knife slipped while he was butchering a goat and slashed his wrist, causing profuse bleeding. Fear resurfaced later when he suffered abdominal pain and a high fever. Emalou's sister had jumped on a horse and galloped ten miles to a cousin's house for help. Much to Emalou's relief, he recovered quickly from an emergency appendectomy.

Among the religious books on the shelves of the Anderson home were a Bible and The Book of Mormon. Emalou was confused. How can I know God? she wondered. She respected her family's teaching but was nagged by an inner emptiness. Perhaps when she turned eight and was baptized, she would know God better. That day came in 1924. She sat on a log by the San Juan River quivering with excitement. When the elders laid hands on her and prayed, she felt nothing. Eager expectation turned to distressing disappointment. Questions and doubts gnawed at her. Is it possible to know God? she wondered.

As Emalou's sister approached her eighth birthday, Mrs. Anderson prepared for another baptism. "Let her wait until she knows what she's doing!" Emalou blurted.

"This is what we do," her mother said firmly, but it made no sense to Emalou. Why subject her sister to the frustrations she herself had experienced?

That year while Emalou's parents and two youngest siblings lived in a tent across the river to be closer to her dad's job, another baby brother arrived amid complications which left him mentally challenged. Nine-year-old Emalou and the older children continued to live in the small cabin their grandfather had built. Temperatures dropped to 25 degrees below zero that winter. Emalou's thirteen-year-old brother sustained crippling frostbite in a blizzard while herding the cattle. Even so, he bravely scrounged for firewood, sometimes bringing in fence posts to burn, but his efforts produced minimal heat.

"I'm glad we're sleeping in the same bed," Emalou said to her sisters one frigid night as they snuggled under a pile of covers. The next morning wood still smoldered in the fireplace, but the water in the bucket beside their bed was frozen solid. Bitter cold was not Emalou's only misery. Repeatedly at night she sensed a huge black cloud descending over her. The experience was frightening. Time and again she resisted it, always grateful to awaken to the light of another day.

The children managed admirably through that grueling winter, but proper nourishment was lacking. School lunch pails carried little more than a biscuit or two. Sensitive to her students' hunger, Emalou's fifth-grade teacher supplemented their meager diet by cooking pinto beans in a pressure cooker while the children studied.

Emalou's first exposure to the "outside world" came at age twelve. "Please go back to Walsenburg (Colorado) with us and help me take care of our twins," her married sister begged while visiting her family in New Mexico. The days in Walsenburg were difficult. Emalou never knew what to expect as she walked to and from the mine to deliver her brother-in-law's lunch. Nor did she understand why the schoolchildren laughed at her when she drew the name of a black child at Christmastime.

The following summer Emalou returned to New Mexico. She helped her mother and thrived on her parents' compliments about her cleaning and laundering abilities. Stealing watermelons with friends from a neighbor's patch enlivened the long days, that is, until the neighbor scared them away with his shotgun.

That fall a cousin informed Emalou's parents, "A family in Aztec has a daughter who was paralyzed by polio. They need an eighth grader to live with them and bring homework to her. Emalou could do that."

Emalou went, but the experience was not a pleasant one. Eating mashed potatoes every day and living without meat or goat milk was nearly intolerable. Occasionally she caught a ride with her cousin on Sundays, walking the last five miles to her parent's home. If she missed her ride back to Aztec, she had to walk the whole eight miles, a stressful experience, especially after dark. Every time she heard a car, she dashed out of sight. Despite her fear, she was conscious of God's presence and protection. One night as she stared into the star-studded, moonlit sky, it seemed to her that His hands were reaching toward her. "God," she murmured, "I want to be whatever You want me to be."

That winter Emalou attended a revival meeting with a friend. The only church she had ever been in previously was the Mormon church her parents sometimes attended. She did not know what to expect at the revival, but she hoped to learn the secret of her friend's happy spirit. There, for the first time in her life, she heard about God's holiness and justice, about mankind's sin and Jesus' sacrifice for it. "If anyone will come and take this," the preacher said, waving a dollar bill, "he may have it." Finally, someone strode to the front and took it.

"God is as loving, merciful, and gracious as He is righteous and just," the preacher declared. "He gave us a whole lot more than a dollar bill. He gave us His Son, Jesus, who provided forgiveness and salvation by dying on the cross for our sins. Just as our brother did not earn the dollar I gave him, so we can do nothing to earn salvation. It's a free gift! If you have any questions, talk with me after the service."

This had to be what Emalou had been yearning for. This must be the way to know God. She was keenly aware that she needed forgiveness. Going to the designated room after the service, she waited . . . and waited . . . and waited. Voices mingled, feet shuffled, then all was quiet. Finally the pastor's wife appeared. "Now, dear, when do you want to be baptized and join the church?" she asked, sitting down beside Emalou with paper and pencil in hand.

"Baptized and join the church?" Emalou stood to her feet, indignant. "I don't want to be baptized! I don't want to join the church! I'm a Mormon!" At that she marched out. She longed for the salvation the preacher had talked about. It was the best news she had ever heard. Surely it meant more than baptism and church membership. If baptism and church membership could have brought forgiveness and peace, she would have experienced that already. She was puzzled. Were these people trying to trick her? Her yearning turned to an agonizing ache. Was there no way to know God?

Returning from Aztec at the end of the school year, Emalou lived with and did housework for a widow who owned a small store and orchard. The widow bragged about how well she cleaned the kitchen and shined the wood stove. As often as possible, Emalou visited her family. During one visit her mother went into labor. While her father was fetching a midwife, labor intensified. "Put some water on to boil," her mother directed. "If the baby comes before the midwife does, there's string in that drawer to tie the cord. The blanket is in the dresser drawer." At age fourteen Emalou was not eager to become a substitute midwife. Nervously she followed her mother's instructions, relieved that her dad and the midwife arrived just in time.

High school loomed ahead, but none existed locally; neither did transportation to one anywhere else. "I really want to go to school," Emalou told her father.

"You'll have to stay with a family somewhere then," he replied. "I'll see if I can find one in Aztec where you can work for your board and room."

The family he found was disorganized and dysfunctional, both parents gone most of the time. Getting the undisciplined children to bed was Emalou's exhausting responsibility. Her hardest assignment, however, was simply survival. At Thanksgiving she was more than ready to go home.

The day after Thanksgiving Emalou's parents dropped their two youngest by the home of their married daughter and went to play cards with relatives. Emalou went to bed before they returned but was startled from a deep sleep sometime later. "Jessie, what's the matter?" she heard her dad call frantically. She bolted out of bed and ran to her parents' room. Her mother lay unconscious, struggling for air.

Emalou grabbed her robe and sprinted a quarter mile to the nearest neighbor. "May I use your phone?" she asked breathlessly. Unable to reach the doctor, she bounded two miles down the road to her sister's house. Her sister and brother-in-law were just getting in their car to take the young Anderson children home.

"What's wrong?" they asked.

"Something's . . . wrong with . . . Mother!" Emalou announced, breathless.

"Hop in!" they urged. Within minutes they found Mrs. Anderson lifeless. Emalou slipped out of the house and cried bitterly. It's Dad's fault! He expected Mother to work much too hard. And what about my baby brother . . . three months old and breast fed. Why didn't God take me? Doesn't He care? How can He be loving? Maybe that preacher doesn't know God any better than I do. Angrily she swiped her clenched fist across her tear-drenched face and returned, grief-stricken, to the house.

Emalou's sister took the baby with her to Walsenburg, but a bottle could not pacify him. He wanted the comfort of his mother's breast. Gradually, he adjusted but not without trials for both him and his new "mother."

Meanwhile, Mr. Anderson went to Utah to find work, leaving the children on their own. Because of the various limitations of her older siblings, Emalou assumed responsibility. Her siblings were cooperative and the farm supplied sufficient milk, chicken, and eggs. For variety they made soup from broken pinto beans they found in nearby fields. Eventually, extended family members came for the youngest five, and Emalou and the older children continued to fend for themselves.

Before long Emalou accepted an invitation to live with Mr. and Mrs. Hawkins, managers of Navajo Methodist Mission School's farm in Farmington, New Mexico. She attended the school and, for the first time in her life developed real friendships with Navajo children, but she worried constantly about her family and her future. Three months after her arrival, at fifteen, she left unannounced, taking the Bible Mrs. Hawkins had given her. She liked the Psalms, but they held little meaning for her. In Aztec she found her sister's family ready to leave for Nebraska. "Want to go with us?" her sister asked. Emalou felt honored.

From Aztec to Santa Fe to Walsenburg and on to North Platte, Nebraska, her sister drove the car and she rode in the pickup with her brother-in-law. Could it be they wanted her to go with them so she could hold the pickup's ailing gearshift in place? It was in the midst of the Depression, and there was no money for eating in restaurants. Each morning, noon, and night during the week's journey, the travelers stopped to make pancakes. In North Platte the family moved into a relative's shack and Emalou into a garage. I can't stay here forever, she reasoned. I have to get a job. Entering a small cafe, she ventured, "Do you need any help?"

The manager looked at her thoughtfully. "We can't pay you anything, but you may wash dishes for your meals."

Emalou welcomed the offer, and soon the manager was paying her a dollar a week. When he left for vacation and failed to make arrangements for her pay, she approached the cashier. "The manager gives me a dollar a week, and I need it before he gets back." The cashier gave her the dollar. When the manager returned and learned what had happened, he accused Emalou of taking money from the till. "You're fired!" he said, refusing to listen to her explanation.

Disgruntled, Emalou considered joining the circus with a younger friend who was also dissatisfied. Instead, she found employment at the Chicken Inn caring for the teenage daughter of the restaurant owner. Since the Chicken Inn's dinners often included bootleg whiskey and police raids were a constant possibility, the daughter was not allowed in the restaurant. Emalou's responsibility was to stay upstairs with her. Two years later she quit the job. A concerned friend offered to buy her a ticket to Salt Lake City to be with her dad.

Refusing the offer, Emmalou found a job caring for two children, ages five and seven, whose parents managed a restaurant and a brothel. Since the restaurant was without refrigeration, the chickens were slaughtered each afternoon. If more were needed than anticipated, Emalou was called from her baby-sitting post to help butcher. With her bedroom directly above the dining room and dance hall, getting adequate sleep was impossible. She was intrigued by the music, dancing, and cigarettes. Because she was a minor, her employers dismissed her when she began to participate.

For a brief time Emalou found housing with a friend. Her friend's husband, a former Bible school student, delighted in enumerating to his card-playing guests the reasons the Bible was not trustworthy. A feeble attempt to justify his lifestyle, Emalou suspected.

Before long the managers of the Chicken Inn asked Emalou to come back to work for them. She worked there only briefly before the owner approached her. "Emalou, Pastor Tulga, a friend of mine, needs help. He pastors the First Baptist Church, and his wife and baby are sick. Would you like to work for them?"

In Emalou's seventeen years, God's unseen and often unrecognized hand had been ever present, protecting, guiding. The new position the manager offered was readily accepted. Never had Emalou experienced such kindness and patience as she did in the Tulga home. The five Tulga children were a joy. Willingly she complied with Mrs. Tulga's gentle request: "We prefer you don't smoke in the house, but you may smoke in the furnace room."

Some months later an evangelistic team from Biola visited the church. God's invisible hand was at work! Since Mrs. Tulga was the church pianist, Emalou stayed home with the baby each evening. One afternoon Mrs. Tulga confided, "Emalou, I'm not feeling well. I'll stay home tonight and you go with the children. I think you'll enjoy the music." The children had raved about a quartet, and Emalou was eager to hear them for herself.

There was a chill in the air as Emalou walked to the church with the children the evening of January 23, 1934. She enjoyed the music and heard the same awesome story she had heard before. At the invitation, she went forward and talked with one of the Biola students. Using the Scriptures, the student clearly explained God's plan of salvation. Emalou was overcome with joy! Walking home, she sensed God's presence even more than she had that moonlit night she had walked from her parents' home to Aztec. Never had she felt so clean, so free! That something had happened was unmistakable. She finally knew God and was deeply satisfied, though she longed to know Him better and to tell others about Him. Tears flowed in the darkness.

At breakfast the next morning Mrs. Tulga inquired, "Did anyone accept Christ last night?"

"I did!" Emalou confessed enthusiastically.

"Praise the Lord!" exclaimed Mrs. Tulga, giving Emalou a warm hug. Emalou felt sure that Mrs. Tulga had been praying for her. She was just as certain that God had sent her to this family. Her desire for dancing and cigarettes suddenly disappeared. Remnants of anger, cynicism, and self-reproach, however, did not. She had become adept at putting herself down before someone else did. As she sought to know God more intimately, she struggled with this kind of behavior. After all, was she not a beloved daughter of her Heavenly Father?

Now, not only was baptism acceptable, it was desired. Emalou wanted everyone to know that Christ alone had cleansed her from sin and that she was living a new life. His free gift brought joy she had never imagined possible! She was baptized the very next Sunday. It was not just a formality; it was an obedient witness to the satisfying change within.

The inner change manifested itself immediately. For some time Emalou's non-Christian boyfriend had been telephoning her daily. "Baxter," she said when he called the morning after her conversion, "I accepted Jesus Christ as my Savior last night. I'm not the same person anymore."

"More power to you," he responded. "I hope you'll do good." She was not disappointed that he never called again. She knew now that they were more incompatible than ever.

Mrs. Tulga stood ready to assist Emalou in her Christian growth. "Why don't you read the Gospel of John?" she suggested. "I think you'll find it exciting and helpful."

Emalou devoured the truths from that portion of Scripture, and her delight defied description. She considered herself a "wild heifer" needing lots of training and help from others who knew God. Max and Vanita Kronquest, First Baptist's youth leaders and graduates of Denver Bible Institute (DBI), began at once to teach and encourage her. Despite their recent loss of an infant son, they were calm and confident in the Lord, and Emalou loved and respected them.

"I want to become a missionary and serve the Lord somewhere," Emalou confided one day.

"Maybe you can go to DBI for training," they suggested.

"I haven't finished high school yet."

"The Lord is able. We'll check it out."

They did, and Emalou was accepted for that October; however, both the Kronquests and Pastor Tulga felt she should start immediately. They recontacted DBI and, upon their recommendation, DBI admitted Emalou for the April-June quarter.

Although the economy of the early 1930s was ailing, the church people rallied, giving Emalou a train ticket; quilts and other bedding; towels; a few long, dark dresses and skirts to meet DBI's dress code; and personal items. The ladies lengthened the clothing to the required eight inches or less from the floor. Emalou was both excited and humbled as she watched God provide. She was exhilarated yet frightened, happy yet sad when members of the church family waved goodbye to her at the train station. Leaving these mentors was difficult, but she was eager to prepare for whatever God wanted her to be and do. She was on her way to Bible school, although she had been a Christian less than three months.

Sleep did not come that night. As the train rumbled its way across the plains and up into the mountains, Emalou reviewed her bad habits and unrefined ways. She was ill-prepared in every way except one–her longing to serve her new Master. Who will meet me? What will it be like? Can I handle Bible school work? Will I fit in with students who've been Christians for a long time? As dawn broke, the train screeched to a halt in Denver and Emalou stepped off hesitantly. A pleasant-looking woman approached her. "Hello," she said. "I'm Hazel Johnson, Dean of Women at DBI. Are you Emalou Anderson?"

"Yes," Emalou said shyly, shaking hands. Was there a fleeting look of surprise in Mrs. Johnson's eyes?

"I'm so glad you came! I've been telling the other girls about your coming. They're eager to meet you."

Meeting seasoned Christian peers was uncomfortable. Emalou had always fended for herself, trying to survive but not caring if she did. Rebuff after rebuff had bred self-consciousness, self-centeredness, defensiveness, and an outspoken manner that often annoyed others. Her motto had been "Hope for the worst and you won't be disappointed." Her metamorphosis as a Christian had only begun, and failures loomed large. Nevertheless, she had learned that God had chosen "the weak and the base and the foolish[2]," and she identified with all of those.

In spite of her rough edges, Emalou was excited about learning God's Word. For one so unfamiliar with Scripture, however, writing a 200-word paper on Law and Grace appeared insurmountable. She drank in knowledge as cotton absorbs water, but her papers were too brief, her grades discouraging. A low grade in "Christian Demeanor" brought her in tears to Hazel Johnson's office. She longed to imitate Christ but had failed miserably. Through heaving sobs she poured out her life's story. No longer just the dean of women, Mrs. Johnson listened with her heart and became a mother to this young lady who desperately needed her.

In the atmosphere of Christ-like love evidenced by both faculty and students, Emalou steadily matured. Her new friendships differed greatly from past relationships, and she felt more comfortable than she had in her own home. Classes and required Bible memorization consumed large amounts of time. Study halls were sandwiched between cleaning, laundry, office work, and preparing desserts in the dining hall. Mother's Day that year was particularly difficult as she grieved over the impossibility of ever sharing Christ with her own mother.

Six weeks into the fall quarter a scarlet fever epidemic closed the school. Emalou was among the first to be quarantined. For eight days she and seven other girls played games, read to each other, and studied and memorized Scripture together in a little house at the edge of the campus. Emalou worked on Bible Survey, her favorite class, summarizing chapters and learning the theme and main characters of each. Occasionally, the school nurse dropped by to ensure that no one broke quarantine. Many of Denver's residents died, but by God's grace, DBI students and faculty were spared.

Emalou thrived on the songs that music teachers Jesse and Florence Jones chose for chapels and her music lessons, songs that focused on spiritual growth and sacrificial service. She did not advance far in piano, but she learned an enormous amount about the Lord. "You were to practice 'Jesus, Lover of My Soul,' weren't you?" Mrs. Jones asked one day during a piano lesson.

"Yes," Emalou replied.

"Play it for me, please."

Emalou played it through once. As she lifted her hands to play it a second time, Mrs. Jones interrupted. "Just a minute, Emalou. Read the second verse."

Emalou read, "Thou, O Christ, art all I want; More than all in Thee I find."

"Could that apply to each of us?" Mrs. Jones questioned.

Emalou nodded thoughtfully. "Emalou, you have a real heart for the Master, and I know that you long to know Him fully. May I share something that might be helpful?"

Emalou lowered her eyes and listened intently as Mrs. Jones gently continued. "I've noticed that you often respond defensively and even belittle yourself. Emalou, the Lord loves you deeply. He is greater than whatever may have caused you to develop such habits. With His help, you can replace cynicism with joyful confidence in Him. You can love others unconditionally as God loves you, even those who are difficult to love."

It was all too true. Emalou sobbed, but her tears sprang as much from joy as from embarrassment. Mrs. Jones had cared enough to point out lovingly the painful reality of her attitude and actions. The words of the song had spoken deeply to her, and she determined to give herself more fully to Christ than ever before. As she and Mrs. Jones prayed together, they asked that God would reveal Himself increasingly to Emalou and help her to grow in His ways.

Emalou's life was filled to capacity. She took Bible and non-Bible courses and worked for room and board. With her small income and $5 a month from the little church in Nebraska, saving $50 for the year's tuition was impossible. The tempter reminded her of that fact frequently. "Emalou," one of her friends announced one day, "I'm quitting and going to California. My boyfriend wrote that I can get a job there and that the weather is great. Want to go with me?"

Money, warmer weather, no worry about grades or tuition fees, time for more sleep–California sounded enticing. Then the Holy Spirit reminded her that she was not her own; she had been bought with a price. "Lord, I'll stay," she responded. "You have placed me at DBI, and I won't leave unless You lead me to."

Summers found Emalou at the school with other students painting, cleaning, sewing for the school's Gospel team, and canning thousands of jars of fruit and vegetables. It was hard work but fun. Occasionally they exchanged a hard-earned nickel for a treat at Daniel's Ice Cream Parlor. The camaraderie was beneficial, especially for Emalou. During a Christmas break she stayed with friends in North Platte, earning a dollar a day at a temporary job. It was God's gracious provision for a much-needed pair of shoes.

At DBI only brief greetings were permitted between male and female students on campus sidewalks. Coed communication occurred almost totally in the dining room, with seating arrangements revised weekly. If a couple desired to become better acquainted and sought permission from a dorm director, they could meet in the lounge with the drapes open, the fellow on one side of the room, the girl on the other.

Chapel times were rich. Missionaries often served as guest speakers. The need for translation workers in Belgian Congo tugged at Emalou's heart, but lack of a high school education disqualified her. Some of her friends gave themselves for work in Colombia after hearing thrilling accounts of God's working in dangerous situations there. To Emalou, that was real missionary work, the kind she wanted to do. As she sought God's will for her life, however, she could not shake childhood memories of drums and chants, dancers with hideous masks, and digging with her brother in the remains of burned hogans. The Navajos definitely needed Christ. Only He could free them from their innumerable fears. But, she saw nothing alluring about being a missionary in the same area where she had grown up. Nevertheless, when missionaries to the Navajos visited the school, Emalou became as intrigued with their stories as she had been with ones from Africa and South America. She also learned that the Joneses spent summers among Native Americans at Southwest Bible and Missionary Conference in Flagstaff, Arizona, and she enjoyed hearing of their experiences.

Gradually the Holy Spirit revealed to Emalou that God had uniquely prepared her. She was already familiar with many of the Navajo ways. "Lord," she prayed, "if You want me to go to the Navajos, please help me to be joyful about it." The moment she relinquished her will, she knew that was where the Lord was leading. Excitement escalated. Eagerly she began to gather more information about Navajos and their needs.

The spiritual toddler moved toward adulthood, her spiritual muscles tortuously exercised as she approached the spring of her senior year. Graduates needed $150 for end-of-year expenses, and summer work at DBI was not permitted beyond graduation. How could she possibly come up with the required amount? She acknowledged that the Lord had provided many times before, but waiting on Him worry-free was difficult.

Emalou (right) and Betty Hess at 1938 DBI graduation

This time His provision came as a loan from a friend. To her, even that was nothing short of a miracle.

As graduation neared, the unlikely Bible school graduate was eager to learn details of the Lord's next assignment. Although she had long perceived "a real missionary" as one serving on foreign soil, now she was primed to proclaim the Savior on familiar ground. Immediately after the June 1, 1938, graduation ceremony, Florence Jones asked, "Emalou, would you take care of our two younger boys for six weeks while Jesse and I travel with the school quartet? After our tour we're going to Flagstaff, Arizona, to direct music at the Bible and missionary conference. You could go with us if you'd like."

Overwhelmed with the trust that the request implied and understanding the responsibility entailed, Emalou nevertheless agreed. Going to Flagstaff would provide opportunity to rub shoulders with Native American Christians! Until conference time, her biggest challenge was keeping the boys from eating too many cherries from the Joneses' tree. When the parents returned in mid-August, she packed her few belongings and accompanied the family to Arizona. Since she had no funds for room and board, she served tables at the conference, working alongside other young people. Several times she noted one of the young male missionaries looking in her direction. She heard he was Canadian and had been serving among the Navajos for six months. He's quiet, but a real gentleman, she thought.

The conference was uplifting! If worshiping God among Anglos and Navajos, Apaches and Papagos, Pimas and Hualapais was so awesome, what would worshiping with every tribe, tongue, and nation be like in the future? Emalou was eager to help as many Navajos as she could to participate in that glorious event. During the conference she spent every possible minute with them, attempting to learn Navajo words.

Harry A. Ironside and other outstanding men of God taught daily from Scripture. Their teaching was devoured by work-worn missionaries and native believers. David Clark, son of missionary Howard Clark, was home from John Brown University and enthusiastically spearheaded conference activities for singles. The excursions, including camping and climbing Mt. Elden and Sunset Crater, were enjoyable, but for Emalou the highlights were the evening campfires and testimonies, especially those of native Christians.

One afternoon toward the end of the conference, Howard Clark sauntered over to Emalou. "Hello, Miss Anderson. I understand you just graduated from Denver Bible Institute."

"Yes, a couple of months ago."

"I've watched your interactions with the Navajos. You seem to have a deep interest in them."

Emalou nodded. "I wanted to be a foreign missionary, but I grew up near the Navajo Reservation, and I believe the Lord wants me to serve among them. First, though, I have to pay off a school debt. I'm praying that God will provide somehow."

"Well, we're in the process of starting Navajo Bible School and Mission to train native people for the work of the Gospel. Our family has been living in Fort Defiance, Arizona, but we're moving a few miles south to Tse Bonito, New Mexico, across the state line from Window Rock, Arizona. That's the capital of the Navajo Nation. If you're interested, we'd be happy for your help with the move and with our children. I'm sure there are other things you could do as well."

Emalou was overwhelmed by the sudden thought of all God had done in her short life. Was this His direction for her now? A confirmation that the Navajos were indeed her people? She accepted Mr. Clark's offer, certain that somehow God would provide for the payment of her school debt.

8
Following Obediently

".. . as for me, the LORD has guided me . . ."
– Genesis 24:27b

Emalou accompanied the Clarks to Window Rock and busied herself studying Navajo and assisting Mrs. Clark. She milked the cow, cleaned house, washed dishes, butchered chickens, and cared for the Clark children. Using a clean garbage can and a plunger, she did laundry, then heated a flatiron on the cook stove and ironed mountains of clothes. Though not yet an official missionary, she visited Navajo camps and sanitarium patients in Fort

1939 NBSM staff
Back (L-R): Howard Clark, Alma Clark, Tsehe Notah
Front (L-R): Mattie Ward, Helen Stamix, Emalou Anderson, Faye Edgerton, Dorothy Siversmith

Defiance as often as possible with Miss Poinsett, one of the missionaries.

Twenty-three-year-old Emalou shared a 12- by 24-foot one-room cabin with two Navajo ladies and three other white missionaries. Their room boasted six army cots, two chairs, suitcase "dressers" under the beds, and "clothes closets" consisting of nails on the walls. The "bathroom," minus a commode and running water, was curtained off in one corner. Bath water was carried the distance of a city block and heated on a small wood stove, the only source of heat. Down the path stood an outhouse.[1]

"By the way, Emalou," a staff member said one day, "a young man helped me roof a building over at the conference grounds in Flagstaff last week."

"Oh? Who was that?"

"Arthur Norris. He asked about you. Wondered what you are doing."

"Oh, yeah, I remember him." She could still see Art carrying pans in the kitchen at the missionary conference. Recently while reading a certain Scripture, God had impressed upon her that He would provide a companion. Was Art the one? "Lord," she breathed, "I want Your will."

Two months after Emalou arrived in Window Rock, Navajo Bible School and Mission was dedicated. For six months she volunteered her services, loving every minute of it. Like most of the other staff, she called Mr. Clark "Papa" Clark; and, to her, Mrs. Clark was the embodiment of Christian womanhood. She preferred to continue serving alongside them, but her school debt hung over her like a shroud. She had to find employment; mission headquarters was no place to earn funds.

Encouraged by Florence and Jesse Jones to find work in Los Angeles, where they had become involved in ministry, Emalou boarded the bus. She found a job as a nanny and determined to work only until the Flagstaff missionary conference later that summer. Every week on her day off she attended a girls' fellowship at Biola and practiced Navajo with a girl she had met in Flagstaff. She could think of nothing but the people to whom God was calling her, and she talked endlessly of their spiritual needs. The group's sponsor was annoyed, but Iris Schwartz, a student preparing to serve among the Navajos, listened eagerly.

Emalou

In July 1939 Emalou returned to Arizona able to pay her DBI debt and buy needed clothing and equipment. She applied to Navajo Bible School and Mission, was accepted, and returned to Window Rock after the Flagstaff conference. Studying Navajo under Faye Edgerton, a missionary proficient in the Navajo language, she fluctuated between exuberance over her improvement and discouragement over her lack of progress.

That fall Papa Clark suggested, "Emalou, the Pine Springs area really needs the Gospel. You could spend the winter there with Alice Curley, a new Navajo Christian who could learn from you as you do visitation together."

Vast distances, isolation, and nomadic ways dictated that most spiritual work be done via home visitation.[2] Emalou was eager to follow Papa Clark's suggestion. Alice and her small son came from Crystal, New Mexico, and the three of them walked daily from one Navajo camp to another, Emalou sharing the Gospel in English and Alice interpreting.

One morning not long after their arrival in Pine Springs, Alice awoke visibly frightened. "What's wrong?" Emalou inquired with concern.

"I haven't slept all night!"

"Are you sick?"

"No." Alice shook her head slowly, her eyes avoiding Emalou's in traditional Navajo manner. Hesitantly she ventured, "Did you . . . did you . . . hear an owl hoot last night?"

"No," Emalou responded, wondering why an owl hoot was so disturbing.

Alice was reluctant to say more; this white woman would not understand. Finally, with misgiving, she ventured, "The owl talked to me all night. I've got to go home!"

"Why?" Emalou asked, puzzled.

"A hooting owl means that something awful is going to happen, like somebody dying."

"But, Alice, you're a child of God. You don't need to be afraid." Even as Emalou spoke, she remembered from personal experience that spiritual maturity does not come overnight. Gently she tried to calm Alice's fears with Scripture. As soon as convenient, she sent word to Papa Clark.

When Papa Clark came for Alice, he said, "Emalou, I think it's best you return to mission headquarters instead of staying here by yourself." Emalou loved being among the people, but she respected Papa Clark's decision. She could continue language study in Window Rock and do hospital and sanitarium visitation.

The following summer Emalou returned to Pine Springs with Berniece Capitan as interpreter. Trying times were ahead. One evening Berniece answered a knock at the door. "Come and help me get my daughter back!" a young woman pled.

"Where is she?"

"She went with some people."

Emalou joined Berniece at the door. "We don't have a car," she explained.

"It's not far. We can walk. I know where they are."

For the two women who had already walked all day sharing the message of salvation in hogan after hogan, sleep sounded more inviting. "Let's wait until morning," Emalou suggested.

"No. They'll leave early tomorrow morning for Keams Canyon and I'll never get her back."

"What happened? Why did they take her?" Emalou inquired.

The woman did not answer. It was 9:30 p.m. when Berniece and Emalou stepped out into the darkness and followed the woman. They did not know where they were going or why. "Lord, show us how to help this woman," Emalou prayed silently. From time to time she asked, "How much farther?"

"Not far," was the standard reply.

Near midnight, amid incessant barking of dogs, they approached a hogan. The woman knocked and a man let her in. Outside, Emalou and Berniece waited, listening, wondering. A child cried. Finally the door opened and the woman emerged holding a five-year-old girl, her cheeks smudged with tears. She continued to cry as they walked.

"Why is she crying?" Emalou ventured.

Berniece talked to the woman in Navajo then answered. "She gave her daughter to relatives from Keams Canyon then changed her mind. The relatives gave the girl some jewelry but took it back when her mother came for her."

At 3:00 a.m. Emalou and Berniece fumbled their way into their trailer and fell, exhausted, into bed. Did we really help that woman? Emalou wondered as she pulled up the sheet. When she awoke, the question lingered. As she prayed for insight, she remembered how God had opened doors for her with a trader's wife who had confided the ugly details of her life. The unpleasant situation had given Emalou opportunity to share with the woman how one could experience victorious life in Christ. Convenient or not convenient, understood or not understood, she determined to let

God mastermind her circumstances without questioning.

The two ladies visited many families within walking distance of the Pine Springs Trading Post and Day School. Berniece was an excellent interpreter and enjoyed proclaiming the Good News as much as Emalou did. They did not always see visible results from their efforts, but some people were responding positively and the ladies knew that God was at work. At summer's end when Berniece returned to the mission school in Farmington, Emalou returned to mission headquarters for language study, hospital visitation, and to help wherever needed.

9
God's Good Hand

". . . the good hand of his God was upon him."
                                              – Ezra 7:9b

O n an August day in 1939 Art pulled into the grounds of Navajo Bible School and Mission (NBSM) in Window Rock. He surveyed the pinyon- and juniper-covered hill on which the Howard Clark home stood overlooking ridges of red sandstone rocks. Sheep nibbled grass near a dry gully which meandered along the road at the bottom of the hill. Beautiful! Art thought. Once again he felt he belonged. To his great relief, a letter from immigration personnel indicated that neither his change of job nor his move would endanger his status as a Canadian citizen working in the U. S. God had cleared the way for him to continue ministering among the people he loved and would undoubtedly provide the funds needed.

Art shared a two-room shack on the hill with Tsehe Notah, a Navajo evangelist with whom Papa Clark had asked him to work. On foot, by horseback, or by pickup they visited people in the hospital and Navajo camps. Well-versed in Scripture, Tsehe was Papa Clark's right-hand man and the main interpreter for the NBSM missionaries. Though he was quite capable of preaching, Tsehe urged Art, "You go ahead and talk; I'll interpret. But, don't talk about death. Navajos will think you're putting a curse on them or wishing they'd die." In view of that cultural reality, Art wondered how one preached "the terror of the Lord" as Papa Clark requested.

One morning at nine Tsehe and Art set out to visit homes, but their horses were nowhere to be seen. They searched everywhere they could think of, but by one o'clock the horses still had not been found. They

Art and native evangelist

returned to their quarters, cognizant of precious lost time. A young Navajo couple was waiting for them. "Preach to us," the couple requested. Like most Navajos, they did not recognize one great spirit, but as they listened to Scripture and several illustrations, their minds were divinely enlightened and they responded. "We've been praying to the sun and earth and other things," they said. "We didn't know we were sinners, but praying to created things instead of to the Creator Himself must be sin. We need the Savior, too!" The morning had not been lost after all. God was so good! The horses had not been located for a reason only He had known.

As Art and another missionary, Mr. Entwhistle, visited in the Fort Defiance hospital, they began teaching three men to read Scripture in Navajo. "Teach us the first chapter of John," the three requested during a succeeding visit.

Answering their questions pushed Art to his limit in language ability. With weary brain, he returned to mission headquarters and sat down to write his support team about the experience: "Speaking carefully, using many gestures and illustrations, and with the help of the Lord, their hungry souls were fed. I will surely appreciate your prayers as I struggle with this difficult language." His tribal knowledge and language ability increased every time Tsehe's good friend, Alfred Hardy, the Navajo judge from Crystal, New Mexico, came to visit. Art heard politics, tribal affairs, and spiritual truth animatedly discussed in an avid mix of Navajo and English.

Whenever Papa Clark was away, Art fed the cattle; milked the cow; and separated, sold, and delivered milk and cream. In February 1940, three days after Papa Clark left for California, a call came from Pine Springs. "Miss Anderson is pretty sick. Looks like appendicitis. Someone needs to come for her." Art was the only one available. He drove to Pine Springs for her and took her to Rehoboth Hospital in Gallup, New Mexico.

A couple days later young Navajo workers Mattie Ward and Dorothy Silversmith begged, "Mr. Norris, take us to Crystal."

"I'd have to drive Papa Clark's pickup, and I'm not sure I should do that," Art countered. "It's been raining so long that the roads will be quagmires."

The ladies persisted and, against his better judgment, Art yielded. The twenty-five miles seemed like 250. Repeatedly the pickup became stuck. Repeatedly they shoveled and struggled. Six hours later they reached the mountain pass road near Crystal, but the pickup's mud-laden wheels refused to turn any longer. "Well, that's it for tonight," Art declared. Exhausted, they abandoned the pickup and made their way on foot through the last two miles of mud.

Returning to the pickup the next morning, Art discovered that the mire had frozen around its wheels. He plodded back to Crystal Trading Post and asked the trader to pull him out. As the pickup was pulled, one of its wheels skidded instead of turning. That worried Art. By then it was two thirty in the afternoon, too late to return to Window Rock before sunset. They'd have to wait until the next day. The following day they endured twenty-five miles of muck, a blowout, and a wheel falling off. The return trip had consumed not six, but seven, precious hours.

When Papa Clark later inspected the damaged wheel, he was not happy! Repairs would cost at least $20. The experience was both a painful and an expensive one, but Art was grateful for lessons learned at the hand of a wise and loving heavenly Father.

Ten days had elapsed since Emalou had been admitted to the hospital for an appendectomy. When Art returned to Gallup for her, she was not yet released. Two days later he returned again, only to learn that she had left with Mr. and Mrs. Carl Harwood, her supporters who had suggested a month's recuperation at their California home.

Back in Window Rock, Art picked up Tsehe Notah and went to Pine Springs for two weeks of home visitation. They used every opportunity to speak of Christ, but few people were interested. They even experienced some opposition. However, since Tsehe was a member of the Navajo Tribal Council, many Navajos willingly discussed politics with him. One day Tsehe saw a couple that had professed faith in Christ the year before. "Where do you stand with the Lord now?" he asked them.

The husband responded. "Giving up ceremonies and squaw dances isn't so bad, but we can't give up our sacred corn pollen. We have to have it when we pray to our gods."

The wife agreed. "Our leaders don't treat Christians good. Besides, the ceremonies are fun." Such a response was discouraging, but the men determined to press on, giving out God's truth and leaving the results to Him.

At a Bible conference in Crystal, Art's cultural awareness continued to broaden as a young Navajo Christian challenged him and several young summer missionaries to a sweat bath. "Come on, you guys. You won't be able to stand it very long, but you ought to try it."

The group gathered at a small mud hut in a private area of a pine forest. The Navajo spokesman explained each step. "First, we've got to find wood and make a good bed of coals. Then we'll find some big stones. While we're heating them, we'll gather cedar bark to put on the dirt floor."

After covering the floor's periphery with bark, they transferred the hot stones to the center of the sweat house by shovel. "Time to go in," the Navajo brother said. Shedding their clothes, the men entered the small sweat house and sat in a circle, skin to skin, their backs toward the wall of the hut. One man stayed outside to hang a blanket over the entrance and shovel dirt over the bottom edge of it. "Have to make things as airtight as possible," the leader explained. Hot dirt trickled around the blanket's edge and fell on Art's back. He flinched. That must have been straight from the center of the fire! he thought.

The men sat in darkness, sweat streaming from every pore. "Good for your body. Cleanses you," the Navajo man declared.

It ought to do something! Art agreed mentally. He had never been so hot or so wet with sweat in his whole life. Though his Navajo friend didn't expect him to stick it out, he was determined not to move until someone else did. Finally, the blanket was pushed aside and, one by one, the men crawled out.

"Now, rub yourselves with sand to dry off." Art cringed, but if that were the routine, he'd do it. Actually, he felt relaxed, and his friend's respect for him and the others seemed to have increased. It was doubtless worth the discomfort.

At the Bible conference Art learned that 25,000 square miles of desert and mesas was home to approximately 50,000 Navajos. That number was increasing 1000 per year despite the high death rate due to tuberculosis and malnutrition. Though the Navajos were the largest Indian tribe, no more than five percent of them were Christian.[1] Art was glad to join Papa Clark and a team of Navajo evangelists after the Bible conference for an initial ten-day visit to the northern part of the reservation. With a grant from R. G. LeTourneau,[2] Papa Clark had purchased a new GMC Suburban truck large enough to accommodate such a team. Off they went to Round Rock, Rock Point, Rough Rock, Dinnehotso, and Shiprock.

Native evangelists

The trip was fruitful in several respects. Not only did the witness of the Navajo evangelists impact their people, but the men themselves were taught and trained in evangelism during morning Bible studies and messages. "Art," Papa Clark declared, "I plan to send more teams to unreached areas of the reservation. I'd like for you to be their driver and assist them however possible."

For two to four weeks at a time Art accompanied the evangelists. He enjoyed the sparsely vegetated landscapes of the lower elevations and the ponderosa pine forests of the higher elevations. Squatty pinyon and juniper trees, sagebrush and cacti, mesas and buttes, rock formations and red earth bordered the primitive roads the men traveled. In many areas this was the first time the Gospel had been heard or a white man seen.

Art wholeheartedly supported Papa Clark's vision to indigenize the Navajo church by training Navajos as pastors and lay leaders. Ministering and having fellowship with Tsehe Notah, Daniel Taylor, Harrison Moore, Joe Yazzie, Chee Wilson, and John Peshlakai brought him sheer joy. Mutual respect developed among the team members. With a tent and other supplies, they traveled over rough rocks, deep sand, and washes to towns as far as 100 miles away. Sometimes they pulled a trailer. Other times they stayed overnight in borrowed hogans. As Art's friends conversed, preached, sang, joked, and teased, he became more and more familiar with their thought processes and language. However, he hadn't mastered it yet. Thinking one day that he was telling some Navajos he wanted to *see* their beautiful jewelry, he discovered that he had told them he wanted to *steal* it. The tone of the word made all the difference.

In September 1939 Art's diary detailed his involvement: "Prepared prayer letters all day. Studied Bible after supper. To Crystal with Tsehe for a week of camp work. Harrison comes to study Bible right after putting the sheep into the corral. Religious instruction classes at Crystal Day School. All day in camps . . . no response."

As schedules permitted, Art began spending more time with Emalou. Then one day Papa Clark announced, "Art, I want you to move to Rough Rock. You've been there with the evangelists and have some idea what it's like. Those people need the Gospel." Art was more than willing to go, but he wondered if the move was a result of Papa Clark's concern about his relationship with Emalou. He would enjoy being nearer her and learning to know her better, but he was confident of God's goodness and knew He would work things out if she were the one for him.

10
A Committed Way and a Faithful God

"Commit your way to the LORD, trust
also in Him, and He will do it."
– Psalm 37:5

Art, it might be well for you to buy a trailer to live in at Rough Rock," Papa Clark recommended. Since Art's $20 a month could not cover such a purchase, in March 1940 he again turned to his former

pastor's California termite business for the needed income. By November God enabled him to purchase a used masonite travel trailer from a missionary to the Hualapais in Peach Springs, Arizona.

Art on his way to Rough Rock

Art pulled the small trailer across miles of dusty, rugged terrain with his well-worn Oldsmobile. From the top of a low rise near Rough Rock, he stopped to view the broad valley. A long, red mesa extended across the horizon, fields of pale green grass and scrub brush stretching before it. Behind the red mesa rose a higher one, horizontally ribboned in tan, brown, and charcoal layers. Fan-like piles of dirt and rock, accumulated over decades of weathering, lay at its base. Cows and horses munched sparse grass along the road. Sheep nibbled at broom grass, and here and there a billy goat rose on his hind legs to chomp at the top of a saltbush.

Pulling into the area near the Rough Rock trading post and school, Art parked the trailer. The trailer had been jostled so badly in transit that the roof sagged and Art could no longer stand under it at full height. It was parked in a prime location for observing culture and community life. People came and went from the trading post–women in full, brilliant skirts; men in broad hats and bright-colored shirts; women and children bent under 50-pound bags of flour and sugar. Tied to nearby cedar trees were several horses, their saddles sporting colorful blankets. Other horses pulled wagons carrying water barrels. The horses were so thin and tired that they refused to run even downhill. Swinging a lasso, a man on a black horse cantered leisurely to the trading post and stopped to share the latest news with another horseman. Interesting people, Art thought, and they all need the Savior.

The magnitude of the spiritual need was overwhelming, but Art determined to do what he could and leave the results with God. On cold winter mornings he read Navajo Scripture portions to the people who waited at his trailer for the trading post to open. Over and over he played phonograph records of Scripture and short Bible messages, memorizing Navajo verses and messages in the process. Some visitors were uninterested; others gave rapt attention to the message they had never heard before. Art knew that the people often said whatever they thought was pleasing to the listener, so he did not press for decisions concerning Christ. Elderly Mr. Weeping Willow walked the three miles from his camp more than once to hear what Art was teaching. "I believe it, but I must hear it often, for I am old and forget," he explained. He listened for five hours one Sunday, starting home at dusk in the snow.

Art discovered that the public school allowed weekly religious classes. Parents had to designate either Protestant or Catholic instruction for their children. Few families claimed to be Protestant and those who did, hesitated to make it known, but Art was soon teaching a class of boys. One day a priest appeared at the classroom door. "Boys, you're in the wrong class," he announced. "Come over here." Not a boy budged and Art continued teaching, eager to expose these young Navajos to the truths of God's Word.

The ministry was both exhilarating and exhausting. In March of 1941 Art wrote, "During the past two months I have tried to work the field alone. The Rough Rock area, with a radius of about thirty miles, is surrounded by three other large areas, each with as many Navajos as are in the Rough Rock area. [Some of the people] are too superstitious to speak their own names. Fear of evil spirits holds them to their religion, which claims power over such spirits through a variety of ceremonies. I have only penetrated the fringes. The need is dire. Every time I ask if anyone has ever told them the story of Jesus, the answer is always no."

Art had to have help, and native co-workers seemed the best solution. One man who wanted to help was drafted into the Army. Even if he were available, how could I pay him at least $30 a month? Art wondered. With the war going on, I can't ask my Canadian friends for that much. Besides, what little money leaves Canada is subject to an 11 percent exchange fee. Art did ask his friends to pray. In response, God sent John Peter Yazzie for several months. Art had taught him to read Navajo when he was a patient in the Fort Defiance Indian Hospital a couple of years earlier. Now confined to a wheelchair, John Peter did much of the inside work and Art managed outside duties. Working as a team, they prepared Bible messages in Navajo and shared the Gospel in their home and in others in the area.

Pondering the enormity of the work, the lack of workers and funds, and his own limitations, Art quoted the words of George Matheson's hymn "Make Me a Captive, Lord" in his March 1941 newsletter:

"Make me a captive, Lord,
And then I shall be free;
Force me to render up my sword,
And I shall conqueror be.
I sink in life's alarms
When by myself I stand;
Imprison me within Thine arms
And strong shall be my hand."

Now and then other Navajo workers came to help. Daniel Taylor, Tsehe Notah, Harrison Moore, Joe Yazzie, and Lorenzo Iashie preached in Navajo wherever they found an audience. Many Navajos listened—some four to five hours—and asked questions. Art prepared meals, provided transportation for the men, encouraged and trained them, and did whatever he could to facilitate the advancement of the Gospel. The Holy Spirit directed in all

Lorenzo Iashie
Navajo evangelist

the evangelistic efforts.

One day Tsehe Notah, Joe Yazzie, and Art visited the Big Legs family not far from Rough Rock. Mr. Big Legs was a medicine man. His long hair was tied in a traditional knot, and a red band encircled his head. When the men arrived, he and his wife laid sheepskins on their dirt floor, which they had swept with a grass broom. Neither spoke English, but they settled down to listen as the men sang hymns in Navajo to the accompaniment of Art's accordion. Tsehe and Joe preached. "We never heard that Story before," Mr. and Mrs. Big Legs declared.

Sometime later Art set out with Daniel Taylor for three weeks. At a remote log cabin they found a woman sitting on a sheepskin spinning wool, her many offspring playing around her. Several dogs lay panting and snapping at flies under nearby saltbushes. When Art and Daniel appeared, the family gathered to listen. "Have you heard about Jesus?" Daniel asked.

The nineteen-year-old daughter had heard about Him from some missionaries. Everyone sat absorbed as Daniel spoke. "This is good news!" the mother exclaimed. "I never heard anything like it before." She was not yet ready to trust Christ, but she urged the men to come back and tell them more.

Four adults and three children occupied the next hogan. Soon Mr. Rough Cheeks dropped by to see why a car was parked outside. Then the man of the house walked in and took his place on his favorite sheepskin. John Billy, a head man in the area, was the next to arrive. All listened intently. John Billy liked what he heard. "Bring your trailer house here by my place and teach me," he urged Art.

Before long Mr. Big Nose came in and sat down cross-legged on the dirt floor in front of the stove made from a gas barrel. The turquoise bead tied to one side of his broad, black hat indicated that he had had a ceremony to protect him from evil spirits. A small deerskin pouch containing corn pollen adorned the other side. Nonchalantly he removed his moccasins from his bare feet, shook out the sand, and replaced them as he listened. Finally he spoke. "If you'll teach me this Gospel, I'll go tell others."

Finally, Mr. Rough Cheeks rose to leave. "I must go break a friendship with my brother-in-law, then I will become a Christian and follow God," he said.

What an afternoon! So many open doors! So many unreached

Navajos! Art depended on the prayers of his support team and on the Holy Spirit's continued faithful working on his behalf and the behalf of those to whom he ministered. The Navajos were much more open to the Truth when it came in their own language from one of their own.

A Rough Rock family to whom Art (center back) ministered

Often Art walked as much as twenty miles a day visiting one family after another. At one home he found Yinuzbah, a seriously ill woman, and told her about the Savior. She begged him to come back and tell her more. Two weeks later he returned with Daniel Taylor and Tsehe Notah. The family was separating the lambs and sheep, and the bleating of the animals was deafening. Near the entrance of a cedar bough shade sat a five-year-old girl weaving her first rug, her tiny fingers pulling the yarn into a pleasing pattern. Coffee boiled in a big black pot sitting over glowing coals. Yinuzbah lay on a bed of sheepskins and quilts, emaciated and in the final stages of tuberculosis. Her mother held her hand. Speaking Navajo, Daniel and Tsehe learned that Yinuzbah had previously trusted Jesus while in a sanitarium. Her eyes sparkled as they read Navajo Scripture portions and enumerated the glorious things God had prepared for those who love Him. "I believe. I believe strongly!" she whispered with great effort.

"Let's invite everybody in the other hogans in this camp," Daniel suggested to Tsehe. Before long, several had gathered around Yinuzbah, and the men preached, pleading with everyone to accept God's gift of salvation.

Yinuzbah's mother gave evidence of the Holy Spirit's working. "I trust my daughter's Savior, too," she asserted.

Art seldom had Anglo visitors, but one day several young men, prospective missionaries, visited him. They were full of zest. "We'd like to climb Black Mountain with you," they said.

After a wearying climb, the men sang Navajo hymns at a hogan at the top of the mountain and Art gave a memorized message in Navajo. On to other hogans they went, gratefully accepting offers of coffee and fry bread.

Near dusk one of the families offered them a place on the dirt floor for the night. Art shared the Gospel there, then the men lay down, exhausted. What seemed only minutes later, the old grandmother called, "Get up! Get up! The sun is shining. Somebody go after the sheep."

The family stirred and the guests enjoyed more coffee and bread. "Where are we going today?" one of the young men asked.

"I think we'd better go back to my trailer," Art replied. "We're not prepared for such a trek. Besides, we've already been to all the hogans on the mountain."

Grateful for the privilege God had given them to preach the Gospel, the men started down the mountain. Coming to a pool of cool water, several of them flopped onto their bellies and drank deeply. "Probably not a good idea," Art said. "Look at the white alkali around the pool." A Navajo man appeared with a team and wagon and offered the men a ride. The trail was steep and as the horses ran down the hill, the wagon hit a stump and tossed the men into the air. Providentially, no one was hurt. The men were glad to get home, but those who had drunk from the bitter pool suffered miserable consequences that night.

Navajos who came to Art's trailer were fascinated by his possessions: a stove, a radio, a sofa bed, and even salt and pepper shakers. "My life would be happy if I had those salt and pepper shakers," one man hinted. Art was grateful for what he had and for the things he could buy at the local trading post, but he missed fresh produce. The Toggenburg goat he had purchased to provide milk followed him like a dog. People called him "The Man with One Goat." He took the goat with him on every overnight trip.

Abaho (back left)
and his family

Most of Art's time, however, was spent in Rough Rock either receiving visitors or visiting people in the area. Abaho, a teenager who spoke little English, accompanied him at times to show him where people lived. Art relished those occasions as opportunities to learn more Navajo and interesting cultural tidbits. "See these?" Abaho said one day pointing at tracks in the dust. "A woman walked here. She sat over there to put her moccasins on."

One part of the culture that saddened Art, however, was the frequent use of alcoholic beverages. He longed to see the people enjoying the freedom that only Christ could give from such bondage. He grieved over the tragic death of the son of Man with the Big Nose. Selling liquor on the reservation was illegal, but home brew was easy to find, and the son had found it. The brewing process may have been faulty; whatever the cause, the young man vomited for twelve hours then died. Man with the Big Nose came to Art. "Bikéé' ásdiid" (My son's tracks have run out), he said. "Help me bury him. He's still in the hogan."

Again Art was confronted with the task of burial, but it did provide witnessing opportunities. As he backed the pickup to the door of the hogan, he noticed in the rearview mirror that the men were carrying the body through a hole in the north wall. Taking it through the door was taboo; carrying it at all would mandate their spending a week within a circle of ashes and undergoing a purification ceremony. As he drove toward the grave site with the body, he glanced in the mirror again. The hogan was already in flames. The fear of evil spirits permeated everything these people did!

At the grave site Art waited for the relatives' arrival. They came bringing a shovel and the blindfolded horse of the deceased man. "Should we take off our clothes before we dig so no spirits will get on them?" they asked.

"That's not necessary," Art assured them. After they lowered the body into the newly dug grave, they looked at Art. Not knowing what was expected, he read Scripture and prayed in Navajo. "God loves you," he declared. "His Son, Jesus, died for you. If you trust Him, He'll forgive your sin and take

Traditional Navajo funeral

you to be with Him forever when your body dies." Then a man led the horse close to the grave and struck it between the eyes with the blunt side of his single bit ax. Art shuddered. The horse fell, struggling. The blows continued until it lay lifeless. Then the men ripped the saddle blanket in half and chopped the saddle, bridle, and reins into pieces. "Why do you do that?" Art asked.

"He needs a horse to get where he's going," was the answer.

Once more Art sought an explanation as he watched the men break the handles of the shovel and the ax and place them in the crotch of a cedar tree. "So evil spirits won't harm us," the men replied. "Everything's backward after death. Sometimes we put a dead person's shoes on the wrong feet to confuse the spirits."

The men broke off a tree branch and carefully wiped out their footprints as they backed away from the grave. "So evil spirits won't find us," they commented, anticipating Art's next question.

What a useless end to a young man's life, Art thought. What fear and what hopelessness!

❖

Hearing a ruckus at the trading post one day, Art sauntered over to investigate. An inebriated man was straddling another inebriated man, beating him in the face. "Go to hell! I'll kill you! You should be up north with the other Diné!"[1] he yelled.

Art puzzled over that. His friends, unable to pronounce the double "r" in "Norris," called him "Hastiin Náhookǫs" (Mr. North) and laughed every time they called him that. "Náhookǫs," meaning "the giant dipper," was the term used for "north." He had eventually learned that, according to traditional Navajos, medicine men grab evil spirits and throw them through the smoke hole in a hogan and they go north, the place for everything bad. But what did this man mean? Were there Diné tribes farther north?

With that question lingering in his mind, Art returned to the realities of the moment. His time was never his own. People came with numerous requests: "I need medicine"; "Give me five dollars"; "Would you take me to Chinle?" Many of the requests were war-related, since approximately 25,000 native men between eighteen and fifty were serving in the armed forces in places they had neither heard of nor cared about.[2] The requests seemed unending: "Read this letter"; "Write a letter for me"; "Take my picture so I can send it to my brother."

With so many demands on his energies, Art needed spiritual refreshment as well as physical, and God provided. Art's lifeline was a battery-operated, table model Philco radio on which he found a Christian radio program. This indirect contact with a Baptist church in Garland, Texas, provided a sense of Christian fellowship. Some evenings he took a long walk to enjoy the scenery and clear his mind. He was encouraged occasionally by hearing children sing "Jesus Loves Me" in Navajo as he walked by. They were obviously retaining what he was teaching them.

Sometimes tiring trips to Gallup, New Mexico, for propane and other supplies were necessary. Visits to headquarters in Window Rock for mission business were also required. On one such trip he drove miles in mud, coming about dusk upon several cars that were stuck. Maneuvering around them was impossible. After eating the egg provided by the chicken he had with him and chatting with some of the other travelers, he spent the night in his car.

In the morning he awoke to find that the other drivers had already jacked up their cars, put rocks and weeds under the wheels, and left. Now his car was stuck. Since his jack was rounded on the bottom, each time he attempted to use it, it sank deeper into the mud. There was little to work with. Fetching his ax, he chopped a chunk out of a nearby telephone pole and used that and some tumbleweeds and sagebrush to get out of the rut. He stopped in Chinle long enough to pick up his mail and the mail for the Rough Rock trader and schoolteachers. All non-natives in Rough Rock did favors for each other: fetching mail, transporting batteries to the government garage to be charged, and buying groceries.

Back in Rough Rock, Art befriended a medicine man with the hopes of introducing him to Christ. The friendship progressed to the point that the native practitioner wanted to make Art a pair of moccasins. "Make them real big," Art instructed.

The moccasins were much too small. "No problem, no problem," the medicine man assured him. "Just dig a hole in the sand and bury them. After a while they'll fit."

Lacking a better idea, Art buried them, but after some days they were still too tight. He left them lying in the trailer and later noticed that mice had gnawed holes in them. Laughing, he showed them to his friend. "Destroy them!" the medicine man exclaimed. "The devil has come. Never, never wear them again!" Art never did, though it was not fear that stopped him.

Planting God's Word in virgin soil was a privilege, but Art longed for a companion to share in the work. Certain ministry situations were awkward; others needed to be totally avoided. One day when the tension was unbearable, he left the trailer and started toward Chinle Wash with no conscious destination. He wandered through tumbleweeds, sagebrush, and Indian paint brush; past pinyon and juniper trees; beside mesas; through dry washes; and along a dusty trail. Oblivious to his surroundings, he agonized, "Lord, should I marry or should I give myself wholeheartedly to You like Paul did without being tied down to a wife? Help me to know Your will." Dusk descended. Stars appeared. Seventeen miles lay between him and his trailer. He trudged homeward, sensing that marriage was God's will; the question remained, to whom. God was faithful, and he would know His will in time.

11
His Open Hand

"... Thou dost open Thy hand, they are satisfied with good."
— Psalm 104:28b

In the spring of 1940 Papa Clark presented a new opportunity to Emalou. "Emalou, down on Highway 66 is a place called Defiance, New Mexico. It's near the railroad about ten miles west of Gallup. No one has ever proclaimed Christ in that area. Would you like to take that on?"

The challenge was enticing! Living on site would allow Emalou more efficient use of time and provide the community a living example of a changed life, but no housing was available. She acquired a car and began commuting thirty-five miles from Window Rock to visit the people. In October, after the Defiance trader kindly offered land on which to place a tent, some men from the mission built a wooden floor and frame not far from the rickety trading post and stretched a tent over it. A wood-burning stove doubled for cooking and heating. Water could be carried from a faucet behind the trading post. With a kerosene lamp, borrowed cot, and self-constructed benches and cupboard, Emalou had all she needed and was deeply satisfied with God's provision. Her new home stood near Rio Puerco Wash, impassable during summer monsoons. To the south was U. S. Highway 66 and to the north lay the Santa Fe Railroad tracks.

Emalou by her tent house

Not long after Emalou moved in, a young Navajo appeared at her door. "My aunt said there's a blue-eyed Navajo here who tells God's Word. She wants me to find out about it," the woman explained. She stayed all afternoon listening as Emalou, the "blue-eyed Navajo," taught God's Word.

"Come back Sunday and bring other people with you," Emalou proposed. "I'll teach you more." On Sunday eight Navajos came.

The Jakes family showed special interest. Mary, Nesbah, and Desbah publically declared faith in Christ the Sunday that evangelists Tsehe Notah, Daniel Taylor, Harrison Moore, and John Peshlakai came to explain the Gospel in Navajo. Emalou was ecstatic! So was Desbah, who removed her turquoise necklace and handed it to Emalou. "This is for you!" she said enthusiastically. Emalou treasured the gift, but she treasured even more Desbah's new-found life and joy. Every Sunday and twice during the week the three new Christians, with full skirts, long-sleeved velveteen blouses, and heavy turquoise necklaces, walked to the tent house. Emalou loved teaching from John, her favorite book. The ladies easily understood the analogies of the Shepherd and His sheep.

Although she spent much of her time with people, Emalou combated loneliness. Sometimes she visited with Iris Schwartz, the former Biola student now ministering in nearby Houck, a few miles to the southwest. Occasionally Art Norris came to visit. She was fond of him and wondered if their relationship might become more than mere friendship.

Prior to her first Christmas in Defiance, Emalou was away visiting supporters. Knowing that she would have little time to plan for the Christmas program after her return, she wrote to the trader. "Would you please tell the people about the Christmas meeting and have someone

First Christmas
celebration in Defiance

meet me and my co-workers at the wash with a wagon to take us to the chapter house?" The chapter house was the seat of local government and a popular meeting place for the community.

At eleven o'clock on the scheduled morning Emalou,

Mr. Entwhistle, Papa Clark, and Daniel Taylor waited by the swiftly flowing stream, but no one came for them. Returning to the tent house, they prepared for the people they hoped would come there. Gradually Navajos appeared from all directions, on foot, on horse, in wagons. Soon the tiny tent bulged with thirty-five people. While Daniel was preaching in Navajo, others arrived, forcing the celebration outside into the bitter cold. As gifts were being distributed at the end of the service, a storm approached and everyone hurried to leave. Just then ten newcomers arrived and begged to hear the message. Once again the Story was told!

The more of God's Word that Mary Jakes learned, the greater the changes her husband noticed. He began accompanying her to Sunday meetings out of curiosity. Another man and the younger of his two wives also came. When these two became Christians, Emalou did not know how to handle the situation. She summoned Papa Clark, who explained the scriptural teaching regarding marriage.

"I'll live with my younger wife, since she believes as I do," the man responded, "but I will provide for my older wife and children, too."

The 8- by 10-foot tent house could no longer accommodate the Sunday crowd. Mission personnel prayed about another facility. An elderly gentleman burdened for the salvation of Navajos stopped by one day. "Daddy Vanderwagen," as he was known, listened with great interest as Emalou detailed God's wondrous working in the Defiance area. "The work is growing so fast that my house doesn't hold everyone," she told him.

"You need a new house," Daddy Vanderwagen declared, reaching into his pocket and handing Emalou a dollar. "Seed money," he explained. "Keep praying. God will provide."

Emalou set the dollar aside. A can of milk was a nickel, a loaf of bread a dime, and a box of oatmeal a quarter. Her $20 monthly income was stretched to cover food, gas, household needs, personal items, and frequent car repairs. Only God could make another home available.

Emalou and Berniece Capitan

That summer Berniece Capitan joined Emalou, providing able assistance and invaluable companionship. Daily the two read the Bible and asked God to lead them to those of His choosing. On foot or on borrowed horses they visited homes, singing Navajo hymns and illustrating Bible stories with flannelgraph. Many people came to their home as well, some late into the night. Each heard about Jesus.

After Berniece returned to school, Esther Damon came to assist. Though not full-blooded Navajo, she spoke the language well and was a great asset. She was so captivated by all that Emalou told her about Denver Bible Institute (DBI) that she enrolled for the fall semester. Her replacement was Madeline Beyale. Though blind, Madeline was quite helpful as an interpreter and in other ways.

Emalou's language ability was improving, but her vocabulary was limited and she had difficulty mimicking the tones. Every time she asked those to whom she served coffee if they wanted it with cream and sugar or black, they laughed. "Why do you laugh?" she asked.

"You're asking 'Do you want it with cream and sugar or do you want it naked?'" her friends explained.

From time to time thoughts of matrimony surfaced in Emalou's consciousness, but people were coming to Christ and growing in their relationship with Him. Serving God was her highest priority. She and Art had had a strong disagreement at the train station in Gallup before he had left on one of his trips to California. Their heartbeat for missions was the same, but their backgrounds and dispositions were so different. He always saw things in black and white, unable to understand her feelings. She determined to spend less time thinking about marriage. She certainly was not interested in the proposal she had received from another friend, and she would not pursue any relationship that might distract her from following God's will.

In the summer of 1942 Emalou was in charge of the children's ministry during the annual Bible conference of Navajo Christians from Defiance, Hunter's Point, Many Farms, Window Rock, and Crystal. That fall she returned for a while to hospital and sanitarium visitation in Fort Defiance. Since patients were away from everything familiar and were suffering with incapacitating or deadly diseases, many of them welcomed missionary visits. One such patient was Esther Benally. Esther Benally believed that someone had cursed her, causing persistent back pain. Because her parents refused to provide a traditional healing ceremony for her, she felt like an outcast.

"If you trust the Lord Jesus, He will take care of you," Emalou encouraged. "Do you know that He died for you?"

Esther had been to school but did not know English well. She thought Emalou meant she was dying.

"No, that's not what I meant," Emalou assured her. Circling John 3:17 in an English New Testament, she said, "Here, read this. You'll understand what I mean. I'll come back and we can talk about it."

❖

Each time Emalou visited, she explained the Scriptures. Before long Esther trusted the Savior and wanted to know more. "Would you like to go to Bible school?" Emalou asked.

"I'll tell my parents," Esther responded in Navajo fashion.

Her parents agreed, and as soon as she was released from the hospital, she attended the Bible school in Window Rock. Later as a faithful helper in Defiance, Esther matured rapidly as she and Emalou studied the Gospel of John together. Emalou's throat tightened every time she heard Esther pray. With tears Esther would pour out her heart: "O God, my family is hopeless and they're crying. They don't even know they can cry to You. They're living in darkness. Please bring them to Jesus."

Bonded in Christ, the two women walked many miles to visit Navajo families. Esther eagerly explained the truth she had so recently experienced. Her joy knew no bounds when several family members trusted Jesus as Savior, but her heart ached over her parents' refusal to leave their old ways.

God had been working in behalf of Emalou's need for more space. Eventually enough money was in hand for the addition of a kitchen and a meeting room, and Emalou's tent house was converted into a bedroom. She was awed with the new building, another evidence of her Father's

Emalou and Esther Benally in Emalou's new house in Defiance

83

gracious hand, but He was at work in people's lives as well. A Navajo lady swallowed a needle she had been holding in her mouth when she sneezed. Emalou asked her missionary colleagues to pray, and the next Sunday the lady was at church testifying that God had spared her life!

Emalou visiting a Navajo family

Meanwhile, at DBI, Esther Damon spoke often about the mission work at Defiance, and a student, Pauline Osborn, volunteered to help there the summer of 1943. Due to the hundreds of military personnel traveling by public transportation, it took Esther and Pauline quite a while to reach New Mexico. Esther Damon could stay only briefly, but Emalou and Esther Benally introduced Pauline to the various ministries. About thirty Navajos came to the service the day after Pauline arrived, and she was all eyes and ears. She marveled that the women wore rainbow-colored blanket shawls on such a hot day, and she saw long underwear peeping below the men's trousers. During the week, she accompanied

Emalou with Navajo ladies

Emalou and Esther Benally to various homes to teach Bible verses and "Jesus Loves Me" in Navajo. A number of people also came to Emalou's home to memorize Scripture. "One boy has learned eleven verses already!" Emalou enthusiastically told Pauline. That was just one more encouraging event in the long list of things God was doing in the Defiance area.

Anticipating a visit from Art on July 4, Independence Day of 1943, Emalou invited her friend Iris and her new husband, Charles Girton, to supper. Art arrived early enough that afternoon that the two of them had time together before the Girtons arrived. "Let's go for a walk," Art suggested. His occasional visits and their intermittent lunch dates in Gallup had bolstered their relationship. Talking and laughing, they made their way across the high desert toward the mesa. In a dusty, barren spot flanked by telephone lines and Santa Fe Railroad tracks, Art stopped. He turned toward Emalou and took her hands into his. Looking into her blue eyes, he asked gently, "Would you marry me?" God had already confirmed to Emalou His will in this relationship, and she gladly accepted the ring he placed on her finger. She would miss the work at Defiance, but God would continue to draw people to the Savior in her absence. His hand was clearly discernible. He was building a church where there had been none, and He had prepared and preserved this companion for her. She was deeply satisfied with His goodness and looked forward to what He would do in and through the two of them together.

Art and Emalou on engagement day

12
You, O Lord, Have Done It!

"I will give Thee thanks forever, because Thou hast done it . . ."
— Psalm 52:9a

Emalou awoke from a fitful night, overwhelmed with God's extravagant goodness. It was October 1, 1943, the day she would become Mrs. Art Norris! Her thoughts flitted to the day a single co-worker had made a pie for Art. She chuckled, remembering the meals she and other single missionaries had prepared for him before he had moved to Rough Rock. Then there were the "Norris" brand chocolates she had seen on the table of one of her single friends. She recalled roaming the hills shortly after that, acknowledging before the Lord that her musically talented friend could be a great asset to Art and his ministry. She remembered saying, "Lord, You called me to be a missionary to the

Emalou

Navajos. It would be hard if You put Art and my friend together, but if that's Your plan, You can give me grace to face what the future holds." She marveled that God in His sovereignty had brought her and Art together!

As she dressed and began preparations for the memorable day, Emalou pondered the events of the five years since she had first met Art at the Southwest Bible and Missionary Conference in Flagstaff. Their relationship had been fraught with storms. Because of the scrutiny of both Navajos and missionary co-workers, becoming acquainted had not been easy. Much of the time their courtship had consisted of little more than seeing each other during mission activities: attending classes, eating and washing dishes in the Clark home, doing laundry together, and riding with others to the hospital and sanitarium. "Bless Mr. and Mrs. Entwhistle's hearts!" Emalou exclaimed out loud. "I'm sure they knew how difficult it was for Art and me to become acquainted. That's probably why they kept inviting us to their home."

Emalou began adding items to her partially packed suitcase. As soon as I finish packing, I'll run over and visit Art's mother, she thought. She seems so nice. I'm glad she could come from British Columbia for the wedding and stay for a while afterward. While Emalou packed, she continued to reminisce. With humor she recalled the day Art had asked her to go to Fort Defiance with him to visit hospital patients. His dark blue Oldsmobile had negotiated the narrow road without problems, but during their return to the mission station, a tire had been punctured. By the time the spare was on, it was dusk. They hadn't gone far until they had another flat. Due to the lack of a spare, they had driven the rest of the way on the rim. She blushed, remembering the looks and comments of various staff members when she and Art had arrived home much later than expected. How could she ever forget Papa Clark's "Where have you been?" and his apparent lack of belief when they had given him a truthful answer. That's probably why he moved Art to Rough Rock, she thought.

Closing her suitcase, Emalou sat down on the edge of the bed. "Thank You, Lord, for Your guidance and blessings," she murmured quietly, her heart brimming. She sat looking out the window, reliving a torrent of feelings surrounding her automobile accident the year before. With warmth she recalled how tenderly Art had laid her bleeding head on his lap as they made their way to the hospital and his concern for her in the emergency room. She had been deeply perplexed, however, when he had disappeared as soon as she was admitted to her room and never returned during the three days she was there. When Papa Clark had declared, "Emalou, I'm sure that this is one of those things that 'work together for good to those who love God,'" she had felt nothing but anger and despair. How could he say that when her work had been interrupted, her car totaled, her face scarred, and Art had left for California without visiting her?

In hindsight Emalou saw God's hand in it all. Art had explained later that the accident made him realize how deep his love for her really was, and he had gone to California to break his engagement to a young lady there. Why had she ever doubted God's ability to bring abundant good out of what seemed to be a series of depressing events?

Emalou roused from her reverie. There was much to do before the afternoon wedding. She glanced at her dress hanging on the door and made sure all accessories were ready. Then she walked to Mother Norris' guest room, and for the next several hours the two of them exchanged numerous questions and answers. Emalou was eager to learn more about this godly woman about whom she had heard so much. Mother Norris wanted to hear about Emalou's family, her conversion, and her ministry among the Navajos. "It is so good finally to meet the one for whom I've prayed so long," she said warmly. "What better way to celebrate my seventieth birthday than to be here for your wedding and to get a glimpse of your and Art's mission work!"

Art

Meanwhile Art was making last-minute arrangements for the honeymoon trip and the move to Rock Point, their new ministry site. He could hardly believe that before the end of the day he would have a wife! At times that had seemed an utter impossibility, at least a wife committed to ministry among the Navajos. His heart rejoiced in God's awesome gift of a like-minded companion, but he had only a vague idea of the adjustments this would require. As he washed his car, he too thought about the trip to Fort Defiance and his subsequent assignment to Rough Rock. He and Emalou had experienced many ups and downs in their relationship. They had not seen eye to eye on a number of things, and neither had been able to understand the other.

Art thought about the vacation in California when he had made a grave mistake. It could have cost him the joy of this day and the pleasure of continued ministry among the Navajos. He recalled the advice that Mrs. Smith, his former pastor's wife, had given while he was staying in their home during a break from his ministry to earn needed funds. The scene was as vivid in his mind now as it had been in reality then. "Art, you really need a wife," she had asserted. "The Lord never intended you to be alone on the mission field. I know a nice girl who would make you a good wife."

Art had not had much experience with females, but he had enjoyed Emalou's friendship. She had been as devoted to serving God among the Navajos as he, and he had thought she might be the companion God had for him. However, their disagreement at the train depot as he departed for California that spring had seemed to indicate little hope of a continuing relationship. Based on that, he had pursued Mrs. Smith's suggestion and become engaged to the lady she recommended. He remembered with agony the uneasiness that had set in and his moments of soul-searching to determine if he had made the right decision. How grateful he was that God had shown him his error in time to avoid adverse circumstances!

Art had returned to Window Rock in June 1942 to get supplies before driving on to Rough Rock. While he and another missionary were roofing a mission house one afternoon, they had heard a thundering crunch of metal and breaking glass and had looked up in time to see Emalou's two-door Ford hurtling into the ditch below the mission. It had gyrated across the fence and back onto the road. A pickup load of Navajos had hit the bridge and veered into her car as she and three co-workers were returning from hospital visitation. The graphic memory overwhelmed Art. He now felt the same adrenalin rush he had felt then as he sprinted down the hill, hair flying, and found the top of Emalou's car caved in on her head. It was a wonder he hadn't fainted when he saw the blood running from the long gash across her forehead. Her passengers had not been seriously injured, but they had picked plenty of glass out of their mouths and skin. Art had extracted Emalou from her car and carried her to Mr. Hardy's car nearby, holding her head on his lap all the way to the hospital. He recalled his agonizing certainty that she was the one to whom he should be engaged.

In the emergency room he had stayed by Emalou's side while the doctors cared for the occupants of the other vehicle. When he had notified them about blood pooling under Emalou's shoulders, they had scrambled, placing thirty-six centipede-like stitches across the mountainous lump on her forehead. As soon as she was taken to her room, he had left for California to break his engagement.

As Art finished cleaning and polishing his car, he marveled over God's gracious ways. It had been that awful accident that had solidified his feelings toward Emalou. She was a hard worker, a good missionary, fun to be with, and she could manage on $20 a month. The more he had learned about her, the more he had wanted to learn. How good to know that his mother and the faithful supporters at Sapperton Baptist Church had been praying for God's choice of a companion for him!

Once his car was presentable, Art strolled back to his room to pack a few items. He pictured the encounter with Emalou after his return from California. "You know, I don't like the way we're estranged," he had ventured as they walked across the mission property. "Well, we don't have to be," she had responded. He was glad God had given him insight to his previous behavior toward her and had enabled him to apologize. He had been critical and rigid in his expectations. He must learn to guard against that and to develop as forgiving a spirit toward her as she had shown toward him. He reminisced with joy about the progression of their relationship and grinned to himself as he remembered the time they had hiked up Mt. Elden with a group of young people during a Bible conference. They had become so engrossed in a conversation that they had become separated from the rest. What a look on Mr. Stokely's face when he had met them on the trail! It was then that he and Emalou had realized the importance of avoiding the appearance of evil. With God's help they had maintained a pure relationship and were facing marriage with no regrets.

❖

The long-awaited moment was finally at hand. A gentle breeze from the open window brushed Emalou's flushed face as she donned her street-length dress and shoulder-length veil. By now her co-workers would be assembling in the Clarks' living room decorated with flowers from the garden. She would soon be Art's wife. Could she meet his expectations? Pondering that was a bit unnerving. She glanced at the unscreened window. A momentary thought of escape streaked through her mind.

As strains of "The Wedding March" reached her ears, she turned to walk down the short hall to the living room. "Rachel," she beckoned to the young Clark girl, "go to the living room now with your flower basket." Rachel walked forward, followed by bridesmaid Dorothy Silversmith. Emalou was awed as she entered the living room. Was this happening to her? Art stood at the side of the room, tall, straight, his eyes riveted on her. Beside him was Harrison Moore in Levis and a cowboy shirt. She tried to concentrate while Bible translator Faye Edgerton and fellow worker

Mattie Ward sang: "Savior, like a shepherd lead us, Much we need Thy tender care . . . Be the Guardian of our way . . . Early let us do Thy will."[1] "Yes, Lord," Emalou responded silently to each verse. The words so aptly expressed her and Art's desire.

Papa Clark spoke briefly, committing Art and Emalou to the Lord for His care and guidance. "Do you take this woman . . . ?" Papa Clark asked, turning to Art. "Do you take this man . . . ?" he queried Emalou. Their hearts overflowing, Mr. and Mrs. Art Norris walked out of the living room to enjoy a reception and the good-hearted teasing of friends before leaving on their honeymoon to Gallup, New Mexico.

In spite of war-time rationing, Art had saved two barrels of gas, more than enough for their trip. For $5 a day they stayed at the Log Cabin Motel and ate at a nearby cafe, at least Art did. Emalou's recent tonsillectomy had left her with little desire to eat.

"Let's go explore the 'wild country,'" Art suggested the next day. They saw the sights around Inscription Rock and Ramah, then bumped along a dirt trail northward toward Route 66. "This has to be the quickest way to Gallup," Art assured his bride. "We should be there before dark." Emalou did not relish the idea of spending a night in the wild! Upon reaching the highway, they found a barbed wire fence between them and the pavement. If they wanted to reach Gallup before dark, they had only one option. Loosening the wire, they drove across, replacing it as best they could.

For the next few days the newlyweds shopped for supplies, then drove to Window Rock where Art's mother was staying. "You ready to go see where we're going to live, Mother?" Art asked. "We'll stay in Chinle for a while and commute to Rock Point during the day to work on our house. It's an adobe house the U. S. Government built for Navajos, but they've used it as a winter sheep shelter. Traditional Navajos prefer to live in hogans; hogans don't take as much wood to heat. Pretty logical in an area that doesn't have many trees."

Without love and determination, the adobe house in Rock Point would have remained nothing more than a filthy 14- by 28-foot dwelling with a flat earthen roof. "The owner said the kitchen has a wood floor, but it looks like dirt to me, just like the others!" Art said when he opened the door.

The three Norrises attacked the floor with shovel, broom, and scrub brush. Four vigorous scrubbings later, they indeed discovered a wood floor beneath accumulated layers of sheep dung. The ceiling, black from fly specks, was likewise scrubbed, and the walls were painted with calcimine, a water-based paint. Art replaced one window and washed it and the others until they sparkled. With a small wood stove, a table, and curtained windows, the kitchen took on a homey atmosphere. Art partitioned the large dirt-floored room into a bedroom and a living room, leaving space both above and below the partition for air circulation. Before laying a wood floor in their bedroom, he dug a 6- by 6-foot storage space. "It'll be easier to lift a trap door than to replace firewood and other things that will disappear if we store them outside," he explained.

The morning they pulled their trailer of belongings from Chinle to Rock Point, they got stuck in the Lukachukai Wash. Emalou got out to push. Art took off and she slipped, nearly landing under the wheel. When he reached the other side, he looked back and saw her brushing herself off. They all had a good laugh, but Mother Norris quickly sobered. "I'm going to pray more for you two now that I've seen the kinds of things you face!"

No sooner had the Norrises moved in than Navajos began to come. They wanted to see the Damóo, (Sunday People), as they referred to Art and Emalou. Most showed no displeasure at their presence; some even expressed delight. Among the first visitors were two women and a young girl. "Why are you here?" the girl asked Emalou.

"To tell you about the Savior."

"Well then, tell us," she urged, and the three listened attentively as Emalou told them about Jesus and their need of Him.

Soon ten more visitors crowded into the small kitchen within a thirty-minute period, curious to know what motivated this unusual white couple. Not often did bilagáana (white people) try so hard to learn their language. The unannounced visitors were welcome interruptions. Art spoke about Jesus in Navajo, and the visitors

Visitors at Norrises' Rock Point home

listened quietly, looking at the floor as a custom of respect. After about an hour, most of them rose to leave. One woman lingered. "Why is she staying?" Art heard someone ask.

"Because she believes, that's why!" answered another.

Not long afterward a man with impaired speech came to the door. He tried to communicate with gestures, but neither Art nor Emalou could understand what he wanted. "He wants a needle," Mother Norris said, having observed the interaction. Emalou gave him a needle and he left, satisfied.

Art continually contemplated ways to make things easier for Emalou. He built a rack on the back of the pickup large enough to hold a 55-gallon galvanized barrel. After filling it with water at the school, he rolled it onto the roof of the house and ran a hose from it to the kitchen sink. Under the overhang of the roof he built shelves for butter and other items needing shade. For electricity, he placed a six-volt wind charger on the roof, but it did not produce enough power. The small generator he replaced it with produced sufficient power for lights but not for an iron.

Emalou was grateful for a husband with such God-given abilities. In no sense did the two of them feel deprived. Their humble home was a God-given haven from which they could minister to the needs of these people for whom God had given them such love. It would become a spiritual birthplace for many. No longer working under the restraints of singleness, they would seek to convey God's love in every contact He brought their way. He had made them one, and they delighted in serving Him together.

13
Direction and Redirection

"The mind of man plans his way, but the LORD directs his steps."
– Proverbs 16:9

Immanuel Mission, a Plymouth Brethren group in nearby Sweetwater, had established religious instruction classes in the Rock Point government day school in previous years. The Norrises added a Sunday school. John, the young son of a medicine man, stayed after Sunday school one Sunday. His loop of long black hair was wrapped with white yarn in the traditional manner. "What did you want, John?" Art asked.

Sunday school children
at Rock Point

John fidgeted. "Would you cut my hair?" he murmured, barely above a whisper.

"Cut your hair? Why?"

"I want to go to school, but they won't let me as long as I have long hair."

Art had heard the belief that long, flowing hair represented the wild, dark side of human nature and that traditional Navajos bound it as a means of keeping their wild side controlled. But when he remembered that thousands of Navajo children were herding sheep instead of attending school, he decided to grant the boy's request. He got a pair of scissors and picked up a chair. "Let's go outside," he said.

Before Art was finished, John spied a horse-drawn wagon coming across the valley. "Let's go behind the house," he urged.

"Why?"

"So no one will see me."

Art complied. Breaking tradition was a serious decision for a Navajo boy, especially for the son of a medicine man!

Culture, weather, roads–all affected missionary work. Shopping trips were planned in advance and no more than once a month, sometimes less. During rainy season the Norrises could never be sure if the washes between Rock Point and Farmington, New Mexico, 100 miles away, or Rock Point and Gallup, 150 miles distant, would be passable. And with the dirt trails nearly invisible at times, they could seldom cover more than ten miles an hour. Arriving at Chinle Wash with a load of coal one day, Art and Emalou found the water too high to drive across safely. "We'll have to walk the rest of the way," Art announced. Emalou waded across first and stood waiting for Art, laughing uncontrollably as he sloshed into the water, teetering under the weight of a sack of coal.

Art had hoped to continue the ministry in Rough Rock, but poor roads, distance, and the developing work at Rock Point made frequent trips impossible. God did direct a trip there not long after their arrival in Rock Point. As they prepared to leave, Art put his accordion and the finger-wound phonograph in their vehicle, then placed a broken-handled shovel against the door of their house.

"Why did you do that?" Emalou asked.

"A guarantee against intruders. A broken shovel handle indicates the shovel was used to dig a grave. No one will come near it!"

After the thirty-mile drive to Rough Rock, they spent a discouraging day visiting in widely scattered Navajo camps. Most adults showed no interest in God's Word. "Let's go to the Big Legs camp at the foot of Black Mountain where Tsehe Notah, Joe Yazzie, and I held Sunday services when I lived in this area," Art suggested late in the afternoon.

Barking dogs greeted the Norrises at the Big Legs camp. Mr. and Mrs. Big Legs were away picking pinyon nuts, but their eighteen-year-old daughter and the younger children were home. The children listened and tried to sing along with the Navajo songs as Art played a phonograph record. He explained salvation through Jesus Christ and was delighted when the eighteen-year-old said she believed in Him. It was too late to travel home when they finished. "May we stay here tonight?" Art asked.

"Aoo'" (yes), the children replied. After eating supper cooked over an open fire, the children lay down on their sheepskins and the Norrises settled into their bedrolls. Timidly, one of the children began singing "Jesus Loves Me" in Navajo. The others joined in, but none of them could remember the words. Over and over Art and Emalou sang it with them until they knew it by heart. They taught them several other songs as well before the children dropped off to sleep. Still pondering the children's eager acceptance of biblical truth, the Norrises also fell asleep.

Suddenly, a loud screech pierced the stillness. Everyone awoke with a start and heard a thud, then a meow. The family cat had crawled through the smoke hole and screeched its way down the stovepipe, dropping to the floor. One of the boys grabbed it and shoved it out the door. Again the household slept, but again the cat awoke them. After a third try, the cat won and everyone fell asleep once more. About an hour later, Emalou was startled awake. A rat had darted across her face, followed in a split second by the cat. Emalou bolted upright. She heard a scuffle at her feet, then a steady crunch, crunch, crunch. Mr. Rat would not bother her or anyone else again!

The next morning the Norrises returned to Rock Point intensely burdened for Navajo children. Away from the influence of tradition-bound elders, the children were receptive to the Gospel. Art and Emalou prayed that God would show them how to reach Navajo young people for Christ. When they visited the Big Legs family late in 1943 to arrange for a Christmas program, they found Mrs. Big Legs seriously ill. She had heard the Gospel several times, but they shared it again. "I want to believe," she said, "but I need to have another ceremony first."

"Would you like for us to take her to the hospital?" Art asked Mr. Big Legs.

"No, you had a dead body in your pickup," he replied. "Besides, a medicine man is coming to help her."

A week later the Norrises returned for the Christmas program to discover that Mrs. Big Legs had died and that the hogan had been burned to the ground. The men who had dug her grave sat in a circle of cedar boughs nearby, warming themselves by a pine log fire. "We have to stay here seven days to get rid of evil spirits. The rest of the family is over there," Mr. Big Legs said, nodding and pointing with his lips to a scant brush shelter. What a difference Christ could make! Emalou thought.

Few days were without cultural surprises and challenges. Exploring cliffs near Rough Rock one day, Art found a roughly carved stick of wood nearly six inches long and an inch in diameter. Notched all the way around about an inch from one end, it had two arm-like protuberances extending below the notch on either side. The other end was deeply grooved lengthwise. "What do you think this is?" Art asked a Navajo Christian. "I found it in that cliff."

"Oh, probably a doll some medicine man hid after a ceremony for a pregnant woman. She probably felt her baby twitch and dreamed about a snake. They hid the 'doll' to protect the baby from the snake's spirit."

❖

In January, Art and Emalou took Mother Norris to Los Angeles to visit Art's brother before her return to British Columbia. While in L. A., they talked with Rev. E. C. Eymann, pastor of the church in which Art had been ordained. "Come back with us," they invited when they learned of Brother Eymann's long-standing desire to visit Navajoland. Reverend Eymann was eager to join them. The homeward trip was hampered by an intermittent generator malfunction. Several times Art tried to fix it. In Kingman, Arizona, a mechanic discovered that the brushes were unusable. "You really need a new generator if I can find one," he advised. He found one, but the cost was prohibitive. Instead, Art purchased new brushes for 45 cents and replaced them himself.

Observing the Norrises, Brother Eymann marveled. He had not heard a word of complaint, and the delays did not seem to ruffle them. They moved a step at a time, watching for God's direction, confident that their time was in His hands. This is a lesson I can surely learn from them, he thought. If God isn't in a hurry, I shouldn't be either. I'm sure I miss many blessings by rushing about.

The generator continued to malfunction, and twice the travelers got stuck in deep mud. Near Kayenta, Arizona, the tires were too coated with mud to turn. Numb with fatigue, the Norrises and their guest finally reached Rock Point. Immediately the Navajos began coming. Day and night they came, as many as twenty-five at once, quietly staring into space as Art preached in Navajo.

Back in California again, Reverend Eymann wrote, "I have come to see, I fear only in a small measure, the great need of reaching these people living in heathen darkness and superstition. And, oh! the laborers are few. As I watched that beehive of activity, the home of Brother and Sister Norris, I wondered just how long these dear servants of the Lord can hold out alone. They need help, and they need it badly. May God speedily raise up young people to help. . . ."

God had begun to answer that prayer even before Art and Emalou were married. Art had asked his friend Daniel Taylor if his daughter Effie could help them in Rock Point sometime in the future. Daniel had agreed, and Effie was scheduled to come soon after Easter. In addition to interpreting, she would learn how to give the Gospel in her own language.

Early Easter morning Art and Emalou were roused from a deep sleep. "I think someone knocked," Art mumbled sleepily. They had returned late the night before from an exhausting trip to Gallup and had walked home from the flooded Chinle Wash. Emalou, who was pregnant with their first child, was especially tired.

Art found a young Navajo man standing at the door, his horse nearby. "Yá'át'ééh! " he greeted.

"Aoo', yá'át'ééh!" the young man replied, then fell silent.

After a culturally appropriate time, Art inquired, "Why did you come?"

"My baby went to the place of departed spirits this morning. Will you bury him?"

"We got home very late last night. Can we come a bit later?"

"We can't eat breakfast until baby is buried."

Another death! Art thought. So many Navajos succumb to hunger, unsanitary conditions, and tuberculosis. Half the children five and younger die of a tragic mix of causes. And this family can't even eat until their baby is buried for fear evil spirits will enter them. "We'll come," Art said sadly and returned to the bedroom. "Dear, this man wants his baby buried now so the family can eat breakfast."

They drove to the man's house in the pickup, dust swirling behind them. "Where's the baby?" Art asked the mother. She pursed her lips and nodded up the hill. The tiny body, wrapped in flour sacks, lay by the path in the sun. Beside it were the remains of a small fire and a tin can half full of water.

"Look, Art," Emalou said softly. "I'll bet the mother sat there all night guarding her dying child." Her hand moved lightly over her abdomen as she thought of her unborn baby.

Art carried the body to the pickup and turned to the man. "Come, help dig the grave." The man was afraid even to see what direction Art took the body, but he climbed in. "Where should we bury him?" Art asked.

"Not this way . . . not east. That way." The father directed them several miles west to a sandy place among the bushes. "Here," he said.

They dug a grave, placed the tiny sack-enshrouded form into it, and covered it with dirt. Art had no idea if the father comprehended any of the Scripture he quoted. When he turned to leave, the man cut a branch from a greasewood bush and backed slowly toward the pickup, brushing out his footsteps. With disgust Art thought of anthropologists who advocated the preservation of traditional religion. If only they could see how terrified these people were of evil spirits!

On the way home Emalou brooded over secret fears, the image of that lifeless form etched on her mind. Would her baby be okay? Would the wash be flooded when she was in labor? "Lord, this child is Yours. I know You'll help even if we have to deliver it ourselves."

At the end of May young Effie Taylor arrived, happy that her two favorite bilagáana were expecting a baby. When Art embraced Emalou and kissed her on the cheek while she was cooking, Effie pretended not to notice. But Emalou noticed! "Art, Effie's here!" she'd mutter. "Behave yourself!" He merely laughed.

The month was crammed with activity. Each morning after devotions together the three of them were off and running. Effie helped to clear the table and wash the dishes. Art cared for various needs around the house. "Run to the travel trailer, Effie, and make your bed, then we'll go visiting," Emalou would say.

At the home of the Gilliwood family in Mexican Water, they noticed seven-year-old David lying on the hogan floor staring into space. "The whole time he's home from boarding school, he doesn't go outside or do anything," his parents said, concerned. Art shared the Gospel with the family, wondering if the lad heard or understood. Perhaps God would make a way for him to help the boy someday.

Wherever the Norrises went, they carried first aid supplies, especially salve for impetigo, an infectious skin disease. If they found a child with sores, they cleaned them and applied some of the salve. "Here, take this cream," they instructed the parents. "Take the scabs off and scrub the sores with soap and water even if your child cries, then put some of this cream on them. They may bleed, but that's okay. They'll heal."

When the three of them were not out visiting others, they often had visitors in their home. Some visitors sauntered into the kitchen and lifted the lids off pans to see what Emalou was cooking. Others wanted haircuts or a letter written or read. Many requested medicine for a headache or an ear infection. Some simply sat for hours and watched what went on in a white man's home. Whatever their reason, Art would call, "Effie, come here." With Bible in hand and often with flannelgraph, he would explain in English the need for salvation and how to be saved, and Effie would interpret. A few visitors eagerly agreed to what they heard; most were not convinced. Some said they wanted to think about it.

"You can't wait," Art would urge. "Everyone is bound for hell unless he repents and accepts God's forgiveness. Later might be too late."

"I'm not a sinner."

"God's Word says we're all sinners. I'll pray that you'll trust Jesus before it's too late," Art would reply.

Effie was puzzled. Why does Mr. Norris want an interpreter? He speaks good Navajo. But Art was training a missionary, the kind of training he and Emalou wanted to see multiplied throughout the reservation. They were gratified to see that Effie's grasp of scriptural truth and her adeptness at sharing it were increasing. They loved her as their own and played ball, tug-of-war, and hide-and-seek with her. Together they took walks, went on picnics, and assembled jigsaw puzzles.

"Dear," Art announced one evening three weeks before their baby was due, "I should go to St. Johns and take the U. S. naturalization test. I think I'll go after I drop you and Effie off in Ganado for your prenatal appointment tomorrow."

The day was a blistering one. Since the hospital had no waiting room, Emalou took Effie out under a tree to wait after her appointment. St. Johns was nearly two hundred miles round trip, so it was late afternoon when Art returned for them. About two miles from Rock Point they took a shortcut. "Art, that ditch is too deep!" Emalou exclaimed. "Look at the mud!"

At the bottom of the ditch the car stuck fast. "Guess we'll have to walk," Art announced. Emalou eased her way out and waddled home between her two companions.

With the baby expected soon, the Norrises acquired a folding, screened-in crib. They did not relish the thought of their newborn interacting with the small bull snake they had seen slithering through the house. When labor started, Art drove Emalou to Ganado, then took Effie to her home.

The last day of June 1944 Karen arrived, a tiny white blossom among the black-haired Navajo newborns. While Emalou was still in the hospital, Art visited his Navajo friends, Mr. and Mrs. Manual Denetsoni, at the church in Crystal, New Mexico. The youth group, including the Denetsonis' thirteen-year-old daughter, was playing softball in a nearby field. After a while Mr. Denetsoni called, "Bessie, come here."

Bessie hurried up the hill. "Bessie, do you know Hastiin Náhookǫs (Mr. North)? He'd like for you to help him and his wife for a while. Come, let's go home and pack some clothes."

Bessie had seldom been away from home, but she did not question her father's decision. It probably had something to do with Christian work, and she wanted to serve the Lord. The trip through Wheatfields, Tsaile, and Round Rock to Rock Point was the longest, roughest, most tiring trip Bessie had ever made. When she awoke from a nap, they were still traveling. "How are you doing?" Art asked.

"Okay."

"We're more than half way."

Heat waves ascended from orange-red, burnt-looking rocks and sand dunes. Bessie had never been in this part of the reservation before. It was nothing like the cool, forested area she was used to. Art pointed out places of interest: Pistol Rock, Kissing Rocks, rocks with "windows" in them. Quietly she listened. When they arrived in Rock Point, a young couple, Claude and Pauline Fondaw, greeted her. "Come, Bessie," Mrs. Fondaw said. "I'll show you the small travel trailer where you'll sleep."

"Where is Mrs. Norris?" Bessie asked.

"In the hospital. She just had a baby girl. I'll show you some things you can do to help after she gets home."

The first morning Bessie watched Art. "Here, Tłʼízíʼ" (goat), he called, rattling some corn in a coffee can. Tłʼízí ran to him and jumped onto a large wooden box to eat while he milked her. "Sometimes Tłʼízí wanders off looking for sparse green grass," Art commented. "If that happens, you may have to find her." Bessie soon learned to stand on tiptoe to see over the tall wildflowers while following the tinkle of Tłʼízíʼs bell.

Ten days after giving birth, Emalou returned to Rock Point with baby Karen. The busy days were soon organized into a routine. Karen often lay contentedly in a recycled Pet Milk box looking at colorful canisters on the kitchen counter. One

Karen and Art's goat

morning Emalou picked her up and went down the path to the outhouse. As the two returned, a bull grazing near the house spotted Emalou's brightly-colored housecoat and decided to investigate. Holding Karen tightly, Emalou covered the distance in record time!

Bessie enjoyed helping the Norrises and knew she would miss them when her month with them was over. Sometimes she cleaned the house or hung clean, white baby clothes in the sun; sometimes she rocked Karen to sleep. The Norrises included her in all activities just as they had Effie. One day after she had interpreted for Art, he said, "Bessie, you tell these people a Bible story and sing and pray with them." Several times a week the four of them drove out among the rocks and hills, across washes, and into valleys to visit homes.

On the days they stayed home, they did not lack for things to do. One day a medicine man came to the house looking ill. He was dressed in jeans and a dirty shirt, his long hair tied back in a knot. Emalou checked his temperature and was alarmed to find that it was 104 degrees! No wonder the lice were crawling off him! He lay in the shade while Art prepared to take him to the hospital. As the men drove off, Emalou wondered what deadly disease he possibly might have brought and quietly committed Karen to her merciful heavenly Father.

With a baby, supply trips to Gallup took on a different character. Such trips required a minimum of a day each way, plus a full day of shopping. Ever gracious, their Gallup friends, Andrew and Esther Peterson, kept them overnight and baby-sat Karen. "You two are as vital to our ministry as our prayer and financial supporters are," Art and Emalou assured them.

❖

Art and Emalou continually sought God's direction for their contacts and use of time. That fall an elderly Navajo man stopped by the Norris home. "Who's winning the war?" he asked. Art told him about the German buzz bombs, the conquest of Normandy, and the allied airborne invasion of Holland. Quiet for a moment, the man asked, "How can bombs fly without someone inside to think for them?"

Art tried to answer his questions, then started talking about Jesus. "I was baptized in a church fifty miles from here," the man stated. "Our priest said you folks might be behind the Germans. He told us we should put you out of Rock Point. Our church accepts our ceremonies and the way we pray to our gods, but you Protestants preach against our way of worship."

"If you saw a friend about to walk across a rotten bridge, would you warn him?" Art asked.

"Sure!"

Using Scripture, Art showed him that trusting in other gods was like trusting a rotten bridge. "Jesus Christ alone offers forgiveness of our sin. Trusting in anything else will bring the judgment of hell about which He spoke."

"If you teach that, the people here will make you leave," the man declared.

Rock Point released-time class

The Norrises sought every opportunity to share God's love, especially with the children. Rock Point Boarding School students frequented their home after school, singing songs and listening to Bible stories. Art longed to see them become

Christians, be taught biblical truth, and learn to share the Gospel.

Desiring to establish a more permanent facility, the Norrises had some land surveyed and applied for a piece of property. While awaiting approval from the Navajo Tribe and the U. S. Government, Art had Bill Scott, a Navajo Christian, help him build a storage shed and shade house. No sooner were they finished than Bill wanted to move into the shed with his new wife. Art consented. A short time later he called Emalou to the window. "Look, dear. What a soft life you have!" Bill's bride was hard at work chopping wood. Tenderly Art embraced Emalou and murmured, "What a gift God has given me in you! Our ministry has blossomed since the Lord put us together."

When Art and Emalou first came to the reservation, peyote, a hallucinogenic drug found in the mescal cactus bud, had just been introduced to the Navajos. The tribal council had declared it illegal and incarcerated anyone involved in Peyote ceremonies, a strange mix of Christianity and traditional native religion. The Peyote religion, also known as the Native American Church, was on the rise. During ceremonies participants ate mescal cactus buds and smoked Bull Durham tobacco lit with a burning ceremonial stick. Allegedly, eating the cactus bud brought a feeling of holiness. Some adherents said they could see Jesus, others that peyote was the Holy Spirit, bringing enlightenment and knowledge of God. Many said that the Peyote religion was almost the same as Christianity. Though those using peyote prayed for material blessings, they knew nothing of sin, salvation, heaven, or hell.

"Is it true that Peyote and Christianity are the same?" asked a couple of medicine men who had seized peyote, rattles, feathers, a gourd, and a drum in a raid on a Peyote ceremony.

"Definitely not," Art replied, and proceeded to clarify the difference, happy for the privilege of declaring the preeminence of Jesus Christ.

The Norrises had had many such opportunities to declare biblical Truth in the nearly eighteen months of their marriage. Every

Visitors at the Norris home

day and many nights had been filled with meeting people's needs, building relationships, and sharing God's Word. By March of 1945 Emalou, pregnant with their second child, was exhausted. A miscarriage seemed likely. "You need to go somewhere for rest and regular medical attention," the doctor advised. Their hearts were still in the work, but both she and Art felt that it was time for a year's furlough. If the war were over when they returned and the government granted a land permit, they could build a mission station then. Entrusting the work to Howard and Helen Montgomery from Immanuel Mission, they left for British Columbia. At thirty-five miles an hour, the trip seemed endless.

In New Westminster Art's mother welcomed the family. The luxury of time for rest, reading, and prayer brought improvement in Emalou's condition. They reported on the Lord's work in Navajoland and helped the Canadian Sunday School Mission to plan for summer vacation Bible schools. Feeling the need for additional language study, Art returned to the States for a Wycliffe Bible Translators course in Oklahoma and was there when Paul Stanley Norris entered the world. Three weeks later Art was back in New Westminster with Emalou to dedicate their newborn.

While in British Columbia, Art and Emalou decided to resign from Navajo Bible School and Mission. The distance from mission headquarters was troubling, as was some lack of agreement on theological issues. In March 1946 they resumed their ministries among the Navajos in Rock Point, happy to see that the Sunday meetings and vacation Bible school had continued to bear fruit and that seventy-five children were attending released-time classes.

L - R: Emalou, Paul, Karen, Art

It was good to be back in their own little rental house which they had worked so hard to make into a comfortable dwelling. They were disappointed to learn that the owner wanted it back. The August heat was intense, but with their two small children and expecting a third, they prepared to move to Immanuel Mission in an area known as Sweetwater. The ministry at Rock Point would suffer, since travel from Immanuel Mission took an hour each way. Art loaded their refrigerator onto a trailer and started out, pulling the trailer with his two-door Ford. Twenty miles of hills, sand, and rock lay ahead. On the way out of Rock Point he met the medicine man he and Emalou had befriended.

"Yá'át'ééh!" Art greeted him cordially.

"Aoo', yá'át'ééh!" the old man replied, his wrinkled face expressionless. "Where you going?"

"We're moving to Sweetwater."

"Good. I'm glad."

Smarting at the unexpected reply, Art began the torturous climb up the craggy hill. "Lord, help me to keep my eyes on You. Bring that man and his people to Yourself." With difficulty he inched the car forward. After a short distance the trailer caught on a rock and refused to move. Art revved the car engine to no avail. There was no help within miles. Unhooking the trailer, he drove the car onto a solid rock above it and attached a long rope to it. He pulled forward then recoupled the trailer and car, continuing uphill for seven miles over an almost solid layer of rock, interrupted occasionally by small arroyos. Some stones had to be avoided, others straddled. Constant decisions had to be made as to which rabbit brush- and yucca-lined trail was the main one. At times he was not even sure where the trail was. If he took the wrong one, turning around would be nearly impossible. Each mile seemed to take an eon.

At the crest of the hill Art turned southward along the wind-swept plateau. Here and there the trail disappeared under small sand dunes. Malnourished horses meandered through the brush. Occasional hogans were visible among the sparse vegetation. Protruding into the sky, long rock mesas and tall, red rock fingers lined the horizon. Five miles later the trail veered sharply eastward, winding rapidly downward into a large valley ringed by red and gray mesas. Afternoon shadow patterns fell on folds of mesa walls. At the far edge of the valley, Immanuel Mission's buildings huddled under cottonwood trees. Four hours after leaving Rock Point, Art arrived at their new home. This move had not been his and Emalou's plan, but even a change in the Apostle Paul's circumstances had turned out "for the greater progress of the Gospel." Surely God's hand was in this turn of events, and He would bring honor to Himself through it.

14
Commitment, Fortitude, and Guidance

"In all your ways acknowledge Him, and He
will make your paths straight."
— Proverbs 3:6

Several months after the Norrises had settled into the rock house at Immanuel Mission, Art and a colleague drove to the top of Carrizo Mountain near Teec Nos Pos. Taking pictures during the war had been risky, but with World War II over, Art wanted photographs to send to supporting churches. As he lifted his camera for a panoramic shot, two Navajo men came running. "Let me have that camera!" one of them yelled. "For all we know, you might be a German spy."

"But the war's over," Art explained. War or no war, the insistent men left with the film.

Other effects of the war were evident as well. "Cho'íinii shá ádin" (There is no one to take care of me.), older war widows complained. Government welfare did not exist. Medical help was available to those with transportation, but people accustomed to ceremonies utilizing feathers and rattles and ashes and sand paintings for healing were hesitant to subject themselves to doctors who did little more than prescribe pills.

Early one morning the Norrises were awakened by hoofbeats. "No one ever comes this early. Something must be wrong," Emalou declared.

Art went to the door. "Your grandmother wants you," the visitor urged.

That has to be the old woman who calls me shiyáázh (my son), Art thought. He found her lying outside her home in the cold near a small fire tended by her daughter. One of her eyes looked as though it had burst. "I'm freezing, I'm freezing," she whimpered. "I have no one to care for me. You're the only one. My son, my son, I'm freezing," she lamented weakly and slipped into eternity without Christ. Tears crept down Art's cheeks. Had he done all he could?

That question came to the forefront often as Art contemplated the spiritual needs of those around him. But, there was only so much one couple could do. "We really need help," he told the principal of the Methodist mission school in Farmington, New Mexico. Their daughter Ruth had joined the family in August of 1946. The care of the children, plus food preparation, laundry, and household duties left Emalou little opportunity to help in spiritual outreach.

"Tom Dennison would be a great asset to your work," the principal asserted. "He's one of our Navajo students, a Christian." Art had met

Tom Dennison (center back) and
Navajo family during visitation

Tom at a Bible conference in Flagstaff and decided to invite him to help them during the summer. Tom and two other Navajo youth, Bessie Denetsoni and Lorenzo Iashie, were godsends in the vacation Bible school, telling the children about Jesus in their own language. A Wycliffe missionary taught the children to read the Navajo Bible. The rest of the summer Tom and Art visited homes in Rough Rock, Chilchinbito, Kayenta, Rock Point, Denehotso, and Many Farms.

Maintaining the desired presence in Rock Point was impossible, although Art attempted to do so for a while. Twice weekly the Norrises traversed the trail to Rock Point for Bible classes. Sometimes the road was washed out by flooding or blocked by drifted sand. Art and co-worker Howard Montgomery even tackled a yawning ditch one day, dumping in an old car and covering it with many shovelfuls of dirt.

The remoteness of Immanuel Mission bred other challenges as well. The Shiprock post office was sixty miles away, and road conditions prevented regular mail delivery. The postmistress, a Christian, assured the missionaries that she would unlock the post office anytime they were able to get there. Anyone making it to town picked up mail for the others.

The nearest telephone, the wall crank variety with constant static, was thirty miles distant. Art wondered how emergencies could be handled. When a man in Farmington offered to teach him to use a ham radio, he eagerly accepted, buying a six-volt battery-powered transmitter-receiver from war surplus. The day he successfully contacted Farmington using the Morse Code, he was elated. "You're more excited about that than you were about getting married!" Emalou teased.

Ham radio provided more than a family safeguard. Art was in contact with the U. S. embassy in Korea, stranded Boy Scouts, South Pole researchers, and a group facing possible death in an ocean storm. To overcome the limitations of the Morse Code, he tried building a more versatile set. Although he tinkered Saturday afternoons until midnight that summer with parts salvaged from non-working sets, his attempts failed.

That summer Art, Tom, and other native workers, John Peter Yazzie and Kenneth Foster, undertook several evangelistic trips. Rock Point, Rough Rock, Many Farms, Chilchinbito, Black Mountain, Pinon: they visited them all, even crossing the San Juan River on foot to preach in southeastern Utah. Several people professed faith in Christ

First Bible camp at Immanuel Mission

during that trip and, through the combined efforts of natives and non-natives alike, many of the children who came to the first day camp that summer also trusted Christ.

Requests for burials were as typical at Immanuel Mission as they had been in Rock Point. Art and Howard Montgomery built a casket for one elderly woman from an old sewing machine case and loaded it into the Ford Mercury. The day was unbearably hot as they drove to the woman's home. Seldom was anything simple, and this day's assignment was no exception. After getting stuck, they finally reached the hogan only to find no one home. They dug a grave in cement-like dirt, then entered the hogan for the woman's body. She lay on a sheepskin, covered with blankets. Loosening her hair from the traditional knot as the family had requested, they prepared to transfer her body to the makeshift casket. "That door's pretty narrow," Art commented. "I'll take the head; you grab the feet." He bent down to pick up the body. Suddenly he jumped back, ashen.

Art with
Paul, Ruth, and Karen

"What's wrong?" Howard asked.

"She moved!" The woman had no pulse and her eyes were lifeless. Baffled, they pulled back the blankets. There lay a cat stretching and licking itself. Weakly, Art sighed and returned to the task at hand.

From time to time other moments of crisis arose, some of them related to the outdoor toilet. Discovering a black widow's web over the mission's outhouse hole, the men at Immanuel Mission puzzled over the best way to terminate the spider's existence. A blow torch worked quite well! On another occasion Karen came running. "Mama! Mama! Paul fell in!" The fifteen-month-old was soon rescued and sanitized.

Early in February of 1948, Emalou was taken 150 miles to Rehoboth Christian Hospital near Gallup to await the birth of their fourth child. Ten days later nine-pound Timmy was born. Back at Immanuel Mission Art baby-sat the three other children, a task with which he was not comfortable. Several times he heard an engine and thought someone was bringing Emalou home, but each time his hopes were shattered. Eventually he learned that the engines he had heard were airplanes piloted by females competing in a cross-country race. No one was happier than he when Emalou found a ride home.

Because of the workload involved in caring for family and visitors, Emalou needed household help. She employed a fifteen-year-old girl to hang the laundry on the line. Looking out a bit later, she saw the newly laundered clothing and linens dragging in the dirt. The girl was not familiar with spring clothespins and had placed them upside down. The next helper, whom Emalou asked to bring the clothes in from the line, had never seen a clothes basket, so she laid a newly washed sheet on the ground and dropped all the clothes onto it. At times Emalou felt it would be less trouble to do all the work herself.

About that time Art, Tom, and John Peter Yazzie revisited Rough Rock again on their way to Téliibito'. They worried their way over the jarring road and through Chinle Wash and set up camp near a trickling spring. Every Navajo that came by for water heard God's Word. After breakfast the next morning the men broke camp and drove on. At a small dugout dwelling with a shade shelter, they found an elderly woman caring for three young boys. "Grandma, could we use your fire to make coffee?" Art asked. He watched the three unkempt and hungry-looking lads as the old lady fanned the coals into a flame. A missionary couple had asked him to keep alert for a Navajo boy they could adopt. "Would you like to give one of these boys away?" he inquired.

"For goodness' sake, why not take two!" the grandmother exclaimed. "Their stepfather doesn't want them and there's not enough food for all of us."

The five-year-old began following Art. "What's your name?" Art asked.

"Tully Furry Cap Yellow."

"I'll take Tully," Art told the grandmother. "I'll stop by for him on our way home."

From there the men went to Chilchinbito to visit John Peter's clan mothers. "My relatives will receive us well," John Peter assured them. However, a four-day healing ceremony was in progress at that camp, and the men wondered if they would be allowed to preach.

The medicine man recognized Art immediately. "Oh, you're the one who helped me bury my daughter. You and your friends may preach any time I'm not working on the sand painting." During the morning John Peter gathered his relatives to hear about God's plan to forgive sin. His people had no word for sin, but as they heard God's Word, they were stirred with a realization of their need. That afternoon the missionaries sat around talking while the medicine man worked on the sand painting. Suddenly, a throat-rattling growl pierced the stillness behind them. Art was startled. The medicine man emerged from the hogan twirling a leather strap to which a stick was attached. As the leather whirled, the stick whirred, vibrating faster and faster, its bizarre tones mimicking the growl of an enraged animal. Toward the east, toward the west, toward the north, toward the south he twirled it. He reentered the hogan and Art looked at John Peter.

"To chase away evil spirits," John Peter explained.

At sunset a naked woman was carried into the hogan and placed on the sand painting. The painting was destroyed, but its beauty allegedly entered the woman's body to bring healing. To Art, the whole ceremony seemed unrelated to one's well-being, yet the pattern was the same reservation-wide: one had to appease spirits to achieve healing and wholeness. All ceremonies and prayers existed for that purpose.

The visit finished, it was too late to return for Tully and get home before dark. The weary men camped on a mesa near the road. At midnight they were awakened by voices and the rattling of wagon wheels. The wagon stopped and a man called, "Will the missionary drive this man to Kayenta?"

Art went to investigate. "This man didn't observe a marriage custom when he was young. He's having terrible stomach pain," the night visitors explained. "The handshaker says he needs ceremony in Kayenta." Deeming the trip useless, Art chose not to take him. As the rumble of the wagon and the cracking of a whip faded into the distance, he tried again to sleep.

Early the next morning as the men prepared to leave, a Navajo man appeared. "How can I get saved?" he asked. "What would I have to do if I became a Christian?" The more he heard, the more curious he became. "Come to my home and tell me more," he begged. The men followed him to his home and answered questions until noon.

"Cook them a meal," the man ordered his wife.

After listening a while longer, the man announced, "I'd like to become a Christian."

The man's wife immediately showed her displeasure with her husband's decision. "If he becomes a Christian, there'll be a lot of things he'll have to do."

The man's countenance fell. He hung his head. "I'll think about it," he mumbled.

Saddened, the men left for Téliibito' to get Tully. While talking briefly with the grandmother, they saw Tully getting into the car. Back at Immanuel Mission, when Art learned that the couple no long desired to adopt, he and Emalou accepted Tully into their home. With four children of their own ranging in age from infancy to four years, some major adjustments were ahead for both Tully and the family. Emalou had just figured out how each of their family of six could have two eggs a week. Her concern grew as Tully devoured everything served to him, plus all that was left after the others were finished. Even what he ate was wasted because his tiny stomach was simply unable to retain such volume. Some weeks elapsed before his eating habits stabilized. The days were trying in other ways as well. To Emalou, the weird whirring of Tully's homemade eight-foot rope whip, similar to the one used by the medicine man, was nearly unbearable, and his mischievous ways were a real trial for the Norris children.

Art had been thinking about the great help John Peter Yazzie had been to him when he lived in Rough Rock. He believed he would be a real asset at Immanuel as well and invited him to come. He did whatever was necessary to accommodate John Peter's needs. To help John Peter to support himself, he bought him a torch, silver solder, jewelry tacks, and rolls of dimes with which he could make jewelry. John Peter could sell $10 worth a day. His joyful smile belied the challenge of his crippling arthritis. Everywhere they went, Art carried him to and from the car. John

Norris family with John Peter Yazzie (Tully beside Art)

Peter had greatly improved in his ability to present the Gospel since Rough Rock days, and he shared it with children and adults alike. The children in Rock Point's released-time classes loved to listen to him.

Returning to Immanuel Mission one afternoon after the Rock Point classes, Art and John Peter had a frightening experience. Summer months often brought monsoon rains. The blue of the early morning sky frequently gave place to dark, angry-looking clouds. By afternoon, lightning would stab the sky repeatedly and thunder would roll. Sprinkles of rain became torrents, sometimes accompanied by hail. This particular afternoon such a storm had just passed. The road was a greater disaster than usual. Art

115

feared a flash flood in Walker Creek or deep holes in the creek bed. He had crossed many such washes. Falling into a hole or getting stuck took absolutely no effort. If the car stalled, he probably could not get John Peter out in time. He stepped into the frigid water. He found no holes, but before driving across, he carried John Peter to the other side. All went well and they arrived home safely. Taking such risks was a small price to pay for the privilege of proclaiming God's life-giving message.

Many times Art had shared this message with a Navajo man living close to Immanuel Mission. Because the man usually wore a long, brass-buttoned World War I Army coat, he was known as Make-Believe Soldier. "I'm following the ways of my mother," the man had maintained. When he became seriously ill, the missionaries increased their efforts to tell him of Jesus. One day as Lorenzo Iashie talked with him, Make-Believe Soldier began breathing heavily and died.

Such events were discouraging. In spite of the missionaries' faithfulness, disturbingly few Navajos embraced Christ and grew in Him. "Many people are coming to Christ in Haiti," Howard Montgomery lamented to Art. "I'd like to go to a place like that."

Knowing that Christ was the only hope, the Norrises kept on keeping on by God's grace. John Peter's uncompromising faith encouraged them. He visited his family during a ceremony for his pregnant sister. His family and friends taunted him when he refused to participate. "Come on. You eat corn; why not take a pinch of the pollen?"

"I'm a Christian," John Peter replied boldly. "Corn is part of my food, but I will not eat something used to pray to false gods."

Jimmy Begay was another encouragement. Like several other Navajo Christians torn from their homes to serve their country, Jimmy had returned from World War II determined to take the Gospel to his people. Their spiritual condition weighed heavily on him. He was only one of two ordained Navajo ministers at the time, having studied at Practical Bible Training School in New York. In Army fatigues, driving an Army jeep, and carrying guns, bows and arrows, cooking utensils, and games for children, he traversed the reservation looking for opportunities to speak for his Savior. At each stop he put up basketball hoops and invited people to gather, providing food and recruiting women to cook it. After the meal, he preached the Gospel in Navajo. Person after person heard and believed, passing from darkness into the light of Jesus Christ.

Art cheered Jimmy on. One day he rode with Jimmy over a road that was little more than a trail, one which was new to Jimmy. "Take a left here," Art directed, or "Angle off to the right." Repeatedly Jimmy lifted his cowboy hat and put it back on. "Jimmy," Art asked after a while, "why do you keep removing your hat?"

"I'm asking the Lord to show me where the road is," Jimmy replied reverently.

Sometime later Art appeared unannounced at one of Jimmy's evangelistic meetings. Jimmy read from the Bible, kissed it, then began to pray. "Oh, how I love You, my Lord Jesus Christ! Oh, how I love You! Thank You for saving me. Thank You for sending missionaries to us with this Good News." Art was touched and wished the scene could be multiplied many times over on the reservation.

One day Jimmy came to Art. "Brother Norris, I want to take the Gospel to the most needy place on the reservation. Can you tell me where that is?"

Without hesitation Art replied, "Lukachukai. Protestant missionaries serve at Chinle, Rough Rock, Rock Point, and a whole lot of other places, but there has never been one in Lukachukai."

Jimmy went to Lukachukai and preached with fervor. Before long he received a letter from the Anglo superintendent of the Navajo Reservation. "Since you are ordained," the letter read, "you are no longer classified as a Navajo. Get off the reservation." Jimmy drove south to the Navajo Tribal Council office in Window Rock and requested permission to speak to the council, many of whom were graduates of reservation mission schools. When he finished sharing the Gospel and showing pictures of his activities on the reservation, the council members clapped loudly. "Jimmy, very few Navajos have gotten a diploma and come back to help our people. You go right on doing what you're doing. Our people need this!" They even passed a hat to collect donations for him.

Nine months had passed since Art had submitted an application for a mission site in Rock Point, and the tribal council still had not considered the request. Obtaining reservation land was seemingly impossible. Art looked for property in Huerfano, Kirkland, and Waterflow, New Mexico, as well as in Cortez and Rico, Colorado. He turned down a position with Wycliffe Bible Translators, knowing that he functioned best in direct contact with people. A decision had to be made: Karen was ready for the first grade and Immanuel Mission had no school.

Both Art and Emalou sensed the Holy Spirit's leading to Cortez, Colorado, but additional funds would be needed to purchase property. God provided jobs hauling mud from well drillers, carrying mail, and doing carpentry and construction work. Early Monday mornings Art drove to Cortez to work. He lived in his old travel trailer during the week and returned to Immanuel Mission on weekends. Finally, there was enough money to purchase three acres, which included an acre of alfalfa, a rock ledge, an irrigation ditch lined with Chinese elm trees, three very crude Indian ruins, and many pieces of broken pottery. The layout and location would permit the development of a Bible camp close enough to the Navajo Reservation to allow endless ministry opportunities. A tent house would suffice for the family's basic needs. They were certain that God would provide whatever else they might need in the process of declaring the eternal riches of Christ.

15
Earthly Concerns, Heavenly Focus

"Whatever you do, do your work heartily, as for the
Lord rather than for men."
– Colossians 3:23

E malou, let's have a Bible camp in Cortez before we move there.
Tom Dennison and some other Navajo Christians could help," Art
proposed in June of 1948. The experience at their first day camp and

with the Big Legs children five years
earlier had convinced him and Emalou
of the effectiveness of children's
ministries.

Art began making arrangements at
once. On the appointed day he drove
their half-ton truck to Sweetwater,
Rock Point, and Mexican Water to pick
up the children. He and the boys slept

1948 Bible camp in Cortez

in a borrowed church, and Emalou coped with her own four and the girls
in a borrowed house. Since the children did not bring a change of clothing,
Emalou scrubbed their clothes by hand every night and hung them on the

line to dry. Every morning the
children heard Bible stories in
their own language, most for the
first time. In the afternoons they
swam or learned Indian history
at Mesa Verde National Park.
Before the camp was over, they
were begging for another one.

Robert and Tully herding sheep

One camper, Tully's nine-year-old brother, Robert, stole Emalou's heart. "Art, let's keep Robert for the summer," Emalou suggested. At summer's end they took him in permanently. Neither he nor Tully was legally adopted, but both took the Norris name.

After Bible camp, volunteers helped Art build a three-foot high frame with high rafters on the newly purchased property. Over the rafters they stretched an 8- by 10-foot canvas tent. The tent house would serve as living quarters and Art's old travel trailer as sleeping quarters. On July 4, 1948, the family moved into their simple home surrounded by sagebrush and an alfalfa field. Tall bronze-colored grass fronds glistened and swayed in morning breezes. Bright yellow dandelions and other wildflowers added splotches of color to the nearby rolling hills. Meadowlarks warbled their gurgling, flutelike songs down by the irrigation ditch. To the south rose the La Plata Mountain Range. Art surveyed the three acres and envisioned a Bible camp center.

With a number of possibilities swirling in his head, Art set to work dealing with down-to-earth matters as well as with ministry plans. The rainy season insured an abundance of bottomless mud. Getting from place to place often took hours. Art did not enjoy getting stuck, but he did enjoy driving in mud, slithering from side to side. "When challenges don't appear naturally, you invent them," Emalou teased one day when he whipped off the road and started up a wash.

Bible camp children

There was so much to do, so little time to do it. Art received several job offers, but he plunged headlong into ministry activities, pursuing part-time employment only as necessary. The spiritual welfare of Navajo children was the primary focus.

At their second Cortez Bible camp Art and Emalou were spurred on by the testimony of a young girl. "Thank you for giving me this Word," she said, holding up her New Testament. "I have taken Jesus as my Savior."

Feeding ravenous campers kept Emalou working overtime. She had barely finished preparing oatmeal on the wood-burning stove before starting on peanut butter sandwiches for lunch. Then it was time to make tortillas and cook stew or beans and rice for supper. Occasionally wild greens added color and vitamins. Whatever the menu, leftovers were non-existent! At week's end the children begged, "Can we

1949 Bible camp
(Bill Craigo teaching)

stay? Can we?" Their pleas nearly broke Art's and Emalou's hearts. Were there other ways God wanted them to minister to these children?

After camp Art turned his attention to securing a warmer home before winter. "If you'll draw up the plans, I'll pay to have your house built," a friend wrote. Soon a neighbor with two mules and a shovel was digging a basement. A cement floor was poured, and sand and gravel were hauled in to make cement blocks for the walls. Their generous friend died before the house could be completed, so the top of the basement was simply enclosed and covered with tar paper.

The basement home was warmer than the tent house, but winter weather brought new challenges. Sliding down snowy wooden steps was inevitable. Frost collected on the ceiling and dripped over everything as it melted. Occasional downpours flooded the basement, necessitating bailing water out by the bucketful. The drying out process was a lengthy one. "Visitors who think our little basement house is so nice haven't been here at the right time!" Emalou groaned after one rain storm.

Both Emalou and Art were masters at making do. A heavy flatiron kept the door of the wood stove shut. Orange crates served as cupboards. There was little furniture, no running water and no electricity. Saturday night's bath water was heated in a tub on the stove. Though grocery money was scarce, the Jersey cow gave plenty of milk and cream. When a guest once asked for a piece of bread and Emalou replied, "I'm sorry, but we don't have any," the embarrassed friend bought them six loaves; then it was Emalou's turn to be embarrassed.

At times the garden produced little more than squash. Although variety was sometimes lacking, God always provided adequate food and often in unique ways. One Thanksgiving the family found a box of groceries by the basement door. "Oh, somebody thinks we're needy!" Emalou commented, chagrined, remembering that her father had thought it shameful to be on welfare. Nevertheless, she gratefully recognized God's gracious hand.

The Norrises began to establish friendships with the Navajos in McElmo Canyon, some of whom were open to the Gospel. Before long a letter arrived from a government official: "You don't have authority to work on the Navajo Reservation. You'd better stop it." What lay behind the letter, Art and Emalou had no idea, but they ignored it. It was obvious that the Lord was laying groundwork for future outreach in the area.

With Art's encouragement, Tom Dennison had attended Prairie Bible Institute. The summer of 1949 Tom brought Rex Winter, Johnny Myers, and Fred Phelps home with him to assist in reservation outreach. The students reveled in the reservation's uniqueness: unfamiliar customs, magnificent rock formations, spectacular canyons, and peaceful desert stillness. Dark-eyed children and infants in cradleboards fascinated them, as did velveteen- and jewelry-clad women busily weaving hand-dyed wool rugs. They saw in the Navajos the same gentle demeanor they had appreciated in Art. Their encounters with reservation sand and mud made them appreciate not only Art's patience but the winch on his panel truck as well!

One day Tom and Fred announced, "We're going to walk to Immanuel Mission and do hogan visitation." Art dropped them off at the confluence of Montezuma Creek and the San Juan River in southwestern Utah. They witnessed to the ferry operator, then set out on the sixty-mile trek. Fred had ignored the advice of a seasoned Navajo and subsequently suffered blisters, sunburn, and dehydration. The gallon of waffle syrup he had brought for energy and nourishment was no substitute for water! Furthermore, the label showing steaming waffles and a grinning man about to eat them mocked him every time he looked at it. Providentially, the men found a windmill, filled their water bags, and pushed on, finally arriving at their destination and fulfilling their mission.

After Bible camp was over that summer, Emalou set out with four-year-old Paul and three-year-old Ruth to take campers home. "Why don't you leave the children here while you deliver the campers?" a friend at Immanuel Mission suggested. Gratefully Emalou accepted the offer, and her gratitude deepened with each passing mile. The ride was long and hot; the car got hopelessly stuck in the sand for several hours.

Meanwhile at Immanuel, Paul and Ruth were put down for a nap, but they did not sleep. "I know how to get home," Ruthie whispered to Paul.

"So do I," Paul boasted.

They slipped out of bed and started down the dusty road. They had not gone far before Ruthie whimpered, "I want a drink." A little farther on, she announced, "I have to go to the bathroom." Step after step they trudged in the hot sun.

Awaking from a nap, the babysitter peeked into the bedroom. No children! Frantically she called, "Paul! Ruth!" No answer. Summoning co-workers, she jumped into the car and tore down the dirt road. "There they are!" she sighed with relief, pulling alongside the two wanderers. Sweat cascaded down their dusty faces. "Where are you going?" the sitter asked kindly.

"Home!" Paul answered. "We would've been there if Ruthie hadn't had to go to the bathroom!"

Later, hearing the story, Emalou nearly collapsed. How gracious of God to care for her precious children and prevent them from leaving the road in search of a shorter way home!

For some time the Norrises had contemplated the benefits of uniting again with others who were evangelizing the Navajos. In fact, several missionaries had met to discuss mutual concerns after the failed governmental attempt to expel Jimmy Begay from the reservation. They wondered if similar attempts would be made to curtail their ministries. Another group in the area claimed to represent Protestant Navajo missions but denied some fundamental Christian principles. Several missionaries, including Art Norris, Charles Girton, David Clark, and Warren and Price Allen, formed the Association of Evangelical Missionaries. The association later expanded to include Navajos and was renamed Evangelical Navajo Fellowship.

Beyond participating in that association, the Norrises had been praying about a combined mission effort with Charles and Iris Girton. Friends since the early 1940s, both couples ministered among the Navajos and shared similar goals. They chose an organizational name and drew up bylaws, but before completing the legal papers, the four of them learned of an existing organization needing experienced leadership. Navajo Indian Gospel Crusade (NIGC) had been founded in 1945 by George and Connie Moore and incorporated in New Mexico in 1947. No longer able to endure the rigors of reservation life due to health, Mr. Moore had asked Charles if he and Iris would assume NIGC's ministries. His invitation seemed to be the answer to prayer for direction, and together the Girtons and Norrises accepted the challenge.

16
The Fringes of His Ways

"Behold, these are the fringes of His ways; and how faint a word
we hear of Him! But His mighty thunder, who can understand?"
$$- \text{Job } 26:14$$

W e really should articulate our goal," Art began as he, Emalou,
and Charles and Iris Girton sat down in the living room of the
Norrises' basement home.

"President Truman's goal is a chicken in every pot. Maybe we should
strive for a peanut in every hogan," Charles quipped, reaching for the can
of peanuts on the coffee table.

It was 1950. Laughter abounded as the Norrises and Girtons, now in
their mid-30s, met to discuss ways to develop NIGC. They agreed that
the mission should be a fundamental, nondenominational, and faith-based
organization fulfilling the Great Commission and training Navajo Christian
leaders. The Girtons would develop the ministry at Pine Haven, New
Mexico, and oversee outreach in the southern part of the reservation.
The Norrises would continue Bible camps and leadership training and
plant churches in the reservation's northern area. Charles and Art would
share the directorship. The mission would be incorporated in Colorado
as well as in New Mexico and would assume ownership of the Cortez
property.

Despite the Girtons' nearly ten years of experience and the Norrises'
twelve, the venture was a colossal one. Before parting that day, the four
trustingly sang,

> " 'Tis Jesus, the First and the Last,
> > whose Spirit shall guide us safe home.
> We'll praise Him for all that is past,
> > and trust Him for all that's to come."[1]

That spring two young men, two ladies, and a child accompanied Tom Dennison from Prairie Bible Institute. "They came to help for six months," Tom explained. Though grateful, Art and Emalou had not counted on housing and feeding five extra people on a pledged income of $40 a month. However, the students had brought a crate of low-grade eggs, a welcome addition to the ever-present pinto beans, rice, and squash.

The students set to work making cement blocks for a chapel which the mission hoped to construct the following summer. They shared the Gospel in Navajo and Ute homes and started a rescue mission in Cortez. As the fruitful summer drew to a close, the Norrises began planning for a visit to supporting churches and individuals. Reporting to them was vital to the continuance of the ministry, but Emalou was concerned. "Art, we don't have enough cash for such a trip."

"We'll have to borrow from the war bond Karen received at birth," he replied. Six-year-old Karen entered the bank with her dad. He lifted her to a high counter and, after she signed her name on the line the teller indicated, the teller gave her dad some money. She didn't quite understand what had transpired, but she knew she had helped the family through a tough time.

When the Norrises returned from their visit with supporting churches, their first major milestone was incorporating NIGC in Colorado in 1951. Board members were chosen and staff members were gradually added. For two decades the funds raised by the Norrises supported their family, sustained the development of Bible-training facilities, and supplemented inadequate incomes of other staff members. Spreading an annual income of $1500 that thin necessitated careful stewardship! That was only one of many seemingly impossible feats orchestrated into reality by the Holy Spirit.

From the outset Art sensed urgency in evangelizing Navajo families pouring into the mining town of Rico, Colorado, fifty miles northeast of Cortez. While surveying the town to assess the advisability of opening such an outstation, he and Charles met a Mormon bishop who had invited them to come to his house Sunday afternoon for refreshments.

"You know, I wonder if the bishop thinks we're Mormon missionaries," Charles mused aloud.

At four o'clock Sunday afternoon they arrived at the bishop's home. A full-course meal graced his dining room table. The two, still stuffed from a steak dinner, dared not glance at each other. "Please sit down," the bishop invited. Turning to Charles, he asked, "Elder Gurpin, would you please give thanks?" "Elder Gurpin" sputtered through a brief prayer while Art was overtaken with a sudden fit of coughing!

The trip netted more than an amusing story to tell. It confirmed the need for an evangelical missionary in the area. Immediately Art and the family began going to Rico each Sunday to establish an outreach among the Navajo mine workers.

Cortez was also a spiritually needy town. Increasingly, the Norrises were becoming aware of the problems with alcohol there. Prior to World War II the sale of liquor to Navajos in Cortez was illegal, but the early 1950s brought a change. Art and Emalou often agonized over the victims of alcohol they saw in the gutters or on the sidewalk. Usually they'd pick them up and seek help for them, sometimes taking them to their own home to feed them and tell them about Jesus.

With the expanding ministries, more facilities were needed. Hearing about Civilian Conservation Corps (CCC) barracks for sale in the mountains north of Mancos, Art investigated. The buildings, which had housed sheep for a time, were full of droppings, but he envisioned affordable mission facilities and purchased all twelve units for

Moving CCC barracks

$4000. "I don't know how you'll move them!" Charles declared, but he had seen Art, with God's help, do the impossible before. Grateful for God's provision, Art sold two of the buildings to pay for moving the others.

God's care for the Norrises was manifested in other ways as well. Clothing for the growing family came via "mission barrels," boxes of used items sent by people from across the country. Mrs. Bud Salter and other mission supporters sent clean, mended, and pressed items. At times, shipments from other sources contained clothing not as presentable. Most of the clothing met a real need, but some items offered little

Mission "barrel"

practical value. The Norris girls spent hilarious hours rummaging through the boxes, attiring themselves in a variety of outfits. One day just as they had the living room floor carpeted with corsets, holey socks, high-heeled shoes, dirty blouses, a grass skirt, used tea bags, and tidbits of ribbon and string, a well-to-do supporter drove up. "Quick, kids!" Emalou directed, horrified. "Get those things back in the box!"

The down side of having their own clothing "store" was that the girls were wearing tight skirts when full ones were in and full skirts when tight ones were popular. Though the children wore mostly hand-me-downs, Emalou insisted that they have new shoes to prevent ruined feet.

Navajos benefited from the mission barrels as well. After a rainy day picnic, Emalou clothed all twenty of the Bible camp children and took their muddy clothes to the Laundromat. At Christmastime Navajos swarmed around the reservation distribution site eager for winter coats. After one distribution, Art's own coat was missing and he had to search the barrel for another.

God often gave Art ideas of ways to solve problems related to daily living. He built a road from the highway into the mission by pulling a scraper behind Emalou's old Ford. When antifreeze rose to $6 a gallon, he substituted diesel fuel, eventually concluding that draining the radiator nightly was best.

One morning as Art prepared to install a septic tank, he warned the children, "You kids go sit on that hay stack while I set off this dynamite."

Standing nearby to count the number of blasts, Emalou overheard five-year-old Ruth. "Sandra," she said to her five-year-old cousin, "if you believe in the Lord right now, you can be saved. If you aren't saved and that dynamite goes off wrong and kills you, you won't go to Heaven."

That summer PBI students came once again to help. George and Edith Palm also came in their small homemade "house on wheels" to teach children's classes and assist in moving the recently purchased barracks to

George and Edith Palm, Tom Dennison

the mission property. To keep food on the table for everyone, gardening was vital, and summers kept Emalou busy canning. Often she canned at night after everyone else was in bed. One morning she put some beans on to cook for dinner and asked Bill Craigo, a PBI student, to watch the pressure cooker while she ran some errands.

"I'd be happy to. Just tell me what to do," he said.

"Well, when steam blows out that little hole, put this weight over it. When the pressure gauge reaches 10 pounds, lower the flame just enough to keep the gauge at 10 for 25 minutes."

Bill placed the weight at the proper time then became absorbed in a book. Before long the lid blew off. Bill jumped to his feet. By God's grace, he was uninjured, but Emalou returned to find beans clinging to the ceiling and walls. For months she swept beans from unlikely places!

From the beginning of their ministry Art and Emalou determined not to give undue attention to demons or stories of demonic activity, focusing instead on Christ. That determination was tested one night when Art was away. A Navajo friend of Emalou asked if she could stay all night. "We don't have a spare bed, but you may sleep on the floor," Emalou answered.

During supper the friend told about a time she had seen a large wolf-like creature coming toward her while she was herding sheep. Uncertain what it was, she had driven the sheep to the corral with the help of the sheep dogs. Leaving the dogs outside, she had locked the door and built a fire. The sheep dogs had barked frantically and backed closer and closer to the hogan. Eventually their barks had turned to yelps of fear and pain. Suddenly, feeling a blast of cold air from the direction of the door, she had jumped into bed and covered her head, yelling "Go into the fire! Go into the fire!" Then her stove had started bouncing.

The Norris children listened spellbound. "O God! Shield them from any ill effects," Emalou pled. By the time the story was finished, all the dogs in the Norris neighborhood were howling, especially those to the north and west. The experience was unnerving.

Sometime later, that friend asked Emalou to take her to the hospital in Shiprock. Arriving in the evening after the doctor had left, Emalou wasn't sure what to do. "You may sleep on a cot in your friend's room," the nurse told her.

During the night Emalou's friend began to mutter. "Are you in pain?" Emalou asked.

"No, he's talking to me at the window."

"Who?"

"You know."

"No, I don't." Emalou was puzzled. Her friend professed to be a Christian, but she was extremely agitated. As Emalou prayed aloud and spoke the name of Jesus, her friend became calm. Whether her friend's behavior had been caused by mental illness or demonic harassment, she did not know, but she was grateful for God's protecting power.

Art and Emalou prayed for God's protection for themselves and their family during physical challenges as well. One fall day Art met a needy Navajo Christian in the Chilchinbito area. Emaciated from tuberculosis, Chris Doctor told Art, "The doctor sent me home from the sanitarium. He said that the sanitarium is only for people who will survive."

The Norrises felt certain that God wanted them to care for Chris, but how? They, their four young children, and the two Navajo boys still lived in the crowded basement house with no modern conveniences. Finally, they decided to set up a bed for Chris in their 6- by 6-foot shed behind the house. Every dish that left that shed was sterilized to keep the dreaded disease from the family. Art spent hours reading Navajo Scripture to Chris and teaching him to read. Gradually Chris gained strength and although he still looked like a ghost, when Art prepared to visit reservation homes the following spring, he announced, "I want to go with you." His witness was invaluable, for in each home he told what God had done for him through Christ. Art eagerly took him on subsequent trips, overwhelmed by God's obvious blessing in and through his life. When Chris was well enough, he returned to his home, bought an old bicycle, and rode around his home area reading the Navajo Bible to anyone who would listen.

"Mommy," Paul said one day as Emalou put a Band-Aid on his hand, "I love your hands."

"I love your hands too, Paul," Emalou assured him.

"Mommy, you and I were born at the same time, weren't we?"

"Yes, Paul, I was there when you were born."

With all the demands on her time, Emalou needed assistance. Eleanor

Beverly arrived in 1951 to minister to the Navajo women and the Norris family. She taught ladies' Bible studies and helped care for the children and household chores.

Eleanor was not the only answer to Art and Emalou's prayers. As the Cortez facility developed, God continually sent equipment and workers. Someone donated a gasoline-fired cook stove into which one had to pump air before lighting. Although grateful for the stove, Emalou was relieved when it was replaced, since its flames sometimes blazed to the ceiling. From the government surplus warehouse in Denver, Art obtained trucks, tractors, lumber, printing presses, and paper cutters at discount prices, all items that contributed to the expansion of the ministries.

In 1952 Art assigned Eleanor and newcomer Pat McIntosh to the outreach efforts in McElmo Canyon near the John Ismay Trading Post on the Colorado/Utah border. He decided to move the family's old tent house to McElmo to house the ladies. He and volunteer Al Miklos loaded it on a truck and started the twenty-eight miles through the canyon. En route, the back tires broke through a spot which had been undermined by water. The men took a 55-gallon barrel off the truck and rolled it into the small cavern beneath the wheel. By placing a jack on the barrel

Pat McIntosh (left) and Eleanor Beverly in McElmo Canyon

and jacking up the truck, they were able to pull the truck forward. The tent house was delivered unscathed.

A few months later when Eleanor married Paul Afflerbaugh, the couple remained at McElmo; Pat was reassigned to Rico. Life in Rico was hard and the work slow, but Pat enjoyed the challenge. One Sunday

Pat's home in Rico

morning she suggested to two Navajo assistants that they all visit a family that had previously shown interest in Scripture. At the hogan, she prayed while the girls gave testimonies and read from the Bible in Navajo. As they rose to leave, an old woman gently enfolded Pat's hands in hers and spoke to the girls in Navajo. Pat turned for an explanation. "She wants to know if she has to know English to be a Christian," the girls explained. "We told her no." The following Sunday the woman became a Christian.

Hearing of people who were coming to Christ brought great joy to the Norrises. The birth of Faith, their third daughter, and opportunities for the growing NGC staff to share the Gospel were other events that gladdened their hearts.

L-R: Paul Norris, Tom Dennison,
Mr. and Mrs. Big Legs

In the spring of 1953 Art and Tom Dennison visited a ragged, 9- by 12-foot canvas home. A dying goat, two cats, and an active puppy shared the dirt floor with nine children younger than fifteen years of age. Four adults soon joined them. No chairs, no table, no beds. As Tom preached the Good News in the family's heart language, Art leaned against a broken sewing machine and surveyed the poverty-ravaged scene. These people definitely needed the Gospel, but their lack of creature comforts was also great.

Later, back at the mission at a staff prayer meeting, Art said thoughtfully, "I believe God wants us to have a Bible reading school. Young people are clamoring to stay after the Bible camps are over. They have little to do at home and should learn to read and write. The new way of writing the Navajo language that the government and Wycliffe Bible Translators developed is easier to read than the old one, so we could teach students to read Navajo Scripture and ground them in the faith. Properly trained, they could minister to their own people better than we can."

"DBI meant so much to me when I was a new Christian," Emalou added. "I'd like to see a full-fledged Bible school here to train those who really want to serve the Lord. Of course, we'd have to have more workers for that."

The staff concurred that some kind of Bible-training ministry was desirable. Prior to World War II Navajos had balked at the government mandate to send their children to boarding schools. To them, leaving the boundaries of their four sacred mountains meant trouble. During the war, Navajo men had lived far beyond the sacred mountains, where some had died. Those who returned, however, demanded education. Now many parents coveted education for their children. Government and mission boarding schools were burgeoning on and near the reservation like desert flowers after a spring rain.

With that in view, Art sought parental permission for campers to stay after the 1953 Bible camp. That fall Navajo Bible Reading School (NBRS) was launched. Students boarded on campus and attended the local public school during the day. Afternoons and evenings they studied Bible and Navajo Reading.

About that time Von and Edna Stillhammer joined the staff and moved to a small dwelling on the mission property. They brought with them a contagious sense of joy. Von, a gifted carpenter, transformed the CCC barracks into a warm, useful educational center. He even placed one

Edna and Von Stillhammer with Bible school students

building over the Norrises' basement to provide additional room and an improved view.

Gradually, the staff felt that students would receive greater benefit from attending school full time at the mission, so plans were made to add English and mathematics to the curriculum in 1954. Anyone twelve years and older could attend NBRS without previous schooling. Soon seventeen students were enrolled. Art taught Bible and Navajo reading; Von Stillhammer, Tom Dennison and his Mohawk fiancée, Arlene Isaac, also taught Bible. Each afternoon students worked on campus for tuition, room, and board. With the distinct advantage of knowing both language and culture, students were taken to the reservation every Sunday to proclaim Christ.

Staff schedules were heavy. Rosemary Foote, who had joined the staff in late 1953, although not trained as an educator, briefly observed a first grade teacher in the public school, then began teaching. Her kindergarten to ninth-graders ranged in age from eleven to twenty-two. Teaching English and math to teens who had had only a smattering of formal education was a major challenge.

Emalou had her hands full cooking all the meals for the student body as well as for her own family. Often the family ate in the dining room with the students. Rosemary helped all she could, but Emalou was grateful when Dorothy Hecker arrived early in 1954 to cook for the school.

The stresses of ministry and family, a prolonged remodeling project, and constant wind, heat, and dust, left Emalou exhausted. Usually she endured trying times with quiet patience, but she had reached her limit. While Art and Von were away on an extended trip, her cupboards became bare, her wallet empty. Heatedly she poured out her soul to Edna, whom she perceived as far more godly than she. "How could Art leave me like this? Robert and Tully are out with their relatives right now, but I still have five hungry mouths to feed. What am I supposed to do?"

"Emalou, you'll just have to trust the Lord," Edna said gently.

Trusting the Lord was the farthest thing from Emalou's mind. "I'm mad, and I want to be mad!" she bellowed, regretting it even as the words spilled from her mouth. Edna prayed with her, asking God to intervene. He did, not only by prompting people to bring food but by enabling Emalou to relinquish her anger.

After one of the summer Bible camps Art loaded jabbering children into the Suburban to take them home. As he drove, he pondered their meager circumstances. Suddenly he saw a ditch across the road. He jammed on the brakes, but it was too late. The front wheels dropped into the ditch and the tie rod buckled. The children fell silent. The front wheels were turned inward. There was no garage within miles. "You children look for some big rocks," he directed. Jacking up the front wheels, he stacked rocks under the bent rod and gently lowered the jacks, repeating the process until the rod was relatively straight. He delivered the children safely to their homes but returned to Cortez with threadbare tires. God's handprints were evident even on vehicles!

Anticipating the second year of NBRS, Art turned to prayer supporters. He wrote: "Many weighty problems confront us. How will we feed twenty new students who will arrive in about ten days? What will we do about our inadequate water supply? How will we discipline and lead the students in their walk with the Lord? It all seems like a mountain of impossibility, but God provided before and will again, I'm sure."

That fall Art added classes in witnessing and Scripture memory to his teaching load. He supervised the boys' dorm devotions and work projects, guided the mission's northernmost church-planting ministries, prepared radio broadcasts, fixed vehicles, hauled coal, maintained furnaces, and shouldered other maintenance and administrative duties.

In wintertime, the whimsical furnace tested the resolve of the students. It was supposed to drop coal automatically from the top chamber into the burning chamber, ashes filtering to the bottom. However, the coal repeatedly solidified and failed to drop. Time after time the furnace quit in the middle of the night and the students awoke to freezing temperatures. "Oh, we'll get it fixed," Art cheerfully assured them. He and Mr. Stillhammer worked long hours, each time believing that the problem was solved. Eventually it was discovered that a different kind of coal worked better, but even a working furnace could not prevent frigid air from seeping in around the windows of a non-insulated building!

As the facilities expanded, so did the challenges. To ease the problem of internal communication, Art purchased crank-style telephones for $2 apiece and devised a primitive intercom system. He and volunteers Al and Norma Miklos installed a water heating system using a couple of boilers Art found. Students and staff

Art teaching a class

hauled donated coal from the mines in two-ton trucks. As long as coal was available and the furnace worked, things went well. At times the boilers created so much heat that blankets had to be thrown over the blistering pipes to decrease the room temperature. During one severe cold spell, the coal supply became critically low. Both trucks were down for repair. After supervising students in the furnace room one morning, Art trudged home for breakfast. "Well, we just put the last shovelful of coal in the hoppers," he announced. "If we can't get more, the waterlines will freeze and we'll have to send the students home. Trouble is, I'm not sure they can get home safely." He prayed with the family and left for his classes.

Emalou prayed as she washed the dishes. Answering a knock at the door, she found a family friend from neighboring Durango. "Emalou, the Lord impressed on me that you could use some coal," he said. In the driveway stood his loaded pickup.

"Indeed we can!" she exclaimed. That load lasted until the mission's trucks were repaired.

Gifts from God's people and many hours of hard labor brought gradual campus improvements. A used institutional-size gas range was acquired, and the installation of another septic tank made an indoor bathroom possible in the girls' dorm. At four degrees below zero with five inches of snow on the ground, trotting to an outhouse at midnight had not been the girls' idea of winter recreation!

Bona fide winter recreation did occur occasionally, such as the time Art rented ice skates at 35 cents apiece for a school outing to Frazier Pond. On another outing, students and staff retreated to a ski slope, sharing a single pair of skis loaned to the school.

As often as possible, Art enjoyed special times with his children, though those times occurred less often than both he and they desired. "If I had black hair and darker skin, Dad would have more time for me," Paul commented once.

Progress toward mission goals was slow, but bright spots did exist. Preaching the Gospel and enabling native men to preach were Art's greatest loves. Having Tom Dennison, an able preacher, as a vital part of the developing mission was highly satisfying. After Tom's marriage to Arlene in 1955, both worked diligently alongside the NBRS staff. Both willingly assisted with radio broadcasts by sharing their singing talent. Monthly days of staff fellowship and prayer together with the Girtons and Wanita Sheagley from Pine Haven was another morale booster.

The work grew faster than the list of prayer and financial contributors, but there was no thought of retreat. "We are much cast on God for the supply of every need, knowing that He will not fail us," Art wrote supporters. He and Emalou always recognized them as indispensable to the evangelization and training of Navajos. "With the mansions of Glory waiting for us, we feel no need or desire to lay up riches here. Whatever money is raised will go directly into the work of the Lord." Considering the sacrifices of supporters like the couple who kept their kerosene lamp turned low in order to give to missions, the Norrises sought to utilize all donations carefully and prayerfully. To keep supporters abreast of NIGC's progress, they initiated *The Crusader*. This twice-yearly newsletter became a bimonthly in the spring of 1955 and continued for a year. Much later, *Mission News* was launched to report on NIGC's northern work.

In the fall of 1955 NIGC's staff voted to change the name of the Colorado corporation to Navajo Gospel Crusade (NGC), a change made in the New Mexico corporation papers seven years later.

Bible school activities continued in Cortez, but the facility was becoming cramped for space. When the farmer from whom Art had bought the original Cortez acreage offered to sell more land, Art's knowledgeable real estate friend urged him to buy. Art considered the benefits.

Student body in the early days

The buildings were so close together that they presented a fire hazard, and the city was creeping closer. The property for sale had irrigation water rights and a small creek. More land would allow room for a recreational area, a large garden, and livestock, the latter providing both food and jobs for the students. Funds became available and the purchase was made.

Art felt that the staff needed to learn to read Navajo. It was a slow, challenging process and included lengthy words such as Ayóó'ádanihó'nínígíí, meaning "The One Who loves us." For some words, special markings were vital to tone and meaning. Shinii', for example, means "my face"; shiníí', "my waist"; and shíníí', "my nostrils." Without appropriate markings, neither tone nor meaning was discernible, at least to non-Navajos.

By teaching an early morning class, Art, affectionately called by some "The One Who Speaks Navajo Well," gently prodded the Bible school staff in their efforts to learn Navajo. Sometimes he pushed them beyond their comfort zones. For example, he took George Fletcher to the reservation to announce upcoming Bible camp dates. The two bumped along the dirt road, stopping at a Navajo camp where Art was well known. Art greeted the family and fell silent, waiting for George to speak. George sat on a sheepskin, his hands sweating. He struggled through the announcement and rose to leave. As they drove to the next group of hogans, he asked, "How will they know what time we'll come for the children?"

A smile crept across Art's face. "I've been coming here so many years that they just know. The important thing is the date." Then he suggested better phrasing in Navajo.

One hundred nineteen campers showed up for Bible camp. George was encouraged by this evidence that he had been understood. Nearly one-fourth of the campers, taught largely by NBRS students in their own language, trusted Christ.

After the American Bible Society published the Navajo New Testament in 1956, Wycliffe translators Faith Hill and Faye Edgerton instituted annual short-term language schools for the missionaries. Learning as many of the language intricacies as possible enabled the missionaries to read Navajo Scripture to those yet illiterate.

Rosemary Foote, who had replaced Paul and Eleanor Afflerbaugh in McElmo Canyon, attended the first session of the Wycliffe training and was impressed by the large number of missionaries working among Navajos. Earlier she had felt God's call overseas but had been hindered due to health concerns. Now she discerned again His tugging at her heart. "Trust me with the health issue," He told her. She determined to obey His leading, but she loved the Navajos and knew Art was counting on her help. After the language session she summoned courage and went to him. "Art, I've thoroughly enjoyed my time here, but I believe that God wants me in Laos now. He has used this ministry uniquely to prepare me."

Art was not happy. He quoted Jeremiah 12:5: "If you have run with footmen and they have tired you out, then how can you compete with horses? If you fall down in a land of peace, how will you do in the thicket of the Jordan?" Though saddened by Art's response, Rosemary valued the Norrises' mentoring, having learned from them how to accept hardship, resist discouragement, and rely on God's provision. Those were invaluable lessons for the days to come.

Art always endeavored to put beneficial written material into the hands of the Navajos, including Ha'asíidii, (*The Watchman*), a bimonthly Navajo/English paper published by missionaries Warren and Norma Davis in Mexican Water. Its Navajo articles were summarized in English to entice English-reading Navajos to learn to read Navajo. Eventually the publication became Adińdíín, meaning "light." Mrs. Olive Lawrence, a mission associate, took over the publication, and Art contributed articles and checked the material for

Olive Lawrence,
Listen editor and printer

cultural appropriateness. Following the issue announcing the completion of NBRS's dining hall, kitchen, and dormitories, NBRS's enrollment increased. Support literature had been successful in many cultures, but Navajos preferred English reading material, so Adińdíín eventually became *Listen* and was produced in English only.

In the late 1950s when the first contingent of Navajo tuberculosis patients was admitted to the Cragmoor Sanitarium in Colorado Springs, Art contacted a local pastor. "Some of those patients became Christians through our ministry, and someone needs to minister to them. Navajo songbooks and Scripture are available on records." Some Anglo Christians, as well as some Navajos, responded to the challenge. By the time the U. S. Government terminated the TB program several years later, many patients had heard God's Word.

The work expanded further in May of 1957 when the Christian Reformed Church transferred their Aneth, Utah, ministries to NGC. In addition to the Norrises, God sent a succession of Navajo and Anglo workers to proclaim the Gospel there.

In 1959 the week-long summer Bible camps were replaced by a two-month summer Bible school to accommodate youth who attended government schools during the school year. Mary Askey, a newer member of the NGC staff, ably directed these sessions. Initially, Robert Norris assisted her. In lieu of tuition fees, the students laid waterlines, set up a

1958 Bible camp at Cortez

laundry room, constructed a storage room for the kitchen, and planted a garden. Two months allowed more time for instructing students in the Word and challenging them to witness. Most of them accepted that challenge; one of them was even the catalyst for weekly prayer meetings in her reservation church.

Mary Askey (left) and summer Bible institute students

NBRS's fall/winter sessions ran September through March. Gradually the number of students exceeded the staff's ability to accommodate them. As God sent additional staff, Art and Emalou rejoiced at seeing their vision becoming reality. Art could think of no greater privilege than teaching God's Word. He was elated to have access to Old Testament portions in Navajo from translators Warren and Norma Davis which, although unrefined, aided the students greatly in their understanding. In exchange for the students' help as language informants, the Davises provided further assistance by teaching Navajo reading and writing at the school.

Warren Davis with student language informants

Every aspect of the Norrises' ministry and personal lives was dependent on God's provision–materially, physically, emotionally, and spiritually. Visiting Emalou one day after Daniel had been born, Norma Miklos was horrified to see a Navajo visitor hand her fever-stricken baby to Emalou, then gather Baby Daniel into her arms. "How could you stand to see her pick Danny up?" Norma exclaimed when the lady left. "What if her baby has a contagious disease?"

"I just have to turn such things over to the Lord," Emalou replied. "If He cares enough to provide coal in a moment of dire need and to help the ministries expand in the face of many odds, He can handle things like this."

That attitude prevailed among the entire mission staff as they faced difficult and unique circumstances in the development of the Bible-training and outstation ministries. The Ancient One had revealed many "fringes" of His ways in the past. No obstacle was too great for Him!

17
Upheld by His Hand

"The LORD delights in the way of a man whose steps he has made firm; though he stumble, he will not fall, for the LORD upholds him with his hand."   – Psalm 37:23-24

The challenges that the Bible school faced were many. Even with the increase in staff, more missionaries were needed. Additional funds were essential. The most critical need, however, was a good, adequate water supply, a need about which mission personnel prayed often. Tom Dennison and Art had dug a cistern in 1953 and hauled water regularly to fill it, but it sprang a leak. Then they dug a well, but it was too shallow and its alkaline water not suitable for cattle or even for flushing toilets. A deep, commercially drilled well was urgently needed. When Clarence Harwood, a friend and supporter, learned of the need, he offered to finance a well from his Spurgeon Memorial Fund. The Norrises marveled at the incredible support team God had orchestrated!

Knowing that many in Cortez had drilled for water unsuccessfully, Art contacted a geologist. "You'll get water," the geologist assured him. At 600 feet water was struck, but the flow was inadequate. "Keep drilling," the geologist urged. "I'm sure you'll get enough water."

Most of the earmarked funds had been spent. Concerned, Art phoned Mr. Harwood. "Keep going," Mr. Harwood insisted. Mission supporters sought God's blessing as the drilling continued. At 935 feet an artesian well was struck. Water rose rapidly to within 125 feet of the top, necessitating placing the pump and casing no deeper than 130 feet!

Miracles continued. The Warren Davises, who lived on a nearby hill, allowed a metal storage tank to be placed on their property in exchange for water. The mission also sold water to a small slaughter/packing house across the road to help offset expenses. Joyfully Art contacted supporters: "The elimination of the water barrier is an indication that the Lord wants us to advance for Him. We want to press the battle to the gates."

Art's determination to advance resulted in a new outstation in Bluff, Utah, where missionary Dorothy Hecker and a Navajo co-worker lived for a time. They witnessed to many Navajo employees of the uranium, sawmill, and oil industries and taught some of them to read Navajo. A nearby Ute village provided exposure to yet another culture.

Cato Begay awaiting flight to preaching assignment

Then Ralph Sharsh, a Christian pilot, proposed an exciting new option for the Bible training ministry in 1958. "Art, I give flying lessons to several Christian businessmen here in Cortez. I'm sure they would help me take students to various ministry points without cost just to get more flying time. It would be faster and mean less wear and tear on the missionaries who drive over such horrid roads every weekend to get student assistants. What do you think?"

Think? Any way to get the Gospel to more people! Many reservation missionaries wanted Navajo-speaking assistants. Some of them drove as many as 200 miles round trip each weekend to utilize NBRS students. Flying to their assignments would allow students longer weekend ministry time. The prospects were energizing! In the wake of oil discoveries, reservation roads were being built, but few of them were good. Airstrips had appeared in out-of-the-way places. Students could reach Aneth,

Von Stillhammer and Tom Dennison at fledging Aneth church

Blanding, Navajo Mountain, Sweetwater, Mexican Water, Rock Point, Oljeto, Kayenta, Round Rock, Huerfano, and Thoreau in a matter of minutes. Art's head spun. Soon students were traveling a total of 3000 miles each weekend. When Mr. Sharsh was no longer available to provide the service, missionary pilot Paul

Wilson stepped in. Eventually, roads improved and the flying program ceased; the students' weekend ministries, however, did not.

Feeding the students and her family took much time and energy, but Emalou was equal to the never-ending task. She prepared Navajo fry bread, mutton stew, beef stew, homemade bread, beans, and squash. Cows, pigs, chickens, turkeys, goats, and orphaned lambs provided meat, milk, and butter. Leftovers usually appeared in soup or stew; anything unfit for human consumption benefited the animals. Ladies in Grand Junction and Paoli, Colorado, canned fruit and vegetables for the school, and Cortez farmer and board member, Gaylord Gardner, as well as several Grand Junction farmers, offered peaches, apples, pears, and raspberries. Under Emalou's watchful eye, every female on campus learned the art of food preservation. Even with the home-canned and donated food, funds were so meager during one school session that the budget had to be cut. Twenty-one students were fed for a whole week on $15.

The winter of 1959 the Norris family developed severe headaches every time they ate peaches. Puzzled, Art reviewed their peach-picking excursion to Grand Junction. He recalled finding at a road construction site just the right size boxes for picking fruit. They even had convenient rope handles. Suddenly it dawned on him: Those were dynamite boxes! The peaches had absorbed residual powder, apparently, but throwing them away was unthinkable. "Perhaps you could boil them," their doctor suggested, but that failed to alleviate the problem. Each time peaches were served, the children would moan, "Are these the headache peaches?"

Providentially, there was sufficient food that did not result in headaches. Supporters in Dove Creek butchered and donated a steer. Someone else donated twenty-five hens past their prime. With Paul and Faith's help, Emalou built a fire to heat a 55-gallon drum of water. Paul worked with a hatchet; young Faith watched in wonderment as her mother grabbed hens and wrung their necks as though she were snapping green beans. Scalded and plucked, the hens were carried to the school's kitchen and wrapped for the freezer.

Sometimes God provided in novel ways. On a trip to Denver, Art and some students heard about a truck accident near Wolf Creek Pass. Reportedly, the truck was "loaded with meat, free to anyone willing to pick it up." Near the 11,000-foot summit, 140 miles from Cortez, the men spied a truck cab at the side of the road. A thousand feet below lay its crumpled trailer. Strewn over the slopes were hundreds of packages of pork. "Let's get what we can," Art directed. The students scrambled down the mountainside. Hams had rolled the farthest and were no longer fit for retrieval, but roasts and bacon were plentiful. The men formed a human chain and passed packages up the mountain, returning to Cortez with a loaded vehicle. Grabbing containers and rope, they headed back to the pass for a second load. That school year the freezer was full!

Sometime later the mission rented a 160-acre farm to produce additional food for the school. Missionaries Richard and Betty Hellyer oversaw the farming/gardening operation and students provided much of the labor.

❖

Only one person had promised to help with the 1959 summer Bible school, and that person did not appear. However, God had His hand on that session. At the last moment Cato Begay, Robert Norris, and Kee Kohoe offered to teach and counsel the boys. A student did the laundry and cleaned, a high school graduate cooked, and a visiting evangelist and his wife taught classes. The Holy Spirit moved in the hearts of the eighteen enrollees. Some confessed sin and sought forgiveness. Others, unable to sleep, awakened staff members in the middle of the night for prayer. Many of them rose early to study the Bible and meditate.

For three years the summer Bible school sessions continued, well administered and spiritually profitable. However, adding them to the six-month winter sessions left the staff little opportunity for family time, maintenance, visits to supporting churches, or vacations. The missionaries wondered if the summer sessions should be discontinued. NBRS's curriculum was geared to Navajo-speaking students with a wide range of ages and with varying degrees of education. Increasing numbers of Navajos were becoming fluent in English, and some were turning to secular schools with broader curricula. Having sought the Lord's

1959 student body

guidance, the staff decided to drop summer sessions, broaden NBRS's winter curriculum, and raise academic standards. Only six men enrolled in NBRS that fall, but those six were eager to learn. They wanted to win people to Christ and establish churches in their respective areas of the reservation. Their courses included Bible, Christian living, child evangelism, piano, guitar, and an introduction to missions. In 1960 the school changed its name to Navajo Bible Institute (NBI) and began developing three-, four-, and five-year courses of study.

As NBI's student body increased, more facilities and a larger support base were needed. One supporter financed a chapel by donating a diamond ring. A Quonset hut became available from the Government, and Art envisioned its usefulness as a shop. He and son Paul jacked it up and backed a mission truck under each end. "Son," Art directed, "climb in the back truck. If you see a problem, just blow the horn." Paul was soon asleep on the seat, his feet sticking out the window. Art wondered why everyone who passed him was laughing.

From the Atomic Energy Commission (AEC) mill in Monticello, Utah, Art acquired an apartment building at minimal cost. Sixteen-year-old Paul helped him saw it in two before he had it moved to the Bible school property. Mr. Stillhammer, with student help, transformed the buildings into olive-green, stuccoed dormitories, a dining hall, and missionary housing. Prayer was being answered!

Monticello building

Students assisting Mrs. Hecker (2nd from right) in kitchen

NBI's students represented several denominations and mission organizations. "Art is more concerned that people love the Lord and share His love with others than he is about fine doctrinal points," one of his friends commented. Art did care about the fundamentals of the Christian faith, but he also cared about people's potential for the Lord's work. In choosing students, he leaned heavily on individual recommendations of pastors, not basing acceptance merely on academic achievement or flawless Christian experience.

1960 NBI students in dining hall

Bible institute costs were kept to a minimum by mandating student work hours to offset the cost of tuition, room, and board. Staff-designed rules were enforced. For Art, the most difficult to deal with were the issues of immorality and disregard for authority. Often with tears he talked as a father with an offending student. "The only way to be strong is to turn away from anything that might hinder your walk with the Lord," he counseled.

On Saturdays the students loved to go into town and enter store drawings, and in the early 1960s one of them won a television set. Since television had not been considered beneficial either in the dormitories or in the Norris home, Art had a tough decision to make. Because the winner's family did not have electricity, Art paid the student fair market value and took the set home, setting the strictest of guidelines for its use. The "snow" plaguing the sole channel did not prevent the family's enjoyment of the Rose Bowl Parade. "Gunsmoke" was out, but, being Canadian and because Mounties did not wear guns, Art enjoyed "Sergeant Preston of the Yukon." "Red Skelton" and "Lassie" were other favorites. The children did not always understand the choices, but they relished every program that was permitted.

Believing that the school would benefit from the addition of Navajo teachers, Art broached the subject at a board meeting that fall. "Has the school been criticized for not having a native worker?" chairman John D. Jess, "Chapel of the Air" radio speaker, asked.

"No," Art replied, "but other missions are adding Navajo teachers to their staffs. It would be helpful, but bringing natives on staff would present unique challenges too. Most Navajos are unable to support their leaders financially, and hiring Navajo teachers when the Anglo staff must raise their own support is difficult. Another difficult issue is finding places for our graduates to serve. Again, few Navajo churches can afford to hire a pastor, and jobs are not always available where pastors are needed." No action was taken. In time, the board believed, God would reveal His will on these issues.

For relief from weightier issues, Art took visitors on reservation trips from time to time. Conservative Baptist ministers composed one such group. A strong wind was blowing the day the entourage arrived at Canyon de Chelly. The visitors were hesitant to follow Art and George Fletcher to an overlook at the edge of an 800-foot sandstone cliff. "The view's better from here," Art encouraged, motioning with his arm in the direction of the canyon. Preplanned, his arm hit George on the back. George yelled and disappeared over the edge. The visitors gasped. Art's peals of laughter were in stark contrast to the horrified expressions on the men's faces. As George climbed up over the rim from the broad ledge where he had been crouching, they visibly relaxed. Art later chided himself for playing such an unwise prank, realizing it could have caused someone a tragic heart attack.

Art's and Emalou's constant responsibilities at the school were physically and emotionally wearing. Emalou chaffed under what felt like constant scrutiny, including that of curious staff members who quizzed the children for information. With no privacy and little time for herself or the Lord, her stress intensified during her early fifties, and she became captive to depression and feelings of worthlessness. How could she escape without bringing disgrace on the Lord or her family? Her many responsibilities left her with barely enough energy to speak. Anger and bitterness over criticism of herself and the family were wasting both her body and her spirit, and she had neither time nor energy to deal with such weighty personal issues. Though recognizing God's blessings, she was unable to summon a pervading thankful attitude. On rare occasions she escaped to a hotel room, but time for writing letters or poetry, working crossword puzzles, or reading for pleasure was minimal.

❖

When mining operations in Rico came to a halt, Pat McIntosh was reassigned to McElmo Canyon. When Aneth and Montezuma Creek, Utah, became more heavily populated and roads in those areas improved, the McElmo Canyon station was closed. The increased activity in Utah and at Pine Haven necessitated more personnel. "I can publicize the need in our radio publication," John D. Jess offered at a 1964 board meeting, "but I believe that personal visits from Mr. Norris to various Bible schools would be the best way to recruit."

NGC board (1960s): L-R: Cyril Norris, Art Norris, Gaylord Gardner, Andy Whitner, Webb McAdams, John D. Jess, Jim Posey, Charles Girton

"True," some agreed, "but he already has too many other things to do."

"We've talked about this for two years," declared another board member. "The oversight of property, staff, students, school, and developing outstations is too much for one man. We must counsel Art to delegate duties so he can spend more time seeking prospective personnel and students."

"That will only add to his work load," others countered.

Holding up a letter, one of the board members ventured, "Our missionaries are also concerned and have submitted some recommendations."

"Let's hear them," Chairman Jess directed.

The board member read: "We recognize and appreciate the many years of courageous struggle and self-sacrifice which the Norrises have made to establish this mission and Bible school. It has become a great burden for one man to direct, manage, and operate the affairs of this growing enterprise with all its varied interests. . . . Mr. Norris might well break down physically and mentally unless the situation is relieved.

"We recognize in Mr. and Mrs. Norris some outstanding abilities as missionaries to the Navajos as well as their burden for the evangelization of the American Indian. Mr. Norris, with his command of the Navajo language and his aptitude to reach and teach Navajos, should be freed from other encumbrances to be used more effectively in this strategic and critical time. He should be free to visit other missions, to coordinate our efforts with those of other Navajo Bible schools, to attend conferences, and to consult with other mission leaders on missionary strategy.

"We have sought the Lord in prayer about these things and desire only to help Mr. Norris and the mission as a whole to overcome present difficulties. We desire to go forward in the Lord's will as He directs, keeping in spiritual unity and fellowship with one another [so] that the Holy Spirit may accomplish through us a greater work among the Navajo.

"We recommend that four key officers be elected and given authority to carry out respective functions. A missionary director, a business manager, a Bible school principal, and a maintenance technician would serve under the direction of the field director. Some of our current missionary staff could qualify for these recommended offices. . . . Art could serve as the field director. However, God is able to send us qualified persons as time goes on and as the school expands to and beyond Mr. Norris' vision of forty Bible school students."

The recommendations, which were approved by the board, took Art by surprise. He and Emalou had not known of such staff discussions, yet several friends, co-workers, and even neighbors knew of the impending proposal. He responded to the board, enumerating issues he felt prevented the implementation of such a proposal. Additional workers would be needed. Also, since the Bible institute's operation depended on funds from the Norrises' supporters, funds for the school would have to be raised if he and Emalou were no longer involved.

A board member turned to Art. "We trust you will seriously consider these recommendations in the spirit in which they were intended and that you'll discuss them with the missionaries to see what can be worked out. It appears that you need to delegate more responsibilities, freeing yourself to do those things that only you can do."

Emalou had never seen Art so discouraged and perplexed. He wept. Was his leadership being challenged? Had he failed? His style of leadership had been to weigh pending decisions for some time without discussing them. Consequently, others were often surprised when decisions were announced. His communication with Navajos was good, but he was not always understood by Anglos. If only the staff had included him and Emalou in their discussions. The situation was tense. Art talked with the staff, but discussion brought no agreement or major change. Some months later he and several board members learned that a few of the staff apparently had been involved in some covert designs. After dismissal of one staff member, the ministry and working relationships became settled once again.

Such times were difficult for Emalou. She was grateful for the Lord's undergirding and the support of Pat McIntosh, whose occasional visits brightened the day. Over coffee they laughed, cried, shared insights from Scripture, and prayed, a healthy interlude in the midst of many pressures. She, as well as Art, was also encouraged by interaction with students such as the one who knocked at the door one afternoon. "How may we help?" Emalou asked lovingly.

"I . . . I don't know exactly," the girl replied. "In the Navajo way we use corn pollen to pray to the sun or mountains or whatever. But now I know that God is the only One I should pray to. I want to get rid of my corn pollen pouch, but I don't know how." A major breakthrough for one so steeped in the traditional religion! After discussion and prayer together, the young lady asked, "Will you go with me to the irrigation ditch?" There, in the presence of her mentors, she dropped the bag into the water. "I feel so free!" she exclaimed as it disappeared beneath the surface.

God graciously led at every juncture. By 1964 the Bible institute property accommodated dormitories, married couples' apartments, dining room, staff dwellings, guest facilities, chapel, classrooms, print shop, office, and radio studio. Although not luxurious, the facilities had been made available with little financial outlay. Other people's junk often became Art's gems. "Beverly Hillbillies!" the family joked, for no matter where they went, they returned with pipe, furniture, or other items sticking out of or tied on top of, under, or on both sides of the car. Many of Art's "finds" were useful; some lay unused, camouflaged by weeds. Whether car and washing machine parts or an old bus, nothing was discarded. Art and the volunteers, including his brother, found ways to fix things inexpensively. Art's wet index finger told him what he needed to know about a light socket when no bulb was handy. A tightly wrapped strip of cloth, known as a "Navajo Band-aid," often stopped water pipe leaks. Opportunities for innovation in the growing Bible training facility were ample.

Students respected Art and looked forward to his chapel messages.

His face glowed whenever he addressed them in Navajo. He explained Scripture, using illustrations from Navajo life. Sometimes he told of missionaries who had served in other parts of the world. "You, too, can preach the Gospel and have the joy of leading people to Christ," he encouraged. One morning he read Luke 9:62: "No one who puts his hand to the plow and looks back is fit for service in the kingdom of God" (NIV). Then he declared, "Following the Lord is not easy, but if you want to follow the One who gave His life for you, you should never look back or give up."

Student Tom Madison took that to heart. In his pre-Christian days he had trained to become a medicine man. Now he bundled up his family on cold Saturday mornings and drove to McElmo Canyon to share the Gospel in Navajo camps. On Sundays he transported people to the church service at Aneth. Throughout his time at Bible school he faithfully "put his hand to the plow," inspired by the Spirit-directed teaching of Art and others.

Students also ministered through five weekly radio broadcasts. This gave them opportunity to preach, pray, and sing publicly. Broadcasts which had begun in the fall of 1954 over a Flagstaff station later expanded to Cortez, Farmington, and Albuquerque. By the fall of 1957, daily broadcasts had covered the entire 25,000 square-mile reservation, plus

Students broadcasting radio program

adjoining towns where Navajos were employed or confined to sanitariums. Charles Girton and several native preachers broadcast in Gallup and Aztec, New Mexico, and in Blanding, Utah. Art also developed a program for the Utes. By 1966 ten weekly Navajo programs blanketed the reservation. Sometimes Bob and Tully made Navajo-language tapes. Even the Norris children read and recorded a play from the *Jack and Jill* magazine, complete with appropriate sound effects.

One of the students who was eager to be involved in the radio ministry was David Paul. God had given David victory over alcohol. One day while he and Art were working on an irrigation ditch at NBI, they found broken pottery, charcoal, and a grindstone—evidences of Anasazi habitation several hundred years earlier. "Were these people related to you, David?" Art asked.

"I don't know," David answered, thoughtfully picking up another artifact and turning it gently in his hands. "Did these people know about Jesus?" he asked pensively.

That same question had plagued Art the time he had discovered a handprint in an old kiva or cache. "Well, David," he replied, "God created Adam, and Adam knew God. Undoubtedly his children also knew Him, yet five-fingered men (the term Navajos used for the human race) turned away from Him. Indians also turned away from Him to worship the sun as their father; the earth as their mother; the stars, mountains, and images that they made themselves. The people who lived here hundreds of years ago probably did not know God. God does not hold us responsible for *them*, but His Word teaches that we *are* responsible for taking the Gospel to those living now."

Sometime later Art ambled around campus after hours to insure that the curfew was being followed. Seeing lights in the chapel, he wondered who was there. It was David. "What are you doing, David?"

"Recording a message for a new station. My people are listening to radio and coming to Christ, so I went to Farmington and got permission to preach over their station."

Art was moved beyond words. How could he discipline a man so concerned for the souls of his people? Every program meant that more Navajos were being exposed to the Gospel of Christ. Several missions used radio tapes with Navajo visitors who came to their facilities. The radio ministry, although expensive, was effective, and Navajo listeners themselves supported about one-third of the broadcast time.

Since broadcasts in Navajo were uncommon, people listened intently as students gave testimonies, sang, and preached. With no concept of air waves, they called radio "Nítch'i halne'í" (the "spirit talker" or "talking through the air"). Reports of the Holy Spirit's working encouraged and motivated those involved in the radio ministries. Art recalled the story of Isabelle, a young girl who had listened to radio while herding sheep near the river. "You can accept the Lord right where you are," she had heard a student say. "Even if you are herding sheep, you can kneel down by a rock and ask Jesus to forgive your sin." Isabelle had done that, and her life had been changed. Every Sunday thereafter she had crossed the river on a rickety suspension bridge to attend church. She grew spiritually and had the joy of seeing her father and two sisters trust Christ. Eventually she attended and even graduated from the Bible institute.

At the Rock Point mission hospital a sixteen-year-old boy had also trusted Christ after hearing the broadcasts. He had begun asking questions the minute he entered the hospital. "My family says that the Christian life is for the white man, but the Navajo man on radio said that Christ died for everyone. He said he also heard that the Christian way is for white people, but he found out that Jesus died for Navajos too. He is a Christian now and happy. Is this way for everybody?" A Navajo hospital worker had talked with him for two hours, after which the boy declared, "I want Jesus for my Savior." He died an hour later. Such was the ripple effect: people accepting the Truth learned from the missionaries, then allowing God to use them in the lives of others.

1968 NGC staff
Back (L-R): Martha Brown, Mary Askey, Art Norris, Ed Felgate, Clara Tohtsoni, Dorothy Hecker, Pat McIntosh
Front (L-R): Tom Dennison, Arlene Dennison, Emalou Norris, Alice Felgate, Iris Girton, Charles Girton

Being a part of that process brought deep satisfaction to the Norrises, as did Tom Dennison's concern for Canada's northern Athabascan tribes after he had been exposed to their needs at PBI. Art had often challenged his students to reach out with the Gospel and was greatly encouraged when Tom, sometimes accompanied by Harvey Betselie, Tully Norris, and others, began evangelistic trips to Northern Alberta in the mid-1960s. James Natachez and Allen Neskahi also ministered in the North. These men hunted, fished, and ate with their hosts. They compared languages, sang, laughed, and played together. "Why did you come so far to visit us?" their hosts queried. In response the Navajos told them about Jesus. Later trips took them to the Beaver and Chilkoot Tribes in British Columbia (BC) and to the Slavey Tribe in Alberta and the Northwest Territories. Art and Emalou bathed each Canadian venture and every development at the Bible institute and outstations in prayer, aware of God's power to sustain and seeking His continued direction.

18

In the Shadow of the Almighty

"He who dwells in the shelter of the Most High will
abide in the shadow of the Almighty."
– Psalm 91:1

A rt and Emalou had poured their lives tirelessly into the Cortez
ministry for twenty-two years. Art was stretched thin. Perhaps
delegating responsibilities would have been beneficial. He couldn't seem
to complete a project without interruptions. At times he walked down the
sidewalk on campus not knowing if he were on his way to fix the furnace
or to check on the progress of the *Listen* publication. Something had to
give both for him and Emalou. Following thyroid surgery and medication,
Emalou's health had improved and her energy level had risen markedly,
but once again her condition had deteriorated both physically and
emotionally. "Art," she declared, "we have to get away for a while. If we
don't, you may have to put me in an institution."

Art had never understood depression but, concerned for Emalou's
welfare and aware of his own needs, he heeded her plea and began
arranging for a sabbatical. Charles Girton would oversee the mission and
staff member Ed Felgate could direct the Bible institute, but more help
was needed. The Norrises visited Bob and Genevieve Miller in Grand
Junction. "Emalou and I have to get away for a while," Art confided to
Bob. "Would you and Gen be willing to come and help fill in?"

After the Norrises' visit Gen and Bob discussed the situation. "Emalou
says they've not had time off in twenty years," Gen stated. "If we can
step into their shoes, we'd better do it. After all, they're the ones who've
taught us that if the Lord calls, we'd better listen." Determined to live by
faith as the Norrises had done, the Millers left the church they were pastoring

and moved their family to Cortez.

In August of 1970 Art, Emalou, Faith, and Dan moved to Colorado Springs. Tim, just graduated from Frontier School of the Bible, joined them. Colorado Springs was an ideal site for a furlough. The Norrises could report to their supporting churches in the area, several of their children lived there, and the town was home to *Listen* Press, allowing them to continue to assist with that publication. Proximity to the reservation would also permit Art to continue some mission involvement.

In the midst of her emotional wilderness, Emalou's attention was captured by Psalm 32: "How blessed is he whose transgression is forgiven, whose sin is covered! How blessed is the man to whom the LORD does not impute iniquity, and in whose spirit there is no deceit! When I kept silent about my sin, my body wasted away through my groaning all day long. For day and night Thy hand was heavy upon me; My vitality was drained away as with the fever heat of summer." How well she identified with the psalmist!

With a more relaxed schedule and refreshing fellowship at Mesa Hills Bible Church, Art's and Emalou's stress levels dropped significantly. God provided four godly women with whom Emalou could talk and pray. For the first time in years she received adequate rest and had time to study, meditate on, and memorize Scripture. Over time, she was able to forgive

Mission site at Montezuma Creek

offenses and release bitterness and anger which had ensnared her in paralyzing depression. In addition to mentoring two new Christians, she enjoyed educational classes with Art and found part-time work in a drug store to be therapeutic. Art thrived on intermittent trips to Montezuma Creek to help build a mission facility on newly leased land.

While still on furlough in the spring of 1972, Art flew to Haiti with his brother, his son Tim, and Tim's bride, Donna. As their missionary friends, former PBI classmates, drove them through Port au Prince, Art was astonished at the absence of trash on the streets.

"People are so poor that anything thrown away is salvaged by somebody else," their friends explained. On a picnic, Art watched children hungrily snatching up discarded watermelon rinds. His friends had warned him not to hand out food, so he simply left more watermelon on the rinds. Seeing a young girl holding a small boy with a toddler nearby, however, he could endure it no longer. He sneaked the girl a piece of melon, which she promptly shared with the two younger children.

All four of the Norris travelers soon were engrossed in sewing, maintenance, and construction projects. Art needed to leave early for a speaking engagement in the States, but before he left, a friend in another part of Haiti radioed him. "Art, if your friends will drive you to the river, I'll meet you on the other side. There's no bridge, but someone will carry you across."

At the river a small-framed Haitian bent down in front of Art. To position his 165 pounds on the man's thin shoulders was nearly more than Art could bear. The barefoot carrier picked his way around boulders and over slippery rocks, setting Art down on the other side. Art reached for his wallet. "No, Art," his friend cautioned, "I've already paid him."

The poverty tore at Art's heart. "When you talk with these people about the Lord, the only thing they have on their minds is food," his friend remarked. "They're more likely to listen if we give them two or three cents first to get something to eat."

Art wept as he boarded the overcrowded bus for the twelve-hour journey back to Port au Prince. Chickens, pigs, and humans vied for space inside and on top of the crowded conveyance. Art pondered the physical and spiritual needs of those around him. Earlier he had counted seven barefoot people going by on the street every minute—people passing into eternity who knew only voodoo, fear, and poverty. He grappled with the knowledge that he had the God-given resources to meet some of their physical and spiritual needs. Reaching the airport in Port au Prince, he waited in turmoil for his flight to the States. Finally, as he walked onto the tarmac to board, he seemed to hear, "You can't leave us in this condition. If you loved us, you wouldn't leave." Choked with emotion, he sank into the seat and buckled his seatbelt. An oil worker plopped into the seat beside him and began prattling about the shrunken head in his hands. Art stared out the window. How could anyone babble about shrunken heads when Haitians were dying without Christ!

Back in Colorado Springs, Art agonized for two weeks, his sobs shaking his bed nightly. Did God want him to leave the Navajos? Why this stupendous burden for Haitians? Gradually he sensed that God was not asking him to leave the Navajos; He was only touching him with the magnitude of worldwide need.

On June 1, 1972, after nearly two years in Colorado Springs, the Norrises returned to Cortez physically invigorated and aware of inner renewal that had occurred at the hand of the Almighty One. While they were gone, NGC's board had labored to increase the mission's efficiency. They had voted to submit to yearly audits and to establish a central office at Pine Haven to receive funds, pay bills, and keep books. They had decided on an 8-percent levy on each missionary's account to cover expenses and asked Charles Girton to serve as office supervisor and treasurer, and Thurley McAdams, wife of late board member Webb McAdams, as bookkeeper.

Art resumed his duties, including preparation for a work project at Aneth. Emalou also reentered the work and was able, with the help of the Holy Spirit, to apologize to a co-worker. Freely she shared lessons learned: "Christians should 'count it all joy' when they go through various testings. No matter how painful, a trial can bring much joy and growth in the Lord." She and other female staff began a weekly Bible study, encouraged to see shy Navajo ladies sharing in the discussion.

When the Berean Baptist youth group from Denver came to help with the Aneth project, they brought a small tent trailer containing kitchen facilities. "Art, come have lunch with us," they invited one noon. As Art sat down at the table, someone outside accidentally knocked the leveling prop from under the trailer. The teakettle slid off the stove, spilling boiling water down Art's legs and into his shoes. Art tried, unsuccessfully, to downplay the excruciating pain. The days of forced inactivity which followed were a blessing in disguise, for he had promptly assumed a heavy workload on his return from Colorado Springs.

Although the Norrises' furlough had been refreshing and the staff and volunteers were diligent, the never-ceasing demands on Emalou's and Art's time and energy took their toll. Their bodies and spirits became weary once more. They were aware of God's mandate not only to preach and to be servants, but to watch and pray. How, they wondered, could they spend sufficient time in prayer when water pipes froze, the furnace went out, and hungry students needed food? Pondering their Lord's remarks to Martha in Luke 10, they longed to sit at His feet. But when? How? "Lord," they petitioned, "help us to be Marthas with Mary hearts." Following a time of meditation, they sent an urgent request to their support team. "Please become Aarons or Hurs holding us up in prayer to the end that glorious fruit may be brought forth in the lives of Navajos."

On trips to keep their supporting churches apprized of their ministries, Art and Emalou reported what the Lord was doing among the Navajos. The simplicity of their person and presentation attracted many who listened. They did not wear expensive clothing or bedeck themselves with turquoise and sterling silver; their one and only desire was to give God glory. They were distressed to hear occasional remarks like, "The Indians worship the Great Spirit and have such a beautiful religion."

Art was quick to counter this misunderstanding. "Navajos worship more than 300 beings, including the sun, moon, mountains, and animals, and their religion is full of fear. Those who don't know Christ know nothing of happiness, current or future. They believe they will go to the home of devils when they die. Unless they know the One who said, 'I am the way, the truth, and the life" (John 14:6a, KJV), they *cannot* go to heaven. The best estimate is that only 2 to 5 percent of them know Christ."

Teaching students who had grasped the Truth was animating. Late in 1973 several NBI students returned from two days on the reservation, radiant from having preached to many Navajos. They had also made plans for a community Christmas gathering at which hundreds more would hear the

1973 - 1974 NBI students

Gospel. Mud covered their car and their gas mileage had been horrible, but such facts were as inconsequential to them as to Art. "In mud, three miles to the gallon is all one can expect," he wrote to supporters. "Jesus went out of His way to save us; the students go out of their way to take the Good News to the reservation. Thank you for going out of your way to give to the Lord's work here."

By 1974 space at the Bible institute was pressed to the limit. Student apartments were full. Even the chapel had been remodeled into an apartment. A nearby barn with a graveled floor was the only place large enough to accommodate the 250 people who came to the graduation ceremony. More staff members were a necessity.

God brought sisters Ruth, Esther, Lydia, and Marie Chatlos, as well as Bill and Mildred Irving, a year later through a transfer from Navajo Bible School and Mission in Window Rock. Bill reestablished the radio ministry which had been put aside for a time due to the lack of personnel. Lydia and Ruth assisted with office work and the music program. Art took Esther and Marie to survey ministry possibilities in Aneth and Montezuma Creek. Leaving the green vegetation of the mission headquarters and driving through the hot, barren reservation, Art pointed to a rock. "See that? Near that rock is a hogan where people need Christ." Pointing in another direction, he continued, "See that hogan? People who need the Gospel live there. Cortez may be greener and cooler, but Navajos here need the Savior. Students come here to teach on weekends, but someone is needed on site." Esther and Marie accepted the challenge and moved to Montezuma Creek, serving there and at Aneth. Occasionally Ruth and Lydia assisted them.

One foggy, dreary morning some months later, Art drove to Montezuma Creek to help Bill Irving replace Esther and Marie's furnace. On the way he picked up a hitchhiker, a man obviously under the influence of alcohol and peyote. Art discovered that he was the son of a former NBI student. Letting him out at the post office, he drove on to the Chatlos home. "I forgot my screwdriver," he commented as he and Bill busied themselves in the cellar. "I'll run upstairs and get a knife." He returned with a butcher knife, and the two of them quickly dismantled the furnace. "Let's carry this outside," Art suggested.

While the men worked, Esther and Marie prepared potato salad and hamburgers upstairs. Suddenly an inebriated man appeared in the kitchen waving the knife Art had borrowed. "I'll kill you!" he threatened, attempting to corner the ladies.

Esther shook so badly she nearly cut her finger with a paring knife. Marie tried to reason with the man. Esther ran to the cellar calling, "We need help!" Art and Bill bounded up the stairs in time to see the man brandishing a knife at Marie. Art recognized him as the hitchhiker. He must have entered the basement and gotten the knife while Bill and I were carrying the furnace out, Art thought. Bill jumped between Marie and the intruder; Art tried to grab the knife.

The man turned on Art. "You and my mother!" he yelled. "Christians! I'll kill you both!"

"If you kill us, we'll immediately be with Jesus," Art responded calmly.

Angered, the man threw the knife. Bill snatched it off the floor and put it out of reach. Grabbing the intruder, he and Art shoved him out the door. "Lock the door!" they hollered to the sisters. The struggle continued. With uncanny strength the man broke loose, ran back to the screen door, and tore it off its hinges.

Esther and Marie prayed. No law enforcement officers were stationed in that isolated area. Desperately Marie tried to phone the tribal police in Window Rock, 200 miles away. It was unlikely that help could arrive in time. Esther glanced out the window. "Marie, look! A patrol car is cresting the hill!"

The patrolman spied the scuffle and barreled in. The offender was well known to him. Snapping handcuffs on the man, he barked, "Get in the car!" As the patrol car disappeared over the hill, the missionaries dropped into their chairs around the table and thanked God for His intervention and a well-earned lunch.

The Bible institute students, supervised by the missionaries, taught weekly released-time classes as a Christian service project and shared the Gospel in homes. They also gained experience teaching children at camp meetings, gatherings serving both the social and spiritual needs of Navajo Christians who were no longer involved in traditional religious ceremonies. These meetings were often held in the open.

Released-time class

People of all ages came by horse, car, or pickup with their lawn chairs, bedrolls, blankets, cooking utensils, and food. Small groups gathered here and there around a large tent or chaha'oh, conversing and laughing. That they represented diverse church backgrounds was, to them, insignificant. "I'm a Christian," many stated, giving testimony to what God had done for them. Fry bread sizzled in hot lard. Freshly butchered sheep, goat, or beef lay on a grill or simmered in a stew over an open fire. Fragrant juniper smoke wafted through the air. Inside, adults listened to sermons and enthusiastically sang Navajo translations of English hymns. "No Dark Valley" was a favorite, perhaps because it expressed release from the spiritual darkness of their past.

The Bible institute was going well, but students had nowhere to exercise in bad weather. "Lord," Emalou prayed as she washed dishes, "we need a gymnasium." Considering their financial situation, even thinking of such a project seemed foolish. "You have not because you ask not," flitted through her mind.

"Lord, if You want us to have a gym, You'll have to send in a lot of extra money."

"Try Me," He seemed to say.

"If You want us to build a gym, please send in an amount we could never expect." Then, wondering how they would know if money received were for a gym, she prayed more specifically. "Lord, if You really want us to have a gym, send an unexpected gift of more than $1000 within the next two weeks."

Days later a check for $1500 arrived! "Art, I think God wants us to build a gymnasium," Emalou said, telling him of her prayer request. Supporters sent additional funds and, on land purchased previously, volunteers Marion and Marjorie Snead supervised the construction. By May 1977 all four walls were up. Eagerly they anticipated adding the roof.

"That wind is really strong!" one of the construction crew remarked as they broke for staff prayers one morning. A few minutes later their prayer time was disrupted by a loud crash. Looking out, they saw the north and south gym walls lying in rubble. Debris was swirling across campus. Stunned, they watched the other two walls collapse. How gracious of God to arrange refuge for the crew before the storm struck!

1976 NBI staff
Back (L-R): Irene Stonehocker, Marie Chatlos, Lydia Chatlos, Ruth Chatlos, Esther Chatlos, Mildred Irving, Emalou Norris, Marie Benally
Front (L-R): Ray Stonehocker, Jim Cook, Bill Irving, Art Norris, George Emmett

But, had they misunderstood His leading regarding a gym?

Certain that this circumstance was a test of faith, the missionaries informed prayer and financial supporters. God sent in sufficient funds not only for a gym/chapel combination, but for four classrooms as well. The classrooms, they decided, should be on the south side of the structure to deflect wind up and over the taller part of the building.

The missionaries looked to God for every need. One morning at prayer time they had just discussed the need for a plumber and an electrician when a knock came at the door.

"Could you use some help around here?" a man inquired.

"What kind of work can you do?" Art asked.

"Plumbing and electrical."

Overhearing the conversation, the staff smiled in delight at God's answer before they had asked for His help.

Educational opportunities at NBI were increasing. Jim Cook, a missionary on loan from another mission, helped to standardize NBI's curriculum and develop four-year English and Navajo study courses leading to either a certificate or a four-year diploma. The 1977 catalog, NBI's first, offered refresher and graduate courses to Navajo pastors and other Christian workers. That fall James Natachez, a Navajo board and staff member, produced art work for publications, directed the athletic program, and taught homiletics and a Bible course.

Art believed, and the staff concurred, that the time had come for a broader, more intensive missions course than the one he had taught in 1960. Vacation and short-term mission trips with his brother in Haiti, England, Ivory Coast, Israel, Greece, Egypt, Guatemala, Colombia, India, and Puerto Rico had broadened his vision and deepened his passion for a lost world. "Churches would be better off to send pastors to visit missionaries than to see the Holy Land!" he declared.

During a recent trip to Ecuador to help a missionary friend, Art had pondered the fate of millions of Ecuadorians yet without the Gospel and the lack of sufficient missionaries to reach them. "Henry," he had asked, "what are Ecuadorian Christians doing about reaching other tribes?"

"That's a touchy subject," Henry had replied. "We missionaries challenge American and Canadian Christians to become missionaries, but we don't challenge the native people the same way. Some Ecuadorians are being trained to reach their own, but pitifully few."

Art had agonized over the implications of Henry's answer. He had encouraged Navajo Christians to preach to their own, but he had seldom emphasized their reaching other tribes or the world. He could not remember having taught them even to pray for the salvation of the world's people. I've failed miserably! he thought. Navajos have had missionaries for years; they themselves should be praying, giving, and going. That realization had prompted him to revamp NBI's mission course. He chose simply written missionary books and even read Don Richardson's *Lords of the Earth* to the students, certain that their traditional beliefs and customs would enable them to relate to the story of a girl thrown into the river for trampling on a sacred site. The Navajos also had sacred places and forbade entrance into "devil hogans," dwellings abandoned due to a death. Richardson's story illustrated the need for Christ's saving and enabling power among the jungle people of Irian Jaya. Perhaps the students would see the spiritual needs among their own tribe and others.

A plan began to form in Art's ever-active mind. "Let's go to Mexico over Christmas vacation," he proposed to his missions class in late 1978. The students were astonished to find Mexican people poorer than the Navajos. Their Mexican host rose early every morning, put charcoal and food in his two-wheeled cart fabricated from car fenders, and pushed it to bus stops. A whole day of selling food netted him a mere $1.25. How, they wondered, could this brother in Christ care for his large family on such meager income? They returned to Cortez determined to send the Mexican brother a used car, but government regulations prevented them from carrying out their intentions.

More than thirty-five years after the Norrises were married, Art, at the age of sixty-three, penned his sentiments and those of Emalou. "As we grow older in the work, we wish we had another life to give to the Lord. . . . What we have done here is very little when we think of what Jesus Christ did for us. These truths spur us on." Their zeal to reach Navajos for Christ had not diminished, but the task was not easy. In 1978, according to Tom Dolaghan and David Scates, Navajos were the fastest-growing ethnic group in the U.S.[1] They had not been very receptive during the first fifty years of Protestant missionary activity, and many were still resistant to the Gospel. The Long Walk in 1864 and the stock reduction program of the 1930s had contributed much to their distrust of Anglos. Rapid changes on the reservation and within the culture created further tension. Few families had had cars or pickups prior to 1978, but now many pickups and some cars frequented the newly paved reservation roads. Salaried jobs often replaced sheep herding. People were no longer dependent upon trading posts and the credit and pawn systems. Though they desired and were acquiring more of the things western culture offered, they feared losing traditional ways.

Many missionaries had flooded the reservation after World War II, and, in spite of the obstacles, progress was being made. More Navajos were becoming Christians and growing spiritually than ever before. Many Navajo Christians who previously utilized the services of medicine men now refused to seek them. The May 1975 issue of *Christianity Today* had labeled Navajos "the most missionaried people in the world," and the recent Dolaghan/Scates study had just revealed that ten times more

Navajos had come to Christ in the previous decade than in all the prior years put together. At one time indigenous churches had been but a dream; now Navajo Christians taught, preached, enjoyed fellowship together, and witnessed to non-believers. The number of new churches with resident pastors, 70 percent of whom were Navajo, had exploded to more than 300. What a change from the former handful of churches pastored by white missionaries! Faithful servants were planting and watering, God was giving the increase, and Christ was building His Church.[2]

Being a part of what God was doing brought great satisfaction to the whole staff and board of NGC. At times, however, details of day-to-day living and decision-making took center stage. In 1973 a rickety house in Cortez, which had been remodeled into a church, had been given to the mission. It had been standing unused, and the board felt it was time to make a definitive decision concerning it. "We could convert it into a mission office," one board member suggested.

"I think we ought to sell it and the lot for $1200 and use the funds toward the Bible school's gym," offered another. That suggestion was approved.

Thinking ahead to retirement, Art bought the dilapidated house. "Our own home!" Emalou exclaimed. "Separate from mission property! And we even have the title!" Instead of the realities of a sagging roof, broken windows, and smashed-out doors, she envisioned a neat, clean haven. When the Girtons came to town, she gave Iris a grand tour. "This will be our living room and that will be the kitchen!" she exclaimed.

Iris shook her head in disbelief. "Emalou, how in the world can you see that in this hovel?"

As Art walked through the rubbish, he spied a hole in the floor. Peeking through, he was amazed to see a two-room basement! The stairway was obscured by mounds of debris. He called in the city inspector. "What codes do we need to follow to turn this bargain into a home?" he asked.

"You'll have to tear it down and rebuild," the inspector told them.

Emalou's heart sank. They could not afford to rebuild. "The LORD gave, and the LORD has taken away. Blessed be the name of the LORD," she and Art reminded each other.

At a later date Art talked with the inspector again. "Well, if you'll put a wall here to keep that one from falling, it might work, but you'll definitely have to rewire everything," the inspector conceded.

Over the next several years while the Norrises continued their ministries, volunteers repaired the roof, added partitions and ceilings, and installed bathroom fixtures. When Art and Emalou moved into their still unfinished house, it was without running water and without washer or dryer.

Returning from the Laundromat one morning, Emalou folded clothes before going to the campus to prepare lunch for the students. She returned that afternoon to find her neatly folded laundry scattered in heaps about the room. Art was at the dining room table studying.

"Art! What happened?" she asked.

Amusement lit his eyes. "Oh, a pack rat ran in and looked me in the eye. I was so scared I threw stuff at it until it left." Emalou failed to share his humor, and she certainly did not relish the thought of sharing her home with a rat!

Art removed mountains of trash and created an office in the basement. His brother, a frequent volunteer and recruiter of other volunteers, installed new kitchen cabinets and built stairs to the attic. A Navajo friend of the Girtons rewired the house. With Emalou's first Social Security check they added a garage. The hand of the Almighty had performed wonders. As Art and Emalou continued to abide in Him, the transformed house became a comfortable home where a steady stream of Navajos received encouragement and biblical instruction.

19
Opening Doors

". . . that God may open up to us a door for the word, so
that we may speak forth the mystery of Christ . . ."
– Colossians 4:3b

As Art celebrated his sixty-fifth birthday, both he and Emalou were beginning to slow down, unable to accomplish all they desired. Who would pick up the reins? How should they occupy themselves? Settling near their children or in a quiet British Columbian coastal town sounded enticing. Perhaps they should take a small pastorate or represent the mission. Maybe they should hold special meetings in Navajo churches. All options were appealing; they waited for the Lord's direction.

Nearly ten years had passed since their prolonged furlough in Colorado Springs and they felt the need of another. However, since the mission board had requested that Art remain as field director and principal of the Bible school, planning for personal needs was difficult.

Art's 1980 report to the advisory board was forthright. "When the mission was small and I was younger, it seemed I could carry on. Since I'm sixty-five and the work is greater, I must begin easing off. Emalou feels she is not able to do what she should and that both of us should resign from this part of the Lord's work. I must regard her health, and perhaps it would be easier for others to take over if we were gone, but I never seem to get scriptural leading for quitting. The only Scripture that God seems to lay on my heart about this matter is one given to Peter in Luke 5:4b (KJV): 'Launch out into the deep, and let down your nets for a draught.' I'm eager to see a work started with Navajos in charge and I wonder what, if anything, the Lord wants me to do about that."

The following March his report acknowledged that some Navajos were coming to Christ and witnessing to other Navajos "but," Art said, "they have evidenced little burden to take the Gospel to other tribes and nations of the world." Candidly, he wrote: "I can no longer carry the never-ending responsibility of directing the northern area of NGC's expanding ministries. I'd like to step out of the directorship of both NGC and the Bible institute and be free to develop work in Canada. I'm willing to work on the mission's financial development and to recruit Navajo Bible school students. The work might become more sharply defined with a Navajo leader. A Navajo might be able to direct things more in keeping with the Navajo mind and heart. Jerry Sloan, for example, comes from a fine Christian family. He's been a pastor for quite a while and is a likeable person. He related well to students when he was here." Art hoped that his proposal would result in more open doors for Christian Navajos to become involved in the Lord's work in both the U. S. and Canada.

After much discussion and gathering of information about Jerry Sloan, NGC's Board of Directors took a bold, new step toward indigenization of the mission. "Jerry," they said, "we'd like for you to consider directing NGC's northern ministries and serving as principal of Navajo Bible Institute." Jerry and his wife, Dolly, were willing, but a Navajo pastor would need to be found for their church in Tuba City before they would be free to assume that position. Rev. Joe Mehesy, with NBI since 1977, consented to serve as interim director and principal.

Meanwhile, Ann Lundquist joined NBI's staff. Assigned to clean the school's guest apartments, she was surprised to see Emalou in slacks and tennis shoes coming to help her. As they worked, Ann asked numerous questions about Emalou's 40-plus years of missionary service. "How in the world could you do all that?" she asked in amazement as Emalou reviewed a number of happenings.

"When things need to be done, you just do them," Emalou responded.

Art continued to teach at the school and Emalou always found plenty to do. Taking Ann one day, Emalou journeyed to Grand Junction for peaches. Ann was impressed by her handling of the manual transmission pickup on winding mountain roads. She had heard about the time Emalou towed the motor home belonging to volunteers Pete and Hazel Klassen sixty miles after they hit a steer. Along the way Emalou told one story after another. Cresting a mountain, she commented, "This is where Art puts the truck in neutral." Noting Ann's quizzical look, she explained, "Coasting downhill saves gas."

Jim and Kathy Ewan, volunteers from British Columbia, arrived in time for the May 1981 graduation. They watched the four graduates butcher a sheep for mutton stew, but when it was time to eat, they opted for the lasagna Emalou had thoughtfully prepared. The Ewans installed a new sewer system, planted donated evergreens, dug postholes, and worked in the print shop and office. On Sunday they worshiped at a Navajo church with Art and were amused when the pastor interjected an English phrase, then stopped and asked, "Brother Art, how do we say that in Navajo?"

The subject of the Norrises' retirement arose during the Ewans' visit. "How can we leave when so many Navajos are still lost?" Art asked with choked voice. They did not leave. In June that year NGC's board asked Art to cultivate support for Jerry Sloan. Seeing Jerry as a "humble man who wants to walk softly before the Lord," Art wrote a letter to Navajo churches in his behalf. "As a young sheepherder, Jerry Sloan ran away to boarding school to acquire an education. He found Christ while there and has led many Navajos to Christ. I'm glad to have this godly Navajo Christian leader and his wife, Dolly, take responsibility as director of NGC's northern work and as principal of the Navajo Bible Institute. Since Mr. Sloan will be working in a mission which serves and trains Navajos, it is fitting that he be supported prayerfully and financially by Navajo Christians. This is a wonderful opportunity for Navajos to pray for and support their own man."

Would the Navajos respond? Many of them were hesitant to support leaders from their own tribe. The task of raising support for an indigenous mission leader would be a formidable one.

In 1980 Art and Emalou had participated in a missionary conference at PBI and been refreshed by the fellowship and condensed courses in Hebrews, Psalms, and counseling. Afterwards they visited a small Bible school in Lac La Biche, Alberta. Art had returned to his missions class with an exhilarating idea. "I want to tell you about a Dogrib Indian lady we met at Key-Way-Tin Bible School," he had exclaimed. "Key-Way-Tin is very much like NBI. In chapel there I told about Navajo Christians and quoted some Navajo Scripture. Afterwards, a Dogrib lady from Fort Rae, NWT, told me that Navajo sounds like her language. She's an Athabascan native, like you, and is training to become a missionary to her people. The Navajos have heard the Good News for years, but very few Dogribs have ever heard it. Just like that Dogrib woman, it's time for you to go share it with others. The Bible doesn't say we're always to receive; it says we're to go and tell."

Three students had seemed to grasp in a new way the concept of spiritual need. After a weekend away, one of them returned belatedly. "You came back late," Art chided.

"Aoo' (Yes)," the student had replied, her face beaming. "My husband and I led two of our family to the Lord. There were so many rejoicings and restorations that we just couldn't leave and run back to school."

After that experience, Art had written, "We have many reasons to praise the Lord. We see Christ's life being formed in the lives of the students, and we see them winning others to Him. We see native churches being started where Christ is worshiped. . . . We praise His name!"

Now, nearly a year later, the phone rang in the Norris home. "Art, I've got a good cheap fare from L. A. to Ontario," Art's brother announced. "I'd like to see the eastern part of Canada. I'll pay your fare if you'll go with me."

"It's a deal," Art replied, "if I can fly on up to the Dogribs in the Northwest Territories (NWT) on my way home." Since meeting the Dogrib student at Key-Way-Tin Bible School and seeing an article on the NWT containing words similar to Navajo, he had wanted to learn more about this Athabascan tribe.

It was October 1981 when the brothers boarded the plane to Toronto. After ten days of sightseeing, Art headed for Yellowknife, NWT. With no contacts and little cash, he used his rental car as a motel that first night, a miserable night at minus 14 degrees Celsius. Early the next morning as he prepared to leave for Fort Rae, a stranger with whom he had been talking exclaimed, "You aren't going to drive *that* road, are you? It's dangerous!"

Art drove through areas of muskeg and stunted subarctic trees. Nearing Fort Rae, he pulled alongside a pedestrian carrying a gun. "Want a ride?" he hollered.

The man climbed in, silent. "Where you going?" Art asked.

"Fort Rae."

"What are you doing?"

"Duck hunting."

"What's your name?"

"Fred."

As they entered the hamlet, Art noted the pilings under the brown frame houses. Permafrost, he thought. Beyond the Catholic church and a general store, Fred motioned for him to stop. "Friend, where can I stay in this hamlet?" Art inquired as Fred got out.

"Oh, just ask anybody."

"How about your place?"

"Sure. We'll have it ready for you in an hour."

With trepidation Art returned at the appointed time. The family quickly warmed to this white man speaking a Navajo word now and then. Similarities of the two Athabascan languages were evident. Art pointed with his lips. They laughed. "Where did you learn that? That's how we point!"

"I live amongst the Navajos. That's the way they point," Art explained. "How else can a person point when he's on horseback and holding the reins with both hands?" he asked, grinning.

The family asked numerous questions about the Navajos and listened with great interest until bedtime. Finally Art asked, "May I use your bathroom?"

He was escorted to a small nook containing a five-gallon bucket lined with a plastic bag. Noting Art's puzzled look, his host explained, "When the bucket's full, we tie the sack and put it on the street in front of the house. A truck comes by to pick it up."

The next day Art took the family to Yellowknife, unaware until that evening that they had purchased alcoholic beverages while in town. The house became far livelier that night. "Guess I'll go to bed," he commented. He did, but not to sleep. The infant in the nearby hammock cried nonstop; the din in the living room intensified as the night progressed. Sounds as though they're throwing dishes at each other! he thought. "Norris," he muttered, "is this the Lord's will or are you crazy?" He consoled himself with the knowledge that God had promised never to leave him.

The next morning when the family was sober, Art remarked, "You know, you don't have to be a slave to alcohol. That stuff will ruin your lives. I have Navajo friends who used to drink, but God changed them."

"Why don't you stay and help us like you did the Navajos?" several asked later as he prepared to leave.

"I'd love to," Art responded, "but I have a wife to care for and classes to teach. Maybe some of my Navajo friends will come and help you." Possibilities sprinted through his mind. Would the Navajos respond to such a challenge? Economically, the tribe was prospering. Many people had responsible jobs on the railroad and in the reservation's oil wells and coal mines. The tribe had its own sawmill, police force, welfare department, newspaper, and telephone system. Surely the time had come for Navajo Christians to pursue mission outreach.

In December Art wrote to Jimmy Mexicano, Jim Begay, George Tohtsoni, Tom Etcitty, Johnson Yazzie, Harry Thompson, and Harold Noble–most of them former Bible school students. "Dear brothers in Christ, I have learned of 17,000 Indians living in a settlement in Canada's Northwest Territories. They call themselves Dene,[1] meaning 'The People,' and use some Navajo words. They have comfortable homes, food, and hospital care, but they do not know Christ. There is no Protestant work in their village. Their spiritual need is desperate. Some asked me to come back and help them. Six Navajo men met December 6 to plan an evangelistic trip up there. I'd like for you men to come to the next meeting."

First group to Fort Rae, NWT
(L-R): Grace and Jones Dehiya, Custer
Lowe, Art Norris, Ryan Gorman

Several Navajo believers began to meet monthly to pray and prepare for the trip. Funds were raised. Food, tents, cooking utensils, sleeping bags, tape recorders, and cameras were procured and transportation planned. On June 15, 1982, following a commissioning service, Jones and Grace Dehiya, Custer Lowe, Ryan Gorman, and Art departed on the historic 2500-mile trek. In Calgary, Alberta, they notified the Dogribs by phone of their impending visit. That evening when the entourage arrived in the tiny hamlet of Fort Rae, they found that the Dogribs had prepared an old log building for them, complete with housekeeper and cook. The chief bantered amiably with them. "I've heard there are Dene people down south and that if we ever get together, there'll be a big fight," he declared, laughing. He and Custer Lowe, playfully dubbed "chief" by his Navajo traveling companions, exchanged hats as a symbol of friendship.

The Dogribs' hospitality was overwhelming. Members of their tribe had made an official visit to the Navajo Nation the year before; now the Dogribs wanted to chauffeur the Navajos, pay for their gas, buy their food, and even provide an interpreter. Several of their leaders hired a float plane in Yellowknife and took the group to the Dogrib settlements of

Float plane in NWT

Snare Lake, Rae Lakes, and Lac La Mart.

The Dogribs changed their Canada Day feast date so the Navajos could participate. On the appointed day the U. S. visitors mingled with the crowd walking along the lake shore to the bustling community hall. There they were escorted to the head table with the Dogrib chief and the

177

village priest. Everyone else sat on the floor on either side of long tablecloths, talking and laughing. The din subsided somewhat when the food appeared. Though cooked by women, it was served by young men. Eating food served by women allegedly brought fur trappers bad luck. The choices seemed unending: apples, oranges, caribou, smoked fish, fish stew, blood pudding, brains, wild rice, bannock, and hot tea. The whole fish set before Ryan startled him. It wasn't that he observed the traditional Navajo taboo against eating fish; he just could not eat something that stared him in the face!

The welcome was gratifying, but sightseeing and feasting were not the reasons for the Navajos' visit. They wanted the Dogribs to be changed by Christ as they had been. The Catholic priest invited them to speak in the church, and they gladly told of God's forgiveness of sin through Christ's death on the cross and of Christ's power to free people from alcoholism. Three hundred fifty Dogribs listened; eleven entered a new life! Art sat on the back steps of the crowded church and wept! Late into the night people asked questions and sought counsel. "We need this!" some of them exclaimed, giving the Navajos money for their trip home and asking them to come again. God's Spirit was clearly at work, and doors were beginning to open for the entrance of the Gospel.

20
A New Era

"'Not by might nor by power, but by My Spirit,'
says the LORD of hosts."
— Zechariah 4:6b

By the July 1982 board meeting, Jerry Sloan was still unavailable to direct the Bible school and mission work. "Perhaps we should merge with an existing like-minded mission," a board member suggested. Preliminary discussion with the administrators of United Indian Missions, Inc. (UIM) in Flagstaff ensued, but in September of that year Jerry arrived. He began to learn NGC's inner workings, recruit students, and hold evangelistic meetings. He was pleased with the Bible school staff but desired the addition of a Navajo teacher. His attempts to raise funds were discouraging. How could he direct the school and the mission with inadequate funds? His was a tough assignment.

The transition was not easy for Art and Emalou either. "We're trying not to feel like 'has beens' but to accept the challenge of what our future holds," Emalou wrote. Art continued to work at student recruitment and fund-raising in Navajo and Anglo churches. A brochure he created for retirees stated, "Don't let these be declining years for you or a time of selfish pursuit. You have developed talents that can be used for God. Now you have a source of income and the freedom to serve Him where He leads you. Your maturity and experience can play a vital part in making our missionary efforts successful."

That winter Art and five Navajos, including Jimmy Etcitty, returned to Fort Rae. This time they met Jimmy Erasmus, a retired Royal Canadian Mounted Police employee and Fort Rae councilman who spoke English, French, and five Indian languages. Mr. Erasmus offered his house to the

L-R: Jimmy Etcitty,
Jimmy Erasmus, Art Norris

group. He listened to their daily Bible studies and was captivated by Jimmy Etcitty's explanation of the Gospel. "You don't look well educated. How did you learn about the Bible and become saved?" he asked.

Mr. Etcitty shared his testimony and answered questions using pertinent Scriptures. "God can change even an uneducated man!" Mr. Erasmus exclaimed.

"Yes," Mr. Etcitty assured, "and if you want to be saved, He can save you."

"How?"

Once more Mr. Etcitty explained, helping Mr. Erasmus to understand from Scripture that he was a sinner. "But when a person repents, God forgives him."

Mr. Erasmus confessed his sin in a spirit of brokenness and thanked God for sending the Navajos. He began at once to read God's Word. "O God, use him among his own people," Mr. Etcitty prayed.

Art Norris (right) with Navajos going to Fort Rae

In their late 60s Art and Emalou were grateful for God's provision, opportunities to serve, and relatively good health. After years of a packed schedule, they welcomed more time to study the Word with Navajos and continued to be active in Bible camps and missionary conferences. Art also accompanied Navajo teams to the Dogribs. "Art and Emalou have white skins but Indian hearts," one Navajo Christian declared.

Art often considered the possibility of an all-native mission organization, one that would focus particularly on northern Canada's Athabascan tribes. While recruiting students on the reservation, he encouraged NBI graduates and former students to participate in the Dogrib ministry. "You've had the Gospel for more than fifty years; it's time you take it to others," he challenged. "There are tribes in Canada much like yours with a similar language. They are as lost without Christ as you were." Many of his former students did become burdened for the Dogribs, and Art sensed the beginning of a new chapter in the history of missions. He was disappointed that Wycliffe missionaries had not yet translated key verses into Dogrib for the Navajos to utilize. He firmly believed that availability of Scripture in one's own language was vital; it had been the key to many Navajos coming to Christ.

Emalou's hands and feet became swollen and painful from gout, and Art wondered if they should retire. The gout was soon controlled by medication and they forged ahead to meet spiritual needs. In May 1983 Art wrote to their intercessory team, "Souls are being saved; many are experiencing great deliverance from bondage, superstition and fear. The power of heathenism is being cast aside, and broken lives and families are being restored. Many Gospel-preaching churches are springing up. We praise God for this. But as we think of Jesus sitting on a hill overlooking Jerusalem and weeping over the needy ones there, we are sure that His heart is also weeping over the unsaved in the Navajo Nation. . . . Were there twice as many churches, multitudes would still be unchurched and on the broad road that leads to destruction. Alcohol is still the number one killer among the Navajos. One reservation area has the greatest incidence of venereal disease of any place in the United States. Can you visualize [these] going down to death, many of them crying out piteously, 'No man careth for my soul'?

"We feel like those pictured on TV in the flooded areas of our country trying to stem the flood with a few sandbags. There is so much to be done here and so few to help. Let's cry out to God who promised 'When the enemy shall come in like a flood, the Spirit of the LORD shall lift up a standard against him' (Isaiah 59:19b, KJV). Let us redouble our efforts to throw out the lifeline." Then, with a compelling heart cry, he added words from Edward S. Ufford's hymn, "Throw Out the Life-Line":

"Soon will the season of rescue be o'er,
Soon will they drift to eternity's shore;
Haste then, my brother, no time for delay,
But throw out the Life-Line and save them today."

Art wanted that lifeline thrown to native people on both sides of the U. S./Canadian border. Efforts to reach the Dogribs, as well as more Navajos, continued. That summer the Dogribs were less cordial than the summer before. Talking about freedom from alcoholism had been acceptable, but preaching about salvation from sin through faith in Christ alone had spawned opposition. "You tricked us," some accused.

Ryan Gorman with Dogrib family

"The spiritual darkness here is appalling," Art wrote. "Conditions make one weep. . . . One would like to take life a little easier, but God has burdened the heart of Navajos for these Dogribs, and I must help while I can." He and Emalou agreed: it was the intercessory prayer of their supporters on behalf of needy Indian people that would bring fruit.

Harvey Betselie was among the Navajos who returned to Fort Rae that winter. "Look!" he exclaimed to his co-workers as he scanned the community bulletin board. "Here's a note advertising lots for lease. Maybe we could build a mission house here. Let's go talk with the chief."

"The people might just give you land and help you build," the chief responded. "If you make a down payment of $35, we'll talk about it at our next meeting."

The feasibility of a Navajo mission organization continued to dominate Art's thoughts. "What do you think of the Navajos organizing to reach Native Americans for Christ, specifically the Dogribs?" he asked Ryan Gorman one day.

"Good idea," Ryan agreed.

"Would you be willing to head such an organization?"

Upon Ryan's affirmative answer, committees were formed and a meeting was scheduled. Much prayer and discussion ensued. Board members were chosen and incorporation papers drawn up. At succeeding meetings officers were elected and trips planned. The group discussed the possibility of a mission station in Fort Rae. The area was predominantly Catholic, but according to an article in *The Vancouver Sun*,[1] the Dene followed "both Christ and the spirituality of their ancient past–which includes beliefs in communicating with the dead, reincarnation, and soul traveling." The salvation of the Dogribs was uppermost in the Navajos' minds.

"We really need to go back to them soon," one of the Navajos said.

"I'm not sure it's a good idea to make frequent short trips," responded another. "When missionaries came to Navajoland, they came to stay."

"Why don't the Dogribs donate money for us to come?" someone else asked.

"We didn't give money to the missionaries who came to us. The Dogribs are no different," another countered.

Art encouraged, enabled, and assisted as asked, but the Navajos planned, banked, wrote letters, and raised funds. He and Emalou followed every development with great interest. On March 15, 1983, Native Gospel Outreach (NGO) was incorporated. Art's dream had become reality!

While attending a meeting at Aneth shortly thereafter, the Norrises listened for hours to

NGO board (L-R): Ryan Gorman, Betsy Newman, Ben Hogue, Custer Lowe

Navajo men preach and believers testify to abundant life in Christ. They eagerly sang the Navajo hymns and savored mutton stew and fry bread with the rest. Their biggest thrill, however, was the $100 offering the Navajos gave to send an evangelistic team to the Northwest Territories that summer! That team presented formal application for land in Fort Rae, and Jimmy Erasmus offered to help them through the lengthy hamlet, provincial, and federal approval process.

The spiritual condition of that northern area was graphically characterized in a local newspaper article. The article told of three men who were sentenced to a week in jail for having sex with a 13-year-old girl who subsequently became pregnant. The judge deemed that the men were merely living their lives in the way life is lived in the high Arctic. Such realities compelled the Norrises and the NGO team to proclaim God's life-changing power as often and as simply as they could. The long trips were tiring and expensive and living conditions in Fort Rae were not what they were used to, but no one complained. Although the Dogribs were slow to accept the Gospel, attitudes were beginning to change.

❖

Art and Emalou were very much involved with the intermittent ministry trips to the NWT, but their interest and involvement continued in the Navajo outreach as well. They were pleased with Jerry Sloan's planning for the future of NBI and NGC's northern area. Preparations were underway for building renovations. One Bible seminar for Navajo church leaders had been held and another requested. These encouraging advances ended when in June of 1984 NGC's board received Jerry's letter of resignation. "I'm sorry I'm in the way of the good progress the mission and school were making," he wrote. "I will do all in my power to help Mr. Norris be successful in making a better training place for Navajos in the future. I would like for him to receive all the support money that is currently coming to me."

The specific reasons for Jerry Sloan's resignation were doubtless complicated and multifaceted. Inexperienced board members lived too far from the facility to provide needed help. Some again acknowledged that leadership responsibilities for both the school and mission were excessive for one man. "It was a mistake to hand it all over to him without some preliminary training or orientation," others contended. Temptations, blame, and accusations all accompanied the failed attempt to place the ministry under native leadership. Disappointment was agonizing, but those involved moved forward trusting the Holy Spirit's leadership. Joe Mehesy resumed interim directorship.

"It's a depressing situation," Art wrote, "but we still have the Lord and will go on with His help in the Bible institute and the outstations." In this bleak moment he was encouraged that NGC's three Utah outstations were under Navajo leadership.

As NGC's board sought a solution for the lack of leadership, one of them turned to Art. "Art, if I were you, I'd sell the mission property and lay something aside for retirement. Take it easy; provide for yourself." But Art and Emalou did not see the property as theirs to sell. They longed for the Bible institute ministry to expand. Retirement funds were nearly nonexistent, but selling the property and taking it easy were simply not options. They had agreed to trust their faithful Lord for every need.

Art knew that he might die before carrying out his dream of developing an interest-bearing fund to help spread the Gospel among natives even after he was gone. He also hoped to distribute inexpensive local news sheets and native language cassettes containing the Gospel to Indian communities in northern Canada. Whether or not those dreams were realized, he and Emalou determined to "run with patience the race" that was set before them in the time that remained.

That "race" included faithful ministry at home. Art continued teaching at the Bible institute and assisted with the editing and mailing of the *Listen* leaflet. He met with leaders of NGO to plan another trip to the Northwest Territories. He and Emalou participated in vacation Bible schools and projects at other missions. They distributed Christmas gifts on the reservation and sought to teach and encourage numerous individuals and congregations. One Sunday they drove eighty miles, preached in Navajo, then rushed back to their home church for the evening service. Arriving home at eight that evening, they collapsed into their chairs and fell soundly asleep, finally struggling to bed at 12:30 a.m. That, seemingly, was the only evidence that they were approaching seventy.

At its February 1985 meeting, the NGC board voted unanimously to turn to UIM for leadership. UIM offered computerized accounting, printing and mailing services, and a recruitment and candidate training system. A merger would also eliminate some of the competition and duplication prevalent among missions on Indian reservations. NGC's sole stipulation, to which UIM agreed, was that the Navajo Bible Institute continue. On April 1, 1985, Art's seventieth birthday, the two missions merged and three of NGC's board members became UIM board members.

The Bible institute was renamed Four Corners School of the Bible for Native Leadership (FCSB) that summer and continued for a time under UIM. Curriculum was upgraded to better prepare high school graduates to serve as pastors, youth workers, and other church leaders. Art sensed it was time for him to leave the classroom. "It's hard to quit giving out the Word in the classroom after spending one's life at it," he wrote. "Like the white pine that puts out a greatly increased number of seeds in its last five years of life, leaving a lot of little trees to take its place, so we must work to leave behind those who have been led to the Lord."

Not only did the Norrises long to see Navajos carrying the Gospel beyond their reservation, they also wanted to see them feeding on God's Word, maturing in Christ, and giving of their resources. For those unable to read their own language, however, the study of God's Word was nearly impossible. With the completion of the entire Scripture translation, the two of them began distributing Bibles and teaching people to read, coming full circle from the beginning of the Navajo Bible Reading School in 1953. "I'm having the time of my life . . .," Art wrote. "Interest seems good, and when we use the Bible as the textbook, it turns out to be a Bible study. I'm thrilled about learning new Navajo words and expressions and thank the Lord for this golden opportunity. God is so good!" He and Emalou counseled pastors, pastors' wives, and other Christian leaders, many of whom were graduates of NBI.

Art with native children

That year was a busy one for the Dogrib outreach also. In June of his seventieth year Art called a friend. "Emalou will stay home to help with VBS, but I'm leaving in a couple of days with eight Navajo men. I covet your prayers. The four- to five-day trip is exhausting."

"How great a grind will it be for you?" the friend queried.

Art laughed. "Well, I'd rather wear out than rust out!"

Ten, not eight, Navajo evangelists accompanied Art in his old van, affectionately dubbed "The Gray Donkey." Several of them had left jobs without pay for three weeks. In High Level, Alberta, the group witnessed to two alcoholic Slaveys from the village of Assumption, one of whom trusted Christ. That contact kindled much prayer for Assumption, eighty miles west of High Level.

While Ryan Gorman and some of the men began work in Fort Rae, Art and three others flew 100 miles farther north to the isolated hamlet of Rae Lakes. Conditions there were grim. Few youth attended school; most mothers were unmarried. "As far as I know, there have been only four conversions here in ten years," the missionary in Rae Lakes commented. That news so burdened one of the Navajos that he could not sleep for several days.

After Art and the others returned to Fort Rae, Art wrote, "I cannot describe the joy that has filled my heart to see the Navajo Christians' response when exposed to the spiritual needs of their fellow tribesmen. They are appalled at the spiritual darkness and were surprised to learn that people are told how much money to give to get rid of a given sin. They ask God to lead them and to meet the need and believe that longer visits are needed. They . . . are discussing how they can provide financial and prayer support [for Navajo missionaries]. Though visible results seem small, they want to press on in the spiritual ministry they have begun. . . ."

NBI graduates Eddie and Betty Benally with Dogrib VBS children

Art tried to learn sufficient Dogrib to enable him to translate hymns and to produce recorded Scripture verses. "It's difficult to try to reconcile people to God who don't feel the need for reconciliation," he wrote to his home church. "They believe the priest will pray them out of purgatory after they die. We all feel very ignorant in presenting Christ. One needs patience, love, and tact and the leading of the Spirit. Last night . . . a man having a heart attack had to be flown 150 miles to Yellowknife in a charter plane costing $1400. How much his expenses will cost the government, I don't know, but trying to reconcile hell-bound men to God costs a lot, too, and that is much more important. . . ."

After a late summer interlude in the States, Art returned to Fort Rae with NBI graduates Jones and Grace Dehiya. "The Dehiyas face opposition as other missionaries do," he noted, "but they don't have to deal with the racial barrier that Satan uses with Anglos." While the Dehiyas taught Scripture, he helped a Dogrib teacher translate songs which expressed the Gospel.

One afternoon Art sat by a window in a tiny loft writing a letter. "Satan seems to have his way here Friday and Saturday nights," he wrote. "King Alcohol reigns, and shouting and yelling and crying go on and on. One is embarrassed by what one sees. Having witnessed a complete reversal of lifestyle in many Navajos, I am confident that God through His Son's sacrifice can make new creatures of Dogribs too, though it looks impossible."

Some of the paperwork for the Fort Rae mission site was completed that fall. While awaiting final approval, NGO discussed fund raising. "Let's have a chili and taco supper and a bazaar," someone suggested.

"Mr. Norris said that Christians shouldn't have to fill their bellies to consider giving to the Lord," one of Art's former students interjected. "We should give because we love Him."

That comment cheered Art. He and Emalou had often encouraged Navajos to support their churches and tribal outreach, but the concept had not been fully grasped. "We missionaries are partly to blame," he admitted, "for most of us have not consistently taught biblical giving."

After waiting more than three years, the Navajos received final approval for the Fort Rae multipurpose building in April of 1986. They were told that unless they started construction by October 1, however, they could lose the property. Funds were needed immediately. A few gifts came in, but Navajo believers seemed reluctant to support a native organization. UIM's director offered to seek financial assistance, but Art felt the Navajos should raise funds from their own people.

Sacrificing time and personal means, six Navajos and Art began groundwork on the Fort Rae mission building. Laboring long, exhausting hours, they accomplished much before returning to Navajoland. Later, Art and Emalou returned with several Navajos to visit the Dogribs and to distribute literature and tell Bible stories. They printed translated hymns, praying that the Holy Spirit would utilize them until Scripture could be translated. Art secured a teacher for a Protestant class in the public school, but the class never materialized.

Emalou in campground near Fort Rae

The Norrises had thought often about the Slavey man whom the Navajos had led to the Lord in High Level the summer before. They were told that Assumption and many other Northern Alberta reserves were in dire spiritual need. In late August they left the Navajos in the NWT, headed southward to investigate, and parked their trailer in High Level. That evening a non-native happened by. Seeing their Colorado license plate, he greeted, "Hi! I'm the Justice of the Peace. You folks vacationing in these parts?"

"We plan to visit Assumption tomorrow," Art answered.

The man's eyes widened. "I'd not go there if I were you! I deal with court cases from there. It's a dangerous place: houses burned, windows broken, drunkenness, violence. They've even shot bullets over the police headquarters."

Undaunted, the Norrises unhitched their trailer the next morning and drove across forest-covered muskeg to Assumption. The conditions were abhorrent. They handed out song tapes and leaflets summarizing the Gospel. People paid attention when Art spoke a few Navajo words. Older villagers gave them dried fish and a tour, but the community in general was hostile. Challenged and deeply burdened, Art and Emalou turned homeward. The light of Christ had penetrated spiritually dark places before. It could do so again.

As the Norrises approached retirement, the pastor of one of their supporting churches saw a change, not in their devotion, but in their focus, especially Art's. He commented, "Whereas Art had been committed totally to the work at Cortez and among the Navajos, his vision broadened to leading Navajo people to minister in the Northwest Territories. Instead of decreasing, his ventures became more daring and more sacrificial. A person would have thought that the old man would back off a little bit; instead, the warhorse galloped a little faster than he did before."

The Norrises had seen the beginning of a new erra in the reaching of North America's native peoples, and they intended to continue being a part of what He was doing. In February 1987 Art wrote to a friend, ". . . on April 1 we will formally retire from UIM International. We don't read anywhere where Paul the apostle quit serving God and we don't intend to either. The message we preach means the difference between heaven and hell; therefore we need to keep busy getting this message out, and this, by God's grace, we intend to do to the best of our ability."

Art and Emalou had understood, erroneously, that they could not receive funds through UIM after retirement; however, their confidence was in a God who could provide beyond their meager Social Security income. "God has given us the Navajo language for a reason, and we would like to use it until 'this poor lisping, stamm'ring tongue lies silent in the grave,'" Art wrote, quoting words from William Cowper's hymn, "There Is a Fountain." "We would like to follow Caleb's example when he said, 'Give me this mountain'" (Joshua 14:12a, KJV).

21
Pressing On

". . . forgetting what lies behind and reaching forward to what lies ahead, I press on toward the goal for the prize of the upward call of God in Christ Jesus."
– Philippians 3: 13b-14

April 1 came and went and the retirement letter had not yet been written. Art and Emalou's yo-yo-style schedule was an arduous one for seventy-two-year-olds. For the first half of 1987 they recruited missionaries at PBI, visited Fort Rae, and surveyed villages in Northern Alberta. Back at home, Art helped NGO finalize plans for the Fort Rae building, then went to help on site. Shortly after he returned from those three weeks, he and Emalou drove north again. Since NGO workers going to Fort Rae were now familiar with border crossings and the use of Canadian money, the Norrises began to focus vigorous attention on Northern Alberta. The village of Assumption was much on their hearts. Though they were not allowed to stay there, they could park their trailer at nearby Rainbow Lake.

Hearing of their plans, a man in High Level cautioned, "I'm on Assumption's school board, and I don't think it's safe for you to go there. We had to evacuate teachers because they were threatened with knives and guns." Ignoring the warning, Art and Emalou again distributed leaflets and music tapes containing the Gospel, assuring recipients that God could give them victorious and eternal life. As a point of contact, they also used photographs of Navajos assisting the Dogribs.

Art spent a total of five months in the North that year, Emalou three. While at home in Cortez they encouraged, counseled, and taught Navajos; served in vacation Bible schools; and visited Bible institute alumni.

January 1, 1988, arrived and, with it, formal retirement. Art and Emalou were awed at the thought of fifty years spent among the Navajos, but the past was not their focus. "The golden years are for being more active for the Lord, not for taking it easy," Art wrote. "Souls are going to hell without Christ; we *must* give out the salvation message as long as God gives us strength." While one in their desire for the salvation of native people, they did not always see eye to eye about the type or degree of involvement they should have. Emalou was concerned about Art's health, especially his cardiac problems. She would have preferred deceleration, not acceleration. Nevertheless, she stood with him in his determination to launch out with renewed vigor.

One Sunday alone in the days of their early "retirement" required fortitude beyond that of many younger people. Leaving home at 8:00 a.m., they visited a native pastor forty-two miles away and answered his numerous biblical questions. Next they drove still further to a house church and spent several hours with native believers there. Before heading home, they searched until they found the home of a man about whose spiritual condition they were burdened and visited him.

NGO building in Fort Rae

In March that year Emalou shared her concern about Art's eyesight. "Art needs cataract surgery. A lot is at stake, for he needs to be able to read the difficult Navajo and to help translate Dogrib hymns." After successful surgery, he was again on his way to Fort Rae with a Navajo team for two months. The team made considerable progress on the mission building, and by 1989 NGO was able to hold two dedication services, one in the States in May and one on site in June.

It was a historic moment when, at the June dedication, Earl Williams and Ambrose and Priscilla Tsosie offered themselves as resident missionaries and NGO pledged to support them. The Norrises were thrilled! Isolation and separation from family deterred most Navajos from such commitment. Less than a week after the Norrises returned home for much-needed rest, NGO leaders asked Art, "Would you take our missionaries to Fort Rae and mentor them for a month?"

"The 2500-mile one-way trip in the truck without air conditioning is hard on the flesh, but the opportunity is too great to turn down," Art told supporters. "The Tsosies have decided to attend Bible school, so three Navajo men and I will take Earl. We'll finish the building, hold children's classes, visit homes, and distribute literature while there. I'm confident that God can bring victory over the horrible conditions in that area. Therefore, we are spurred on."

Some, including Art, were concerned about Earl's serving alone; others asserted, "He's like Abraham and wants to obey the call of the Lord. God will care for his needs." Earl did a good job of handling Bible studies, home visitation, and interaction with the youth. When Art, Ryan, and Jim Taylor (who with his wife, Mildred, had served for a while at the Bible school in Cortez) visited him in February 1990, he was happy and growing spiritually. When they learned a bit later of his sudden decision to leave to finish his education and pay off a debt, they were greatly disappointed.

Three times that year the Norrises traversed the long road to the North Country. On one trip they took Earl's replacement, Gene Holyan. Gene was good at giving object lessons and the Dogribs received him well; however, when the Norrises left, they felt as though they were abandoning their child. "I'll be okay; I'm following God's leading," Gene assured them. Two months later he wrote, "Rae is the land I love most on earth now. There's no doubt that this is where God wants me. I have peace living here." He worked at learning the language. He started a men's Bible study, played Dogrib tapes, and showed the *Jesus* film. The children made friends with him, but some adults avoided him, thinking he was trying to steal them from their own church. His greatest concern was "the icy indifference of people's hearts." When the long, cold winter came, he had to adjust to mid-afternoon sunsets, a smoke-filled blue-gray sky, and a frozen lake and sewage lines. Snow-packed streets came alive with snowmobiles. During the dreary days many Dogribs succumbed to the ravages of alcohol. NGO prayed that Gene would resist temptation.

Among those who responded to NGO's pleas for help with the 1991 summer outreach were three grandmothers with Bible school training who helped in Northern Alberta villages. They were well accepted. Other

Navajos ministered at other sites.

That August at UIM's thirty-fifth anniversary conference in the States, Art contrasted past spiritually barren years on the Navajo Reservation with the increasing occurrence of camp meeting, revival, and church signs scattered across the reservation. At seventy-six he and Emalou were gratified to see many Navajos and a few Dogribs finding freedom in Christ. "We're becoming old and wonder what to do," he said. "Many go to Florida where there's nice water and ocean-side shuffleboard. But Navajo is not spoken there. Besides, what good is pushing a shuffleboard around? These are golden years for us. Dave Breese on one of his radio broadcasts said, 'Some men die in battle, some men die in flames, but most men perish inch by inch playing little games.' May God keep us from that!"

On the afternoon of April 15, 1992, Art was scheduled to fly to the NWT. That morning he entered the doctor's office for a checkup. The doctor examined him and announced, "I want you in the hospital tomorrow for an angioplasty."

How can that be! Art agonized. God has so masterfully arranged the details of this trip! I need to solidify summer plans and encourage Gene. Later he remarked, "The procedure didn't hurt, but canceling the trip sure did!" By June he was able to join Gene in Assumption and Meander River to address children in public schools and to recruit them for vacation Bible school.

Becoming increasingly fearful that Gene was succumbing to Satan's attacks, NGO's governing board mandated that he come home and look for a co-worker. Gene did not want to leave. They sent him an airplane ticket, but he did not come home. In August while in Canada, Art and a Navajo brother learned that Gene was studying at a Baptist school in Edmonton, reportedly struggling with alcohol. Disappointed, they turned their attention to door-to-door evangelism among the Slaveys and Beavers. They noted less opposition in Assumption than previously, but a policeman warned them not to stay there overnight in their van.

At Christmastime Art went back north with Ambrose Tsosie and Jerry Nininger, a missionary from Immanuel Mission, to distribute gifts from the Navajos. Jim Taylor and David Shed, a PBI student considering becoming NGO's missionary in Fort Rae, joined the men in Three Hills and rode as far as Northern Alberta. While the rest went on to Fort Rae, Jim and Art made their way to the hamlets of Assumption, Meander, and Jean D'or Prairie. Despite a less than cordial welcome, they distributed gifts and confidently witnessed. As they worked together, they discovered their mutual interest and experience in camping ministries and discussed the possibility of a Bible camp for native children. They even began praying for a half acre of land. Accepting an invitation to speak at High Level Baptist Church, they shared the vision of a camping ministry. "We've looked for potential sites," they told the congregation, "but even if we found property, the obstacles seem insurmountable." Len Dueck, a member of the church and a counselor in government schools, was cheered by the Norris/Taylor report. He had been praying for someone to reach native children.

On his way back to the States, Art dropped Jim off in Three Hills. "Jim," he confided, "only God knows if I'll see a camping ministry become reality. I'm facing radiation therapy for prostate cancer."

Not long after Art reached home, Mr. Dueck called. "Brother Art, you'll be happy to know that my wife and I have given our 120-acre farm about thirty miles east of High Level for a camp. It has a cabin, natural gas, water, electricity, and telephone service."

Len and Pat Dueck

"One hundred twenty acres!" Art exclaimed. "And we asked God for a mere half acre!"

No one could have foreseen all of the miraculous answers to prayer that would occur in 1993. One Sunday morning that spring Art drove fifty-five miles east of High Level to Fort Vermilion and walked into a small Sunday School Mission church. "Hi, I'm Mark Baer," a gentleman greeted him. "Your name?"

"Art Norris, Cortez, Colorado. My wife and I are involved in outreach to native people, and we're looking for a base from which to work. We have access to a church in High Level, but it would be convenient to have something here as well."

Mark, a Minnesotan, was happy to see a fellow American. "You may use our facility as a contact center if you'd like."

The Norrises rejoiced at this and other evidences of God's working. Back home in Cortez, they learned that two Navajos from their Bible study had become Christians. Two bus loads of Navajos unconnected with NGO were planning vacation Bible schools in several British Columbia communities. News came that Fort Rae was having regular Sunday services, and a van was donated for NGO's Canadian work. With renewed vigor the two of them prepared for summer ministries up north with the Taylors.

Beginning their four-day trip in early June, Art drove the motor home and Emalou their ten-year-old Chevy van loaded with tents, Bibles, and other supplies. Emalou was exhausted. The trip itself seemed an impossibility. How could she survive the hectic weeks ahead? Driving through Montana, she noticed ominous clouds. The wind picked up and rain began pelting the windshield. The thought of driving through a violent storm was too much. "Lord," she murmured, "if You wanted to, You could push this storm away." Immediately the clouds parted, some moving east and some west. Her spirit was renewed as she drove down a virtual hallway between two storms. "Lord, if You're willing to do that for me now, You can give strength for the whole summer!" she cried.

Near Three Hills the motor home engine blew, providing nearly a week of unexpected, God-ordained rest. When the engine was finally replaced, Jim Taylor accompanied them on to High Level, where his camper was parked. Together the three of them made the rounds of nearby villages, sharing the Gospel and recruiting children for anticipated vacation Bible schools. "You know," Jim remarked one day as they ate, "I believe the Lord wants Mildred and me to take our camper into Assumption."

"If God is leading, I won't discourage you," Art stated.

Certain of God's leading, Jim scheduled an appointment with the council and new chief. The previous chief, who had been resistant to the Gospel, was deceased. On the day of the appointment Art drove Jim to Assumption. "Shall I go in with you or stay in the car and pray?"

"Either way," Jim replied.

Art prayed while Jim met with tribal leaders. "I wonder if my wife and I might move our trailer here for a few weeks and help your people with maintenance needs," Jim requested respectfully.

"You'd be welcome," the new chief replied.

Rejoicing over such a miracle, Jim notified his wife, Mildred. She came from Three Hills by bus and helped him paint houses, fix fences, and do other odd jobs. Noticing a man having trouble roofing his house, Jim asked, "May I help you?" The man accepted his offer, and before the roof was finished he had placed his trust in Christ! Gradually, the villagers' attitudes toward the Taylors warmed.

By the time the Norrises returned from a brief break in Cortez for a family reunion and fiftieth wedding anniversary celebration, the Taylors had left. "May we park our RV where the Taylors had theirs?" they asked the tribal council.

"Sure. Just work with the priest and divide your time between Assumption and Meander," the council urged. Art and Emalou were eager to include Meander. They discipled the man in Assumption whom Jim had led to Christ, showed videos of Navajos singing and preaching, and distributed more literature. They were full of awe as they wended their way home that fall. They had been cursed by some, cautiously received by most, and, in some cases, even given a cup of tea, but God had masterminded significant contacts on five reserves.

Immeasurable spiritual need still existed. Fort Rae still had no missionary. Many Navajo Christians, twenty-five that summer alone, had participated in short-term missions, but none had been willing to stay long term. They needed to be challenged to leave home and families. Had not Christ left His Home and endured a wretched, sin-cursed world out of love for the Father and for sinners?

In her letter on behalf of NGO that fall, secretary Betsy Newman stated her amazement at the Norrises' perseverance and joy even in difficult situations. "Pray for these never-tiring servants," she wrote. Then, challenging her own people, she continued, "Just as there was much prayer for us to be delivered from our sins, so we Navajos must pray for the unsaved people of the Far North."

That Christmas Jerry Nininger, Ambrose Tsosie, and Art again took Christmas gifts north, stopping in Three Hills for Jim Taylor. Having driven the 1250 miles from Cortez to Three Hills in twenty-four hours, seventy-eight-year-old Art commented, "I'm going to have to be more careful about rest and exercise if I make this trip again." The trip was worth every effort, for the tribal elders in Assumption were pleased to see Jim and readily agreed to a vacation Bible school in their village the coming summer.

With the blessings of 1993 behind them, the Norrises and Taylors pressed on into 1994 with great expectancy. In April Art rendezvoused with Jim to promote summer vacation Bible schools on several reserves. He even received permission to speak on Assumption's 12-watt radio station! He had dreamed of the possibilities of Christian radio programming as an economical and effective way to reach northern tribes. Radio could accomplish in a brief time what it would take missionaries decades to do. He considered an FM transmitter that could fit in a suitcase and run off a car battery for broadcasting to remote places and understood that such a transmitter was available from HCJB Broadcasting Company in Quito, Ecuador. While pursuing options, he discovered a station, equipment, and tower for sale for $9000 Canadian. Family Life Radio might help, he thought, but Canada required that a portion of the programs be produced in country. Broadcasting from Alaska was another option, as was a Christian station in Bellingham, Washington. Unaware that High Level and Yellowknife were already covered by satellite, he and Jim investigated satellite signals, since such signals were not bound by international borders. One thing was definite: a full-time person was needed to pursue Christian radio.

The men visited Len and Pat Dueck and learned that the donated farm, now Eagle's Nest Bible Camp, was under the oversight of the Shantymen, a Canadian mission organization. An abbreviated camping session was planned for the upcoming summer with the first full season slated for the following year. Children from different reserves would attend each week. Except for the Dogribs, all reserves were within a hundred miles of the camp. Excited about the potential of such a ministry, Art and Jim helped with preparations.

Alert to every opportunity, the men inquired of a guard in a correctional facility in Yellowknife, "Could we visit the inmates and show a video Sunday afternoon?" Not only were they allowed to show the video, but Art was given permission to preach. So many opportunities, so little time, so few workers. Art recruited a local pastor to teach weekly Bible studies at the facility, and soon the guards were taking inmates to that pastor's church. Emalou's previous declaration about Art was proving true: he was like yeast, stirring people up and challenging them to become involved.

Later that summer Art and Emalou returned north together. He again drove the motor home and she the van packed with supplies. The realities of his prostate cancer and shingles and her limited strength were overshadowed by people's need of the Savior. Again storm clouds appeared as they drove northward in tandem. Suddenly a bolt of lightning struck horizontally between the motor home and the van, igniting a tree at the roadside. "Thank You, Lord, for that special reminder of Your power and presence," Emalou breathed aloud, remembering His intervention the year before.

In Alberta the Taylors and Norrises helped to maintain order among the twenty lively campers at Eagle's Nest, then prepared for Assumption's very first VBS by cutting poles and erecting tents.

Jim Taylor (left) with VBS children in Assumption

Local men helped to tidy up the assigned lot. Ever-present inquisitive children, black flies, horse flies, mosquitoes, and barking dogs kept the dedicated seniors on edge. Five Navajos arrived to assist them. No sooner had they pitched their tents than the rain began and everything turned

Navajo Florence Betselie teaching VBS

to mud. The large tent leaked and partially collapsed twice. Nevertheless, team unity was evident throughout the week as they gathered daily in the Norrises' motor home for Scripture reading, prayer, and discussion of their plans.

On the historic morning twenty-four children came late and stayed for lunch, which Emalou prepared. Enthusiastically they sang with Art's accordion accompaniment but continually disrupted classes by running to the store for candy, gum, and pop. In spite of the commotion, God's plan of salvation was clearly explained. During evening services, adults listened no less distractedly than the children. Whether the week was a "success,"

Art telling story at Assumption VBS

no one knew, but at least the villagers had been introduced to Christ and the team was invited to return.

Someone in Meander River heard about Assumption's VBS and asked for one in their village. Though the Navajos needed to leave, the Norrises and Taylors, unwilling to ignore an open door, moved to Meander on Sunday and set up their equipment. On Monday, after dealing with twenty undisciplined, hyperactive children with short attention spans due largely to Fetal Alcohol Syndrome, the couples were exhausted. Two ladies from the Baptist church in High Level responded to their urgent plea for help. The heat was oppressive, the bugs were intolerable, and Emalou was not feeling well. The whole team was frazzled. In weakness they looked to the Lord, grateful for this unprecedented opportunity, and acknowledged that the responsibility for harvest was His.

That fall, a mere six weeks after undergoing another angioplasty, Art, nearly eighty, joined the Navajos for another Christmas trip. Due to frigid temperatures, the planned outing for Assumption's children was replaced by the first-ever Christmas program, an all-day event. There and again in Meander, High Level, Fort Vermilion, Bushe River, Rainbow Lake, Rocky Lane, and Jean D'or Prairie the Navajos distributed gifts and literature and told the Christmas story. As one couple listened, the Spirit of God faithfully drew them to Christ.

Before leaving the area, Art helped to plan for Eagle's Nest Bible Camp needs: shelters, beds, chairs, dishes, a cooking/dining facility, a septic tank, and a well. "Art's burning himself out to see people come to Christ," a fellow missionary commented. "It's just in his fabric. He and Emalou are still pioneers."

22
His Strong Hand and Hearing Ear

"Behold, the LORD's hand is not shortened, that it cannot save;
neither his ear heavy, that it cannot hear."
– Isaiah 59:1 (KJV)

In 1995, within five months of the Christmas outreach, Art, still dealing with shingles, angina, and cancer, was back in Alberta. Again, he and the Taylors encouraged children in several villages to attend summer vacation Bible schools and camp. In Fort Vermilion he challenged Mike and Barbara Shumik, former Canadian missionaries to Indonesia: "How about starting a Sunday school in Meander River? I know it's eighty miles away, but those people need the Lord."

Mike's imagination was sparked. "We could build a portable room and move it to Meander." Plans fell into place. NGO would provide materials and Mark Baer would transport the 12- by 16-foot building. Until it was ready, Meander officials offered the use of their alcohol recovery building.

In July the Taylors and Norrises and the Norrises' granddaughter Olivia returned for a second round of vacation Bible school in Assumption and Meander. Again the children's behavior and constant presence kept the elderly couples exhausted and Olivia in tears, but little by little the Gospel was gaining

Olivia Pearson with Slavey children
in Assumption

Olivia playing with
Slavey children

entrance.

Similar advances were being made at Eagle's Nest Bible Camp, where new plywood shacks housed the children. Slaveys and Crees came, and eight Dogribs traveled 450 miles over gravel road from Fort Rae to attend. Most of the Dogrib children professed faith in Christ, including a girl who had told the missionary the previous summer that Jesus could not come into her heart because her deceased grandfather lived there. Tough times undoubtedly lay ahead for these children; commitment to Christ in the Dogrib culture usually meant sacrificing family ties.

Fatigued but elated, the Norrises returned to Colorado late that summer. "The best summer yet!" Art declared. "We had some harassment and

VBS children in Assumption

things stolen in one village, but that's to be expected, for 'they know not what they do'" (Luke 23:34).

These ongoing ministries took a toll on the Norrises' financial reserves. They were dipping into limited Social Security funds for ministry needs. Learning of this, UIM's director offered to write a letter to their supporters. "We would accept a mild letter to that effect," Art replied.

Although Art underwent chelation therapy for prostate cancer, by December he was again able to accompany Navajos for their Christmas outreach and visit to the Sheds, who had become NGO's missionaries in Fort Rae. For some time he had wanted to visit Garden River, but the road to this small burg, 100 miles beyond Fort Vermilion, was seldom navigable. "I'll take you in my four-wheel drive," Mark Baer volunteered.

That was all Art needed. They loaded gifts and left. "Quite a road, eh?" Art commented.

Mark nodded, gripping the steering wheel. "And quite an expanse of nothingness. Absolutely no sign of civilization for a hundred miles. If you get stuck, you're stuck. That's why I threw in some food and a propane bottle and burner." They spun and slid, slowly clocking off the miles and meeting only two cars the whole way.

"We'd better get permission to hand out the gifts," Art said as they drove into Garden River. Passing several log houses, they pulled up beside the tribal elder's office. Art opened the pickup door and shivered as sub-zero air engulfed him. "Kind of cold for an old man in spite of all my winter clothing!" he gasped.

Uncomfortable circumstances were not insurmountable barriers for the Ancient One. With His help and much determination the men climbed in and out of the warm cab until every home had a Christmas package containing a gift and a letter from Navajo Christians proclaiming Jesus as Savior.

Back home in January of 1996 Art received a letter from his urologist friend. "Dear Art, The brand of cancer you have is prostatic adenocarcinoma—or a glandular aggressiveness. Your stage is D (A is best, D is worst). Though remissions of up to seven to ten years are known, an average remission of about three years can be expected. Let's hope for longer!"

That spring eighty-one-year-old Art returned to a number of Alberta's reserves to advertise summer ministries. He was encouraged to learn that the Meander Sunday school was going well and that the Bushe River chief had opened his village to a Sunday school. While pursuing his God-given task of laying groundwork, he prayed fervently that God would send a full-time missionary to the area.

An opportunity to challenge Christians to involvement came as he spoke in the High Level Baptist Church. Everyone sat expectantly as he stepped to the podium. His once tall form was now slightly bent, his kind, thoughtful face framed by white hair. A smile lurked a mere millisecond from his twinkling eyes. Fifty-eight work- and prayer-filled years had passed since he and Emalou had arrived on the Navajo Reservation. In retirement they had traveled thousands of miles yearly to share Christ with Northern Canada's native peoples. Did God's Word mention retirement? Did it say that cancer and cardiac problems were reasons to sit quietly and wait for death's eager fingers?

Stillness pervaded the sanctuary. "Brothers and sisters," Art began, "I'm grateful to be with you. I understand that you have been praying for the Lord of the harvest to thrust forth laborers to the Indian settlements of this region. God has been faithfully answering your prayers. Our Navajo brothers and sisters in the States have been coming to the North for several years to share the Good News with their Dene relatives. Progress has been slow. Backward steps seem at times to outnumber forward ones, but God is working. A few Dogribs, Slaveys, Beavers, and Tall Crees have trusted Christ and are standing strong for Him in difficult situations. But, brothers and sisters, . . ." His voice broke.

The congregation was hushed. "My fellow believers, the number of those who have trusted Christ is negligible. We have barely begun to penetrate the spiritual darkness, and that in only a few hamlets. In hundreds of isolated villages Jesus is not known nor has His name even been heard. Drunkenness, immoral relationships, high suicide rates, families in shambles. Sin and hopelessness reign."

Distressed by the gravity of these truths, Art continued with quiet anguish. "These people–people for whom Christ died–are enslaved to Satan." Love for North America's First Peoples oozed from his manner and every word. He and Emalou had lived, moved, and breathed for their salvation. With their years numbered, they yearned to see younger missionaries taking the Gospel to these they so loved. Though their prayer focus included the entire world–millions in Africa, Asia, Europe, and South America who had not so much as heard that there is a Savior–their hearts still ached primarily for the native people of North America.

Art continued: "I have never doubted my call to the Navajos. God confirmed it by enabling me to learn that difficult language. It's been a painfully slow and difficult work, but God gave my wife and me deep love for these special people. Now He's privileged us to challenge and assist them in bringing the Gospel up here to their distant relatives. When I hear of other mission fields where people respond more quickly, I'll admit that I'd like to go there too. That isn't possible at my age, but as long as God gives us breath and health, we can work where He has placed us."

Art scanned the attentive listeners, gray-haired saints among them. "Career missionaries are hard to come by these days, but that's not an impossible obstacle for the God of the universe. Many retirees, perhaps some of you, travel in recreational vehicles. Perhaps you could serve the Lord for a month or two where no career missionaries are available. Going just a couple hundred miles north and making friends with Indian people could pave the way for their reception of the Gospel. God can place you, equip you, and enable you to make a mark for Him. Last summer from our RV my wife and I showed many Gospel videos to native people. Videos catch their eyes and ears; the Lord can capture their hearts. One new believer, now into the Word, often sings of God's amazing grace. Imperfect though we and our methods are, God uses whatever we make available to Him. Amazingly, He uses His redeemed ones to bring glory to Himself. It is *He* who is responsible for the increase."

With conviction Art challenged, "Where are men, women, and young people who will stick it out through the sunshine and blizzards of life to tell others of Jesus? Where are the saved who are willing to be as inconvenienced for Christ's sake as He was for ours?

"Friends, do you remember the passage in Deuteronomy 15 about the servants of Hebrew masters who were to be freed in the Jubilee year, the seventh year of servitude? However, if the servant loved his master and chose to continue in his service, he could have his ears punched with an awl signifying his desire to be a lifetime servant. My wife and I heard about the great need in the village of Assumption and were told that it was not a place for white people to go, but we went anyway because those people need Christ. We have recently rededicated ourselves to getting the Gospel to more people in that village and other villages in the area. We love the Master and have chosen to have our ears punched by Him, the King of kings and Lord of lords. We do not serve Him in our own strength. We gladly engage in His work as He supplies our needs. Servanthood is not the prerogative of youth alone. His people are to be ambassadors no matter what their age. Time is short. Multitudes are dying without Christ. What can we do to change that? What can you do? What *will* you do?"

After Art's impassioned plea to the Christians at High Level Baptist

Church, he returned to help Emalou prepare for the summer's ministries. They planned lessons, games, songs, and prizes; purchased food and mosquito repellent; and readied tents. In July they and their twelve-year-

Mildred Taylor with children at first Eagle's Nest camp

old grandson, Kevin, headed to Assumption, joined again by the Taylors.

Despite the usual challenges, several children at the vacation Bible school showed interest. A nine-year-old girl repeatedly questioned Emalou about spiritual things. Patiently Emalou answered, praying that God would accomplish His purpose. They again recruited children for Eagle's Nest Camp, where log dormitories had replaced the plywood shacks. Many children who attended were from villages contacted by the Taylors and Norrises, including the inquisitive girl from Assumption. Before the week was over, that girl had trusted Christ!

Never lacking ideas for spreading the Gospel, Art and Jim made and distributed Slavey tapes. Art also attempted to drive the motor home to the top of a mountain just outside High Level to test for signals on his ham radio, hoping to find another way to disseminate the Gospel. His mission was stymied when the tires spun on the narrow trail and, with Emalou directing from the rear window, he had to back two miles downhill.

In addition to the usual villages, Paddle Prairie permitted a Christmas program and gift distribution that winter; however, at eighty-one, Art was too exhausted to participate. He and Jimmy Etcitty did visit Jean D'or Prairie, though, a visit which opened that village to the Gospel.

Art refused to let the vision of Christian radio for Northern Canada's native peoples die. After praying about his April 1997 trip, he felt God wanted him to take Jimmy Etcitty and check out the potential of a radio outreach in Hay River in the Northwest Territories. Someone told him that a 200-watt radio station could be purchased from HCJB in Ecuador for $3,000. Jim Taylor, who shared Art's vision, learned of another station about a hundred miles from Three Hills that he thought they might be able to buy and move to High Level. Back to the Bible Broadcasters in Lincoln, Nebraska, recommended Bible Broadcasting Radio Corporation, which beamed Christian programming into Canada via satellite.

With still no definite leading on any of the broadcasting alternatives, the men turned their attention to Eagle's Nest Bible Camp. More than 150 children heard God's Word there that summer. Sitting at a campfire one evening, Art pondered what a tragedy it would have been had the camps been delayed until the facilities were modernized.

Staff and children at
Eagle's Nest Bible Camp

The week after camp, some of the Navajo workers who had become interested in the Tall Cree campers initiated a vacation Bible school on the South Tall Cree Reserve. Forty children and several adults trusted Christ during that VBS. The rest of the Navajo/Anglo team divided into groups for VBS in several villages. It rained all week at Assumption, where four Navajo ladies helped the Norrises and Taylors. Mud saturated the carpet of the Norris van. Unruly children ripped curtains off the van windows and confiscated window screens. "We're willing to sustain such damage in order for these kids to hear God's Word," Art wrote, aware that God was the One who had orchestrated their being in that village. He had not known until a short time earlier that his childhood friend, Bill Hardy, had prayed for the salvation of these tribal groups since the end of World War II when he had been assigned to the area by the Canadian government! God was beginning to answer those prayers!

While still in the area, Emalou discipled a new Christian and helped Art to prepare hymn, Scripture, testimony, and sermon tapes for distribution.

Only a few months after arriving home, Art and Ryan boarded a plane for NGO's 1997 Christmas outreach. Again, Jim Taylor accompanied them. The natives seemed less suspicious and local Christians more interested in reaching Canada's First Nations than before. Ryan preached at Fort Rae and gave his testimony at the Yellowknife prison, where three inmates trusted Christ and an Inuit inmate rededicated himself. Traveling on, the men saw a sign: "Kakisa Lake, First Nations Reserve." "Let's go there!" Art suggested enthusiastically. Twelve miles down the road they found a small but friendly group of Slaveys who had heard nothing about either the Bible camp or the Navajos' visits. The tribal leaders approved a vacation Bible school there the following summer, evidence to the three men that the Holy Spirit had preceded them.

"I feel bad that we go in and do a little bit, then leave," Art lamented as the men left. "Oh, that God would send someone long term! If the Lord allows, I'd like to come again next summer." Jim wondered if God would work through Art's presence or his absence.

Back home, Art handed Emalou a real estate photo of the house next to the Taylors in Three Hills. "Emalou, there's so much need and so little time! Do you think we should move to Alberta?"

"I hate to be so far from family, Art. We're in our eighties and need to think about future needs."

"Art knows he is living on borrowed time," Jerry Nininger commented. "He wants somebody to take up this work. He could probably rest if somebody did. He loves people and seems to know everybody. He doesn't waste time just talking with them; he's either sharing the Gospel, working on a connection that will further it, or stimulating others to share."

Four months later Art was back on the road, this time with son-in-law John Pearson and Stephen Christensen, son of former NGC/UIM missionaries and grandson of Charles and Iris Girton. With their satellite receiver, they hoped to pull in Sky Angel, a program providing fourteen conservative TV stations and fourteen FM stations. If successful, they could provide receivers to tribal areas devoid of Christian programming. Unfortunately, their attempts failed.

The summer of 1998, eighty-three-year-old Art took a laptop north with him instead of his usual ham radio. He spent quiet moments at the keyboard sending and receiving electronic mail. "I can always use ham radio when I'm old enough to retire!" he asserted.

Tim and Donna Norris helped with the vacation Bible schools and camp that summer. In Kakisa Lake the chief welcomed them warmly. He gave them moose meat and attended the first class with his wife and child. At Eagle's Nest the team found new cabins, a new wash house, new washroom facilities, an improved play area, and plans for a swimming pool. Nearly 200 children from ten native communities and four towns came, twenty of whom returned to their homes as new Christians.

The results of 1998's summer ministries were heartening but, from Art's perspective, the following summer was the most fruitful one they had ever experienced up north. Fifty-five children trusted Christ. He and Jim had discovered that an Edmonton radio station broadcast via satellite to fifty-five FM stations scattered over Alberta's reserves. Furthermore, every reserve could be reached twenty-four hours a day, seven days a week. NGO had promised to provide taped Gospel messages for a year. Michael and Man Sandstrom, a young missionary couple with Northern Canada Evangelical Mission, had begun serving long term among the northern villages and were eager to pursue radio outreach.

In the spring of 2000 the Norrises, Taylors, Sandstroms, and Chinese Christians whom the Sandstroms recruited in Edmonton and Toronto staffed the vacation Bible schools. Afterwards Art joined his brother, Cy, in British Columbia to visit places they had loved during their childhood and teen years. That trip to Canada was Art's last. On September 30, 2000, he and son Tim departed for Alberta, but Art became ill at Denver International Airport and was admitted to a hospital in Colorado Springs near the home of his daughter Karen. An aortic and two inguinal aneurysms required immediate surgery.

A frustratingly slow recovery did not mean non-productivity for him or Emalou. Back in Cortez, they invited their church youth to a dinner honoring six Navajo women preparing to go north for a VBS. After hearing the ladies' testimonies, fifteen of the youth dedicated themselves to the Lord's service. "That evening accomplished more for eternity than my making another trip could have," Art declared later. "God's hand is not shortened. He will call others to accomplish His will not only among Canada's First Nations people, but among the people of the world."

23
His Gift of Family

"Behold, children are a gift of the LORD;
the fruit of the womb is a reward."
– Psalm 127:3

Art's and Emalou's ministries had been the source of great blessing. Their family had also contributed much joy to their lives. As they reminisced, their 1993 wedding anniversary celebration came to mind. "And now, ladies and gentlemen, 'Life with Mom and Dad from the Beginning'!" Laughter reigned as the Norris offspring took their places. Nearly fifty years had passed since Art and Emalou had exchanged wedding vows, and with the help of their children, they were about to review family memories.

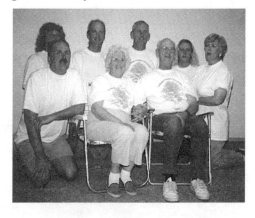

Norris family (L-R): Ruth, Paul, Dan, Emalou, Tim, Art, Faith, Karen

Paul and Karen, as Dad and Mom, seated themselves in the front seat of a make-believe car while the other four climbed into the back. Paul turned the imaginary ignition key and off they went. Talking all the while, he jammed his foot on the accelerator and jerked the pretend steering wheel from side to side. "Daddy, you're getting too close to the edge!" Karen gasped. "Come on, Daddy, you've got children in the car!"

"This is a near-death experience!" a backseat passenger groaned.

211

When the illusory ride was over, the children reminded Art and Emalou of other possible scenarios. They had great fun reminiscing.

Touched by the lovely anniversary celebration, Art and Emalou returned to Alberta, Canada, where they had interrupted summer ministry for the occasion. Enclosing monetary gifts in thank-you letters, they told their children how much they missed them and the grandchildren. "We've consoled ourselves by reviewing the good memories we have of all of you . . . . We would like to share a little of what God has given us. Of course, this material stuff is not nearly as valuable as that which we have always wanted to share with you, that is, the spiritual riches in Christ Jesus. We usually don't find it hard to accept a material gift, but it's really up to us individually to accept or reject spiritual riches.

"Months before each of you was born, we began praying for you. As soon as you were born, we privately and publicly dedicated you to the Lord. You all have treated us very well. You are our greatest possessions on earth. Thanks for this recent reunion and fiftieth wedding anniversary celebration. One of these days the circle will probably be broken. Statistics would show that Dad probably will be the first to go. As our bodies are deteriorating, we see real purpose in the process and rejoice in it, for it means it won't be long until we meet the Lord face to face. What a joy that will be!"

Despite major misunderstandings prior to marriage, Art and Emalou were mindful of God's sovereignty, shaping, and polishing. Though they were from quite different backgrounds, they had, with His help, developed harmony and a deeply caring relationship. They were grateful for the family He had given them. Recalling past years was a blessing.

The years in the basement house were full of special memories, as were the years that followed. Each morning the children heard the squeal of their father's ham radio and the dot dot dash of the

Norris children Back (L-R): Tully, Robert
Front (L-R): Tim, Ruth, Karen, Paul

Morse Code. Timmy, adept at throwing his glass bottles out of the crib onto the cement floor, was weaned early. "Okay, Timmy," declared his exasperated mother, "that's the last bottle you're going to get!"

Art often had to be away. He was gone the morning Ruth climbed up on Emalou's lap after family devotions and murmured, "Mama, I want Jesus in my heart." Can one so young understand? Emalou had wondered, but who was she to question the Holy Spirit's working? She hugged her spiritually awakened three-year-old close as Ruth asked Jesus to be her Savior.

A few years after the family's move to Cortez, Karen entered first grade. "I'm part Navajo,"she proudly announced to a classmate.

"No, you aren't," the classmate responded. "My mother said you can't be. You have blond hair and blue eyes."

"But I have two Navajo brothers."

Bob and Tully were indeed considered family members. Sometimes they attended a boarding school, sometimes the local day school. To help them maintain their identity, Art conversed with them in Navajo and taught them and his own children the beauty of their culture.

After three years in the basement house, the Norrises moved to another temporary dwelling with only two bedrooms, no running water, and no indoor bathroom. Faith joined the family soon thereafter in 1952. It was a tight squeeze, but at least the house was lighter and drier than the basement. The children were excited about a baby sister, especially Robert and Tully. Eagerly they watched her grow. Her first sentence

Back (L-R): Tom Dennison, Alan McHardy, Tim, Art, Emalou with Faith
Front (L-R): Paul, Ruth, Karen

was "Tully, tie my shoes!" When she was old enough, Tully and Robert contrived a fairy tale for her. "Once upon a time an airplane flew real low over the mission and a bundle fell out. Laddie caught the bundle before it hit the ground and brought it to us. Guess what! You were in that bundle!" Faith heard the story so often she believed it.

Faith delighted in sitting on the back of Bossy, the gentle Jersey, while her dad milked. Every drop of the milk was put to good use. All the children loved the butter their mother made, but they did not share her enthusiasm for homemade cottage cheese. For some, even the smell of clabbered milk hanging in the cheesecloth over a drip pan triggered a gag reflex. But for Emalou, homemade cottage cheese with black pepper was a treat. Art preferred store-bought cheese, the sharper and stronger the better. The "aroma" of ranker varieties, which Emalou insisted he store in the basement, sometimes rose through heater vents and permeated the house, triggering marital discussions on "taste" and "good taste."

Art believed in order, and getting up in the mornings was part of that order. Awakened by the six o'clock campus bell or lively polka music, the aroused children raced to the one and only bathroom. The first to arrive was considered lucky by those left standing in line. For anyone not responding to the wake-up call, Art's threat of a cold water treatment was usually incentive enough, but Paul was not a morning person. Occasionally he awoke to sprinkles of cold water.

The children learned early that a Norris does not stand idle. There were chores enough for everyone: dishwashing, ironing, gardening, canning, plowing, milking, or fetching escaped livestock. But there were fun times as well. As a first grader, Timmy accompanied Nancy Stillhammer, daughter of missionaries Edna and Von, to the stream flowing through the mission property to fish. A bit older and not wanting to share the fishing pole, Nancy had hoped to fish alone. She tossed in her line and waited. Just as she whipped the hook out of the water, Timmy walked behind her, and the fishhook lodged in his lip. Soon she was trudging up the hill carrying the pole, Timmy in tow. "Mama, come quick!" she hollered.

Nancy's sister appeared at the door and, seeing the hook with a lead sinker hanging below it, calmly directed, "Let's go get your dad, Timmy. He's the one to take care of this." When Art saw the situation, he laughed and dashed back into the house for a camera. Emalou followed him out, fuming, "What's so amusing about seeing Timmy in pain? How can you take time for a picture?"

Just then Mr. Stillhammer appeared, fetched a pair of pliers, and cut the line free.

"Let's go to the doctor, son," Art said. "What a way to end a fishing trip!"

Whenever possible, the four oldest Norris children spent time with the Howard Montgomery children. What one did not think of, another did . . . like starting a fire in the "kitchen" of the tumbleweed "house" they had built, attempting to walk arm in arm across a flooded river, or crafting a homemade hand grenade for the Fourth of July.

To Art and Emalou, as well as to the children, family times were always highlights. Birthdays were celebrated with homemade cake and a gift. Christmases were also special, tree-cutting a family project. Of necessity, gift-giving was limited, but on Christmas Day the children opened boxes received from supporters, most containing food. The food was a godsend, but writing thank-you notes to strangers for cans of peaches and beans was not particularly exciting.

One year after Christmas while putting the decorations away, the older children discovered that ornaments made excellent missiles. Emalou, away at the time, returned to find her decorative family heirlooms shattered and strewn about the house.

As the staff increased, holidays were usually celebrated with the larger mission family. To the Norris children, the mission *was* their family and they never lacked for playmates. To them, eating a meal without guests seemed abnormal. Family times were frequently interrupted by ministry needs, a reality felt by most of the children. They cherished family picnics, game evenings, reading and eating popcorn together. Camping, panning for gold, and accompanying their dad on errands were also treats, but all such activities were much too infrequent to suit them.

The children loved Art's playful moods, though his antics sometimes embarrassed Emalou. With the family on a ferry in British Columbia he limped across the deck, his hands in contorted configurations. Behind him trotted the children, laughing uncontrollably. He did not intend to make fun of anyone, but Emalou, remembering her own brother's disability and sensitive to passengers' stares, was horrified. She followed, whispering, "No, Art, no!"

Strife was not unknown among the siblings. Tim and Paul locked horns frequently, but they also played together. At times Bob and Tully badgered their Anglo siblings: "Red Coats! You treat us just like the English treated the American colonists." Sometimes to irritate their siblings they rattled off Navajo with their friends.

"Okay, then, I don't want to know your old language!" Karen responded as a junior high student.

At sixteen Paul confiscated Karen's after-school snack one afternoon. "You took my cheese!" she insisted emphatically.

"No, I didn't."

"Yes, you did!"

Pulling the bedraggled hunk out of his pocket, Paul slapped it on the table. "There, take your old cheese!"

Beside herself, Karen doubled her fist, rapped him sharply on the temple, then ran to the bedroom and flung herself across the bed, sobbing. Quietly the door opened. She looked up to see her dad. "What you did to Paul was okay, Karen. He should not have done what he did."

Paul was not always excited about school, but he was anything but dumb. He had his own printing press and even knew how to set type. His dad was proud of his accomplishments and of those of each of the children, though the children often heard his compliments secondhand.

With so many students, staff, and missionary families living close together, discipline of the children was difficult. When the children were younger, Art had applied a belt to their backside; as they became older, he smacked alternate hands, with an extra swat for flinching or pulling back. Emalou elicited "repentance," at least from some, by appealing to feelings. The children often felt that they had to toe the mark because of who their parents were or because they represented the mission. They perceived that more was expected of them than of the other children on campus, and they perceived rightly. After all, they were the director's offspring!

The Norris household was always busy. Seldom did the family sit down to a meal without the phone ringing or someone knocking. There were not enough hours in Emalou's days. One morning as she said goodbye to departing guests, her friend Pat McIntosh came and started on the overflowing basket of ironing. As Emalou prepared to launder dirty towels and sheets, more guests arrived. Little wonder she's exhausted! Pat thought empathetically.

When the family journeyed to supporting churches from time to time, they lived on sandwiches and slept in the car beside the road. Sometimes Art whipped off at mountain overlooks and applied the brakes at the very edge, thrilling some family members and frightening others. To keep themselves from boredom, the children sang or competed in finding the most state license plates. Emalou sat with her hand over the back seat ready to whack whichever child might need it.

As they traveled, Art taught the children to think. "What if . . .," he'd say, then proceed to ask them what they'd do in certain situations. They stopped at museums, a car manufacturing plant, Custer's Battlefield, the Kellogg factory, state capitols, and national parks. He reviewed with them lessons learned on nature walks with park rangers. Friends also treated the children to new experiences. Taking the family to a steak house, a supporter told them to get anything they wanted. Trained to order by price, the children scanned the menu and asked for hamburgers. Another supporter treated the family to a day at Chicago's Brookfield Zoo. Just as the family approached a cage of slithering snakes, someone touched Emalou's arm. Her scream brought hearty laughter from bystanders.

The children sat quietly as Art preached, showed slides, and told about the mission work in various churches. Afterwards they dutifully stood by the display table distributing literature and answering questions, enduring the routine as many as five times a week. Each return to the road was a welcome respite from the unending questions of strangers.

Art often tried to draw the children into conversation. At home at the supper table one evening he asked generally, "How was your day?"

"Tim called Massie a Jap," Faith responded.

Tim hung his head and slid low in the chair. "I'll see you later," his dad remarked. Tim knew what that meant. All the children were acquainted with the biblical injunction to "spare the rod and spoil the child."

Jokesters that they were, Bob, Tully, and their friend Jack Stillhammer devised a prank for George, a young PBI graduate. They would never think of playing such a trick on Mr. Norris, "The Boss Man," as they called him, but George would relish it. Rigging a bucket of water over the chapel door, they watched, ready to yell "Surprise!" but the surprise was on them. They were paralyzed with fear to see Art striding toward the door. What a relief when he emerged soaked but laughing!

At an early age the children had learned to trust their dad by jumping to him from high places. As some of them ventured out on their first bicycle rides, he was at their side helping them. Sometimes he gave them wheelbarrow rides or took them bowling. At picnics he whirled them on the merry-go-round and played ball with them while Emalou set out a fried chicken lunch complete with tablecloth and napkins. Winter activities were also fun. The budget did not allow for downhill skiing, but used skis from an army surplus auction worked great on snowy roads. On occasion Art pulled a toboggan load of children by car, swerving from side to side for extra thrills. Inner tubes tied to sleds provided additional icy excursions. Emalou thought some of the activities a bit dangerous, but she merely required that wet feet be wiped before the fun lovers reentered the house.

Mealtimes were often educational seminars. With a waltz or march in the background Art would tap out a rhythm on the table or on someone's shoulder or head. "Paul, what's that instrument?" he'd ask when an oboe entered or "Karen, what instrument is that?" referring to a trumpet. Not highly gifted in music, he was nevertheless moved by it and wanted his children to appreciate it. He loved classical music but found contemporary music distasteful. When the children were still quite young, he exposed them to Beethoven's "Fifth Symphony." He himself could play piano and accordion and required the older children to learn piano plus at least one other instrument. Karen learned the violin, she and Ruth the clarinet, Paul the trumpet, and Timmy the trombone. He had hoped they could play together, but the required transpositions were too difficult. None fully appreciated his efforts at the time, but years later Karen gratefully recognized the difference between her musical tastes and those of other young adults.

Sometimes the focus was on science. Of English descent, Art drank tea brewed just right and served in one of his mother's china cups. Since letting it cool naturally did not fit his busy schedule, he placed table knives, handles first, in the tea and taught the children about heat conduction while the tea cooled. Conversations about God's awesome creativity accompanied gardening, hunting trips, and rides through the mountains. Attempting to impress the children with God's power, Art had each of them plant a tree, water, fertilize, and pray for it!

With old cars and other items sitting around, the mission property appeared more like a junkyard than a Bible school. Some of the cars worked; some didn't. Some boasted more than 330,000 miles. Art's favorite was a classy 1921 Cadillac whose gas gauge dropped visibly as he drove. His own children were embarrassed to be seen in it. "Daddy, let us out before we get to school," they'd beg. Navajo children, however, piled in at his invitation and he'd take off with childlike glee in a cloud of dust. Emalou just shook her head and wondered if she were the only adult on the site.

One evening during a series of revival meetings Emalou put the children to bed and went to the kitchen. "Mama!" five-year-old Faith called. Emalou went to her bedside. "Mama, I need to be saved." Happy for such bedtime delay, Emalou talked

Art and children with
Grandmother Norris

and prayed with her, rejoicing with Art later that their youngest daughter had trusted the Savior.

Emalou's nights were often short. The children were in bed by nine and Art liked to retire early. That was her chance to clean house, iron, and catch up on other things. She learned to survive with little sleep but was always tired and sometimes weepy. Working around the mission one day, associate missionary Jim Cook heard her singing, "It will be worth it all, When we see Jesus; Life's trials will seem so small, when we see Christ; One glimpse of His dear face, All sorrow will erase, so bravely run the race, Till we see Christ."[1] Jim knew something of her workload and never forgot the lesson.

The Norris children were taught to respect others, but, to Ruth, some things were intolerable. On the school bus one day a boy taunted her and Faith in a singsong voice, "Art Norris preaches to Indians because white people are too smart to listen." Twelve-year-old Ruth drew her fist back and

L-R: Ruth, Emalou, Faith,
Karen, Tim, Art, Paul

whacked him full force. "Faithie," she whispered, "don't you dare tell Mom and Dad. We aren't supposed to fight 'cause it gives the mission a bad name, but that boy can't talk about Dad like that and get away with it!" Dutifully Faith promised secrecy.

Art and Emalou had daily devotions with the children and longed for them to grow in Christ. Tim often wondered as he read Scripture how his mother, without a Bible in front of her, knew the words he stumbled over and even those that followed. Some of the children viewed the devotional times as little more than a legalistic routine, but the older they became, the more they longed to experience a real relationship with God. Some wished their parents would share details of their own spiritual journeys. Convinced of the value of Scripture memorization, especially when she had little time for reading, Emalou involved the whole family in the Bible Memory Association.

Art was willing to make the sacrifices necessary for his children to attend the high school connected with his alma mater. By the late 1950s Robert, Tully, and Karen were all at Prairie High School (PHS) in Alberta, Canada. For Emalou, sending fourteen-year-old Karen was difficult. Paul and Ruth followed in 1960 but before the school year ended, Ruth had had enough of rigid rules. Unable to persuade her to stay, Art and Emalou arranged to meet her bus in Salt Lake City. To their surprise, Paul and Karen were with her.

That winter when the temperature plummeted to twenty-four degrees below zero and school buses would not start, the three of them were exuberant over a day off. "You shouldn't be so happy about not going to school," their father rebuked. At two that afternoon he finally got the car started and took them to school. Embarrassed, they entered their classrooms with the day nearly over.

One day when the Norrises' friend Mr. Harwood was visiting, Emalou served potato corn chowder, cheese sandwiches, fruit, and cookies. "Do you ever have meat?" Mr. Harwood asked.

"Oh, yes," she replied. "Sundays we have chicken or roast and use our best china."

The next morning as Mr. Harwood shared the family's oatmeal breakfast, he buttered his toast and reached for the jam. "We're not allowed to have butter and jam on the same piece of bread," three-year-old Danny admonished.

"Oh, I'm sorry. If those are the rules, I'll stick to them." Mr. Harwood said.

Another morning with company at the table, Art asked, "Danny, would you pray?" Danny bowed his head and blurted, "God, help Faith not to be so mean and stinkin'."

"What was that all about, Faithie?" the guest asked later.

"Don't ask me! I never know what he's talking about!"

Tragedy and death were realities to which the children were exposed. Tim and Danny were shocked the day their friend Tony, a Bible school student, and a missionary were killed in a car accident. "Come," Art said to the boys, "let's go look at the car." Seeing the tangled remains of the VW made a deep impression on them. Years later Tim commented, "I think Dad thought seeing that car would make us more responsible drivers."

"Yeah," echoed Dan. "Once he and I saw a head-on wreck in which the driver was mangled. Dad made a point of telling me that that man had suffered because the other guy was in such a rush."

Concerned about college funds for the children, the Norrises spent the summer of 1962 in Seattle working at a Christian facility which was housing visitors to the World's Fair. Most of the family worked in the kitchen, housekeeping, or office. Art learned how to run a press in the print shop and obtained a used 1250 offset press for the mission while he was there. Back home, he set it up in the basement of one of the buildings and began to learn its idiosyncracies. At midnight one night he was still not home. Emalou found him in the basement, baffled and disheartened. Crumpled paper littered the floor. "Art, what's wrong?"

"Aw, you have to adjust the fountain solution, then you test print some papers and throw them away, then you try a little more solution, and it still doesn't work. Then you adjust the pressure on the ink roller and throw away more test papers. Disgusting!" He was relieved when Jim Cook took over the job and did it well.

The next summer most of the family worked in the vegetable harvest in Milton-Freewater, Oregon. Twelve-year-old Faith's task was to keep four-year-old Daniel busy outside so that those who worked nights could sleep. Looking for ways to increase the summer's income, Art talked with the owner of a nearby raspberry patch. "Faith," he said one day, "the owner of that raspberry patch over there will let you eat all the raspberries you want if you'll pick them for him." Faith set to work, eating the biggest and juiciest, but she had to stop so often to find Daniel that she lost her job. Art also discovered a loaded apricot tree and bought the fruit, which the family picked and sold at a profit. Even with their multiple earnings, the summer netted little. Nevertheless, God provided funds for Karen to attend Multnomah School of the Bible in Oregon and Paul, Calvary Bible College in Kansas City.

In 1964 when missionary Richard Hellyer was insulating pipes under a mission building, five-year-old Danny crawled under to help him. As

Danny and Navajo friend

they wrapped used clothing around the pipes, they talked about many things, including Jesus. "Danny, would you like to receive Jesus Christ as your Savior?" Mr. Hellyer asked after they had talked for a while.

"Yep, I would," Danny answered. Before praying with him, Mr. Hellyer made sure he understood.

Over the years the children were involved in ministry as well as in routine chores and maintenance. One summer Tully assisted with Navajo Gospel Mission's youth program. Most of the Norris children helped with American Sunday School Union's vacation Bible schools, one of which Tim directed before entering college. Some taught at summer camps, and during one break from Bible school Karen cooked, cared for the house, typed letters for her dad, and baby-sat Danny while Ruth assisted Emalou with several vacation Bible schools.

After the older children left home, Art and Emalou had more time to spend with Faith and Dan. Vacationing in Mexico, the four of them pitched their tent on a spectacular white sand beach and spent hours collecting shells. In the mountain villages they noted extreme poverty. Everywhere they went, people clambered to get the Spanish tracts they distributed from their car windows.

Back at home, Faith enjoyed ball games and peanuts, community concerts and operas with her dad. The first time he took her to an auto race, she buried her head in her coat to escape the deafening roar. Soon, however, she was cheering with the rest, and Art knew that he had won another family member to the sport.

One Friday evening he brought home a portable sewing machine and set it on the table. "Faith, if you can make something this weekend, this sewing machine is yours." Faith rushed to F. W. Woolworth Co. for material. By Monday morning she had two new outfits. Art was as proud as she of her accomplishment. In her sophomore year he asked one morning, "Faithie, want to go deer hunting after school?" The two of them drove into the mountains, found an observation point, and munched on snacks as they waited. Finally, a doe approached. Just as she was near enough for Art to shoot, Faith crunched loudly into a crisp apple. The doe ran, much to the relief of both tender-hearted father and daughter.

"Dad's definitely soft-hearted," Tim said years later. "He almost passed out once just telling us about someone whose leg was rebroken so it would heal right. And he always chokes up when he hears Canada's national anthem."

"My friends used to be afraid to come home with me," Faith commented in her adult years. "They thought Dad looked so stern, but he cries over babies, marching bands, and weddings. He doesn't come across as a softy, though."

"Dad was tough," Dan reminisced. "I remember the time the septic line was plugged and he just couldn't get it cleared. He finally took the lid off the tank and threw in a couple of inner tubes. He climbed on them and floated to the spot where the pipe from the house entered the tank. When he poked a stick up the pipe to clear it, stuff erupted all over him. He always taught us that if there was a job to be done, you just do it."

"When I was in a pastorate," Tim related, "Dad told me that, for him, his work wasn't so much a matter of his spiritual gifts, but a matter of what needed to be done. God seemed to gift him for whatever tasks He placed in front of him. Dad was simply available."

A letter Bob wrote after his graduation from PBI encouraged Art and Emalou: "I thank the Lord for leading me to Prairie Bible Institute. I attended Prairie High School also. The Lord taught me many things which

I would have had a hard time learning anywhere else. . . . I don't know exactly what the Lord is leading me to do, but He has the blueprints. This past summer I helped the Stillhammers at the Aneth outstation. Mr. Stillhammer and I baptized several [people]. Whatever I do and wherever I go, it will always be to give out the Gospel." Years later several Navajos told Art and Emalou that Bob had led them to the Lord.

After earning a PhD at Penn State, Bob taught at the college level. Tully earned a masters degree and became superintendent of a public school on the reservation. Sadly, after years of serving the Lord, both men began living lifestyles that brought sorrow to Art and Emalou. At the age of forty-three, Bob died an alcohol-related death.

Thinking of Bob's and Tully's education, Karen commented one day, "Mom, Dad, you must have been disappointed in us kids. Bob and Tully both got higher degrees than any of us."

"You haven't disappointed us," Emalou responded. "We'd much rather you be ordinary people having a relationship with the Lord than college graduates making lots of money."

In 1967 Art ordered a brand new Volkswagen "bug" from Germany. "Faith," he said as he prepared to leave for a deacon's meeting one evening, "go start the VW and let it warm up, but don't move it." Faith, who was just learning to drive, threw on her coat and ran through the snow. She started the car and waited. Would her dad never come? Impatiently she put the car into reverse and let out the clutch. Wham! The five-ton truck behind her looked fine, but the rear end of the VW had not fared so well. As Art strolled out of the house, she crawled from the car, blood draining from her head and neck. Damaging a brand new car would surely warrant loss of life, but all she heard was a quiet, "I thought I told you not to move it."

In 1968 Karen planned a party in honor of her parents' twenty-fifth wedding anniversary. She had begun to notice some changes in them, but their ministry still often took priority. Only God knew if they would show up at the party. At the appointed hour they drove in. "I'm so glad you came!" she exclaimed exuberantly.

"Unexpected guests did just arrive at the school," Emalou replied, "but we showed them the guest room and told them we'd see them tomorrow morning." Things truly *are* changing, Karen mused.

Dan benefited from those changes. He and his dad went deer hunting, and the two of them also spent a memorable week in Rico, Colorado. They drove around in the mountains, found old mining claims, and snagged fish in Trout Lake, fixing them for supper. Those times with his dad were special to Dan. The older children knew each other better than he knew any of them, but he had some advantages that they had not enjoyed. Not only did he spend more time with his dad, but Art and Emalou, thinking that perhaps they had been too strict with the older children, had become more relaxed in their discipline, more willing to take some risks with the younger children.

Dan
with pet lamb

Stockcar racing was Art's special love. "Want to go to the races?" he asked a friend's son in Cortez for the summer. Arriving at the track and learning that one of the drivers had not shown up, Art volunteered, but his offer was ignored. Midget cars also attracted him, as did another form of entertainment he and Dan devised. Marking off a quarter mile near the mission, they took turns taking the old pickup through the gears and timing each other. They also backed vehicles up hills, explored rugged canyon trails, and worked themselves out of impossible predicaments on isolated, back-country roads. The two of them even went to the Purgatory ski area in the Colorado mountains when Art was in his early sixties and stayed on the bunny trails all morning. In the afternoon Dan announced, "Dad, I'm going to try some other trails. I'll see you at four o'clock at the lodge."

At four, Art did not appear. Dan skied a bit longer, then returned to the lodge again. This time his dad was there. "Dad, what happened? Where were you?"

"You'll never believe it, son. I went off a corner into deep snow and couldn't get up. I finally gave up and lay there 'til some kids came along and pulled me out." In spite of his dad's fall, Dan was proud of his efforts.

In 1974 Emalou and Dan planned to go shopping for Dan's school clothes while Art went fishing with a volunteer. Early that morning Emalou went out to pull weeds. When she didn't return, Dan went to check on her. "Mom, are you about ready to go to Durango?"

"What for?" she asked.

"To buy school clothes. Remember?"

"Where's Dad?"

"Mom, you know. He went fishing."

"He doesn't fish."

Dan knew then that something was wrong. "Mom, come in and lie down a bit," he said, assisting her into the house. "Did you eat breakfast?"

"No."

"Just lie still. I'll fix you an egg."

After two bites Emalou lay down again. Dan ran to find one of the volunteers. "Something's wrong with Mom! Can you come?" he urged.

When the volunteer and Dan suggested a trip to the doctor, Emalou became belligerent, but they took her anyway. Her blood test revealed a blood sugar dangerously below normal. After receiving intravenous glucose, she was able to think clearly but remembered little that had happened that morning. Some months later she discovered that her hypoglycemic episodes seemed to be connected with her thyroid medication. Once she ceased taking that, her blood sugar remained normal.

When Bible school and mission responsibilities lessened in the 1980s and the weight of making and enforcing rules was gone, Art became less rigid. His increased sensitivity and spiritual growth were evident to co-workers. Both he and Emalou were aware of past criticism for involvement in missionary work to the detriment of their children. God gave them the grace to acknowledge mistakes and accept the criticism. Emalou confided to a friend that they had spent so much time with the Navajos she had neglected her own children and wished she had given them priority. "In retrospect," she said, "I believe I was too demanding and did not listen to them enough."

Art added, "When they were small, I felt like I knew how to handle them, but when they got older, I didn't know what to do. I regret not having attended their ball games. I really felt the lack of a father role model."

"I missed having a mother around, too," Emalou continued, "someone with whom to discuss things. Having experienced the world's tough realities as a young person myself, I pushed my children toward spiritual things to save them the agony I had known. Some of them rebelled, and I realized that I had pushed too hard. I even apologized to our eldest son for spanking him almost every day. I should have thought of a more acceptable way to train him. In those days I was always concerned about care of the house, meal preparation, and whatever else, and I didn't take time to show affection to the children. If I could do it over, I'd take more time to assure them of my love." However, she and Art concurred–brooding over mistakes gained nothing. They had to move forward in the new light God had given.

Most of the children had felt the less-than-desired parental attention. "At Dad's funeral the Navajos will sit in the front row and we'll sit in the back," they joked in their adult years. "That's the way it's been throughout life. They *are* his life." "But," one of them asserted, "I didn't think of myself as underprivileged because Mom and Dad were in ministry. They were busy, and ministry by nature is a sacrifice. In order to minister you have to give up something."

Prior to a weekend reunion in the 1990s Tim commented to his mom, "I sure hope Dad can just be Dad for the weekend and not look for some Indians to talk with." His statement expressed the longings of all the children for uninterrupted time together as a family.

Commenting in her adult years, Ruth said, "Dad had flaws and was criticized by many people, but he did not let that hinder him from going on with the work that God called him to do. He changed what he could and let the rest go, going forward with purpose to serve God."

"And they reared us in an era when strict discipline was the thing," Paul added. "They weren't alone in their strictness, and I don't hold any grudge for the way we were reared; all our needs were cared for. Each of us learned to deal with whatever emotional concerns we've had, and nothing really bad has happened to any of us."

In spite of imperfections of both parents and offspring, love bound them together. "I have something better than life insurance," Art told some friends during his golden years. "Tim moved to Cortez and told me that any time we need him, he'll come immediately." The other family members likewise expressed such love. "If anything happens to Dad, we'll take care of you, Mom," they assured Emalou. Dan and Ruth also lived nearby,

Paul not far away. Karen willingly came whenever needed, and after being widowed, Faith moved closer to assist her parents.

Art's body and inquisitive, inventive mind remained active. Tim stated, "At age seventy-eight Dad acquired a used desktop computer and began the process of learning to utilize electronic mail. In his eighties he bought a laptop. He has trouble remembering some aspects of operation, but he likes the ease of communication, especially during trips to Canada. He's not ashamed to solicit help from us kids or anyone who happens by."

At one family reunion Art determined to learn how to water ski, although none of the children were accomplished enough to teach him. He did not cover much distance, but he did eventually achieve a standing position. "Art isn't a terribly talented person," Emalou remarked, "but he doesn't know he can't do things, so he tries and, sure enough, something gets done."

At eighty-two, with silver hair, rimmed glasses, and a hearing aid, Art declared, "I still think someday I'm going to invent a solar-powered bicycle. I have a solar panel that would charge a battery, and I could ride around town without buying a license plate!"

In the latter 1990s the phone rang in the Norris home. It was Paul. Since Art's hearing was poor, Emalou handled most of the phone conversations. However, before Paul hung up, he asked, "Mom, may I speak with Dad?"

Art went to the phone. "Dad, I just wanted to let you know I love you," Paul said. Art understood with his ears but, more importantly, with his heart. What he had just heard communicated forgiveness for times past when ministry was his number one focus.

Karen also came to a new understanding of her father in her adult years. She recalled his telling about the discovery of an ancient kiva or storage area and vividly remembered how the imprint of a hand had so profoundly moved him. It had reinforced his calling to bring the Gospel to Indian people. "That story helped me begin to understand Dad in a new way," she commented. "Indians are part of who he is. I no longer expect him to change nor do I feel in competition for his attention.

I believe, without rancor or hurt feelings, that everything and everyone could be stripped from Dad, but as long as he had his personal relationship with God and was relating the Good News to Indians in some way, he would survive. He would hurt terribly at the loss of his family, his church, and his mission affiliations, but he would survive those losses. Without interaction with Indians, however, he would lose his reason for living. This realization has helped me to release him when he goes to the tribes in northern Canada. With his age and health condition, my natural instinct is to want him to stay close to home. Understanding his identity with the Indians and his calling to reach them, I can watch him go knowing that he would not regret dying in the course of working with them. Deprived of these ministry opportunities, he would not fare well emotionally and probably would not last long physically either. He needs to be busy doing what he is all about.

"I also realize that much of what I interpreted as negative attitudes toward me while I was growing up was actually an expression of who he was. It was a product of his being goal-oriented and his sense of rightness rather than about me as an individual. Dad's single-mindedness was not something we understood or accounted for as children."

Karen took a walk with her aging parents one day. The three of them chattered amiably as they ambled across a hill. "We talked a lot about a lot of things, didn't we?" Art commented after they returned to the house.

"Yes, that was special," Emalou responded.

Some days later he surprised her by saying, "It must have been hard on you all those years when I didn't spend much time talking with you. You didn't have much of an outlet then, did you?"

Those days were history. Emalou was simply grateful for her husband's increasing sensitivity. Karen had observed the mellowing process. Increasingly her dad asked family members for opinions and admitted being wrong when appropriate. She sensed his genuine pride in her and her siblings. How thankful she was to see her parents from a new perspective and to establish an adult relationship with them.

Reminiscing about his dad's spiritual strength, Tim recalled, "One morning when I was in junior high, I wanted to talk with Dad before I left for school but couldn't find him. I went barging into his bedroom and found him on his knees. It was then I began to realize where he got his strength and endurance. Living in our home, I saw Christianity from the inside out and wanted my parents' God to be my God. In my opinion, Mom and Dad were successful parents as well as successful missionaries."

As parental personalities were discussed, Dan commented, "Dad helps others, but he also understands that he needs help and that there are people who are willing to help him. Mom is also sacrificial and servant-like, but it's hard for her to receive, even after all her years of missionary service."

Tim laughed. "If I went to the folks' house, Dad would probably say, 'Tim, could you help me hook up this computer?' or 'Will you light the furnace for me?' But I wouldn't be there ten minutes until Mom would ask, 'Can I get you a cup of coffee?' or 'Would you like some ice cream?' That's just Mom; she wants to do it. Both of them in their own way are pretty neat!"

"If I had to grow up all over again, I wouldn't want to do it any differently or with anyone else," Dan asserted.

Remembering her younger days, Ruth commented, "Finding Dad on his knees in the living room early in the morning when I went in to practice piano had a big impact on me. It was obvious he had been reading his Bible. So many people thought he was so strong. It's true that he didn't need other people's approval, but he did have an Authority; He did bow to God. More than anything he ever said, the fact that he didn't know it all and went to God for help impacted my life. Mom spent a lot of time reading the Bible, too. I remember seeing her behind a door near the living room with her apron over her head for a bit of privacy for prayer. I remember her struggling through a particularly difficult time, and when a breakthrough finally came, she listened to 'There Is a Balm in Gilead' over and over. She clung to that truth."

One day in the late 1990s, a friend asked, "Emalou, has there been a recurring theme in your prayers through the years?"

"Yes," she answered. "I have a tendency to speak, then think, then regret. I've prayed much that God would remind me to think and pray before I speak. I'm thankful that He has helped me to a certain degree. I've also prayed all my life that my children might know God and draw close to Him and be a testimony to others. That continues to be my prayer and burden, and I'm so thankful for those who assured us that they were praying for our children."

"That's my daily burden too," interjected Art. "Nearly every day we pray for all our children and grandchildren."

Art's cardiac condition had caused concern for years. He and Emalou had discussed possible bypass surgery, but having heard other people's stories, they decided against it. In 1998 after having had three angioplasties, Art again experienced angina simply from eating. "Perhaps we can put in a stent," the cardiologist suggested, but after examining Art thoroughly, he announced, "A stent won't help. You're booked for triple bypass surgery." With little time to discuss the unexpected turn of events, Art and Emalou asked the Lord to direct them and sensed that surgery was the treatment of choice.

Family members gathered at Art's bedside, praying with him and wishing him well. Their concern grew when during surgery the doctors had difficulty restarting his heart. "We were able to perform only two bypasses," the doctor informed them afterwards.

It was touch and go in the recovery room. As Art emerged from anesthesia, Dan bent over him, his eyes filling with tears. "Dad, you've *got* to make it. We *need* you."

Later Ruth called to see how he was. "Well, at the moment he's singing 'Jesus Loves Me,'" the nurse reported.

The next night Ruth stayed with him. "I heard you were singing 'Jesus Loves Me' last night, Dad."

"Ruth, it has never been so black as it was then," her dad replied soberly. He had always perceived other people's complaints about their ailments merely as an excuse not to work. His own twelve-week recovery and accompanying bout of depression gave ample time to rethink that theory. His pain lessened, but he was too weak to eat or walk. Emalou faithfully cared for him. He saw other patients dealing with similar conditions, and little by little God increased his empathy towards those with physical problems.

"Seems I'm about like I was before," Art noted a number of months after the surgery. "I still have angina after eating or when I'm under stress. But I should be able to go north again next summer." Several months later he did make a quick trip to British Columbia with his brother. Imagining Emalou's concern, a friend called to encourage her.

"Oh, I've just committed him to God," Emalou said. "He belongs to Him, not me."

As months passed, Art gained considerable strength and could rise early and work until late afternoon without rest. With the help of Emalou and nitroglycerin tablets, he could again actively serve the Lord, though not as vigorously as he once did. By the spring of 2001, the little strength he had gained was dwindling. He had spent some months confined to his immediate surroundings, but his heart was still on the Navajo Reservation and with the beloved natives up north. "Dad," Tim volunteered, "how would you like to go visit the Navajo church in Nazlini?"

Art was more than ready! Interaction with Navajo believers was good medicine, as was the adventuresome journey home afterwards over Buffalo Pass in the Lukachukai Mountains. Snow had visited the mountains the week before, and the never-great trail over the pass was less great than usual. The mud was miserable and the truck insisted on getting stuck more than once. Darkness was descending. Surely we're near the top, Tim thought, but if this stop-and-go process continues, we might be here all night. I wonder if Dad has enough nitroglycerin tablets to get him through.

"Are we near the top, Dad?" Tim asked for the second time.

"Yes, we're pretty close."

It was late when they got home, but the exciting adventure and opportunity to be with his beloved people had brought Art momentary renewed vigor.

Art and Emalou thanked God for the children He had so graciously given them. They had indeed been divinely blessed!

Norris family at Art and Emalou's 50th wedding anniversary

24
Shouts of Joy and Victory

"Shouts of joy and victory resound in the tents of the righteous:
the LORD's right hand has done mighty things!"
— Psalm 118:15 (NIV)

After his trip to Nazlini with Tim, Art's health continued to deteriorate. The reality of soon being in the Lord's presence became an endearing thought both to him and Emalou. "With a lump in our throats for heaven" appeared as a closing to a letter. Their lives were lives of gratitude. Quoting John 15:16a (KJV), "You did not choose Me, but I chose you . . . that you would go and bear fruit . . . .," Emalou added, "How I praise God that He, being who He is, would dare to manifest His grace on an unlikely fifth child of twelve in a lowly Mormon home! He has 'chosen the foolish things of the world to shame the wise and . . . the weak things of the world to shame the things which are strong' (I Cor. 1:27). I trust He has been glorified in His choice of this 'foolish' person."

Art echoed that gratitude. "Emalou and I are just a couple of simple redeemed sinners. We both came from humble homes. God gave us the exalted privilege of giving our whole adult lives in His service. We thank Him for this."

Sometimes they expressed their gratitude through Scripture. On one such occasion they quoted Psalm 16:6 (KJV): "The lines are fallen unto [us] in pleasant places; yea [we] have a goodly heritage." Another time they recalled Joshua 23:14b (KJV): "Not one thing hath failed of all the good things which the LORD your God spake concerning you; all are come to pass . . . ."

In spite of that, Art sensed that he was not where he should be with the Lord. He bemoaned the fact that he had not given more time to the study of God's Word. He felt that he had not been properly prepared for opportunities he had had to speak publically to both Christians and non-Christians. "I was always called on to take care of something mechanical or to repair this or that. I got involved in these things and did not study the Word as others did. I'm ashamed of that. Those things had to be done, but I wish I had had the gumption to put more time into study. It comes over me how absolutely far away from the Lord I am. He says, 'Love the Lord your God with all your heart, and with all your soul, and with all your mind' (Matt. 22:37). I just feel utterly undone on that. I recognize that we can have victory in the Lord, but I have not had victory in these matters as I wish I had."

Both he and Emalou recognized God's help, the help of faithful co-workers, and the help of praying, giving friends. Only with such faithful undergirding had a Bible school and several mission outstations been established and literature and radio broadcasts been taken into native homes. Only by God's grace had Navajo Christians been challenged to missions among Canada's Athabascan tribes. Art and Emalou had been mere catalysts and encouragers in the process, a process yet unfinished.

Nearing eighty, Art had written: "We have one overwhelming passion right now. We want to see this same kind of transformation [that occurred among the Navajos] amongst the tribes up north. We wrestle at night in prayer. Our passion is that they may be delivered from their spiritual darkness before our time comes to depart this life. It looks impossible right now, but God is able. The time is short, and the 'King's business requires haste.'" He concluded with Romans 9:1-3 (NKJV): "I tell the truth in Christ, I am not lying, my conscience also bearing me witness in the Holy Spirit, that I have great sorrow and continual grief in my heart. For I could wish that I myself were accursed from Christ for my brethren, my countrymen according to the flesh . . ."

Now Art and Emalou wondered who would proclaim God's Truth among these precious people after they were gone. Jesus Himself had left the glories of Heaven to spend thirty-three years in a human body on a sin-cursed earth for mankind's sake. Would Navajos be willing to leave all to follow His call to the ends of the earth? Art and Emalou ached to see some of them settle permanently among people who desperately needed the Gospel, just as Anglo missionaries had left family and home to move to

Navajoland.

Only weeks into the twenty-first century the metastasis of Art's prostate cancer to his bones and Emalou's rapidly decreasing eyesight demanded ministry changes. Trips to Canada ceased and jaunts to the Navajo Reservation were greatly curtailed, but the Norrises did not cease ministering. With limited strength and mobility, Art found more time for prayer. Many Navajo Christians made their way to the Norris home for Bible study, counsel, and encouragement. Art and Emalou provided teaching tapes and literature for both Anglo and Navajo believers and participated financially in proclaiming the Gospel in the NWT and Alberta. Though their bodies were failing, only death would still their efforts to see their beloved "chosen people" brought to salvation and maturity in Christ.

For Art, that experience came on October 22, 2001. His body had become weak and pain-racked. A week before his death Emalou heard him singing "Love, wonderful love, the love of Christ for me," a song she had heard him sing many times through the years. Then shortly before entering his Lord's presence, he murmured feebly, "I love Jesus!" Attentive family members stood by grieving, yet rejoicing, as he breathed his last. His pain was forever over. Privately they laid him to rest, but nearly 400 people attended his memorial service. "We have something to rejoice about!" Tim Norris declared as he stood to welcome the crowd. Rev. Jim Wince, former associate pastor of Mesa Hills Bible Church in Colorado Springs, testified, "Art, to me, was faithfulness, but I'm sure he would prefer that we talk about God instead of about him." With clarity and compassion Reverend Wince proclaimed eternal salvation through Christ, the same life-giving message that had compelled Art to pour out his life for the First Nations of Canada and the U. S.

In a letter informing their support team of Art's homegoing, Emalou stated, "Since I am eighty-six years of age and have failing eyesight, I have no illusions about further public ministry. I do, however, pray that God will use me in some way to bless others." An added note revealed her lingering burden: ". . . continue to pray for God's enabling and for support of the radio ministry and those who labor in it."

From diverse backgrounds God had brought her and Art together and joined them into a dynamic unit under His leadership. He put the imprint of His hand on them, on their co-workers, and on the hearts of those who prayed and gave for the sake of the Gospel. In the face of a herculean task, it was He who gave joy and victory!

Art and Emalou

25
The Legacy Continues

"Therefore, my beloved brethren, be steadfast, immovable, always abounding in the work of the Lord, knowing that your toil is not in vain in the Lord." – I Corinthians 15:58

We've spent forty-two years on the Navajo Reservation bringing the message of salvation," Art wrote in a *Mission News* article in September of 1980. "Our letters of commendation are Navajos saved and brought to a place of service to God amongst their own people. This is *our* 'Brown Gold.' Texaco, Phillips, Superior, and other oil companies came here about the same time as we, and they hit brown gold, too. Their equipment is the best, their salaries right up top, and their profits astounding. But men's souls are far more valuable than oil. Our equipment is poor, our salaries low, and we don't receive much esteem. But, we are rich unto the Lord."

Art and Emalou did indeed strike "gold." Through them God initiated transformations in the lives of hundreds of native people. Many of those whose lives were divinely changed have poured themselves into sharing the Good News of Christ with others. Ben Lewis was among those touched by God and by the Norrises. Watching Ben, obviously inebriated, chase his wife down the road with a stick one day, Art exclaimed, "What in the world is that fellow doing?" The Norrises never knew how or when the Holy Spirit changed him, but the next time they saw Ben, it was evident that God's hand was upon him. He learned to read Navajo and studied the Bible constantly, asking Art for help with difficult portions. "Brother Norris," he confided one day, "sometimes our pastor says, 'If you love the Lord, put up your hand.' Every time I put up my hand, my heart hurts."

"What do you mean?" Art prodded.

"Well, every time I put up my hand, I remember the bracelets I stole from a trader years ago. And every time I pass the trading post where I stole them, the Holy Spirit tells me that was sin."

Art opened the Old Testament. "Look, Ben. God expected His people to make restitution for things they had stolen."

"That's what I want to do," Ben replied earnestly.

"Who was the trader?"

"Mr. Helms. He has a big house here in Cortez. Will you go with me sometime to tell him?"

"I'd be happy to, Ben."

Ben did not return right away. "Suppose that was just a passing notion?" Emalou questioned.

"We'll see," Art replied.

Three weeks later Ben knocked. "Let's go see Mr. Helms now," he urged.

Question marks lined the face of the tall Anglo man who answered the door. Ben marched in and sat down. Art offered his hand. "I'm Art Norris. This is Ben Lewis. He wants to talk with you about something."

Mr. Helms turned questioningly to Ben. Ben hesitated, then forged ahead. "When you worked at the trading post, another fellow and I stole some silver bracelets. We pawned them in Shiprock. Now I'm a Christian, and I want to pay for them. I can't pay it all at once, but I'll bring you money every time I get a paycheck."

Tears of joy streamed down Ben's cheeks as he and Art left. "You don't know how happy you've made me, Mr. Norris. My heart doesn't hurt anymore."

"I didn't make you happy, Ben. The Lord did!" Art replied.

Another Navajo whom God made "happy" through Art Norris' caring ministry was John Peter Yazzie. John Peter, confined to a wheelchair, tells the story: "In the late 1930s I was in the hospital suffering with bad arthritis. I couldn't walk. I was saved, but I wasn't a very good Christian. Mr. Norris and another man visited us patients. Mr. Norris taught me about the Lord Jesus and how to read Navajo. When he moved to Rough Rock, he asked if I could come and help. We visited people and told Bible stories at school. He talked in English and I translated. A lot of people trusted the Lord.

"Mr. Norris really loves our people. He took care of me, even carried me to the toilet. I stayed with him at Rough Rock. After World War II, I stayed two years with his family at Immanuel Mission. We made visits and taught school kids. Sometimes he taught and sometimes I taught. That is where I learned to tell people how to be saved and live a Christian life. At first I was scared, but Art helped me. My sister, my aunt, my niece didn't know Christ. My grandma hated God's Word and said, 'I don't want that!' but she accepted the Lord when she was old and sick.

"God answers prayer. We prayed about Art having Bible school and that happened. We prayed that my brother would come home from the war and trust Christ and he did! Art Norris taught me a lot about the Christian life. Sometimes we studied the Bible together. If it had not been for his help, I would have gone the other way and not followed the Lord."

Art taught both young and old about the Christian life. He had a life-changing influence on eight-year-old Stanley Hammond in the late 1940s after he and Emalou moved to Cortez, Colorado. The Hammond family lived in a hogan near the John Ismay Trading Post, where Art and Emalou visited them. The family listened quietly as Art shared the Good News in Navajo. Young Stanley was fascinated with this white man and his wife who spoke his language. He attended their Bible camps to learn more about the One they called Jesus.

Later, at the end of Stanley's Army training, his officer said, "You'll get orders tomorrow. Most of you will probably be shipped to South Vietnam."

That night on guard duty, Stanley thought about Art Norris. He nudged his buddy. "A white man taught me that God sent Jesus Christ to die for me. We don't have to be afraid of dying."

"Yeah, I know," his buddy answered. "I'm a Christian, too."

"Then we'd better tell the others. They're really scared."

They sought out the other soldiers on duty. "You guys don't have to be afraid. If you let Jesus save you from your sin, you'll be with Him even if you die in combat." They were amazed the next day to learn that none of them was assigned to Vietnam.

After two years of duty in Europe, Stanley returned to the reservation and visited a relative in the hospital. "The guy next door has cancer," his relative told him.

Walking into that patient's room, Stanley greeted, "Yá'át'ééh. I hear you're having bad trouble."

The man nodded dejectedly. "The doctor said there's no hope."

"I want to tell you something important," Stanley said, sitting down by the patient. "God loved the world so much that He gave His Son. Whoever believes in Him won't perish; they'll live forever even after their body dies." It was the same truth Art Norris had taught his family years before. "Do you know what that means?" he asked the man.

The man shook his head.

"Whoever believes in Jesus can live forever by confessing sin and acknowledging Him as Savior."

"Whoever? That means me!" the patient responded, his face aglow. When Stanley left the hospital, he stopped by the man's room again to say goodbye. "Now I have hope!" the man exclaimed joyfully. Stanley was doubly grateful for having learned about Christ from Art Norris.

Another young man whose future had its roots in the truths he first heard from Art Norris was George Tohtsoni. George had not always understood the things Art taught in the released-time classes at Rock Point in the early 1940s, but he had liked the young white missionary. Later he understood about Jesus and believed.

As an adult, George lived in Aneth, Utah, where missionary Ray Stonehocker taught him how to study the Bible. He loved God's Word and was encouraged by the friendship and prayers of Ray and others whom Art Norris assigned to Aneth. Before the Stonehockers came to Aneth, sermons there had been in English, translated into Navajo. Ray had encouraged George to preach in Navajo and helped him to prepare sermons. George was gifted in explaining Scripture. When the Stonehockers left, Art challenged, "George, you could be the pastor of this church."

"I've never been to Bible school," George replied.

"Pray about it. The Lord will help you."

George accepted the challenge, and Art helped him whenever possible. At first, preaching was difficult for George, but he studied diligently and grew in his knowledge and ability. He loved the people he shepherded and begged non-Christian Navajos to trust Christ.

George preached part in English and part in Navajo. At every opportunity Art and Emalou joined the Navajo congregation to hear his expositions and were greatly encouraged by his clear communication of biblical truth.

Numerous other lives were divinely earmarked at Navajo Bible Institute. One day a

George Tohtsoni (center front) and Aneth congregation

police officer stopped by to see Art. "Mr. Norris, we've apprehended a young fellow who was drinking. He has a charge against him, but if you agree I'll let him come to Bible school instead of putting him in jail."

"That's fine with me," Art responded. Henry Toledo, a professing Christian, enrolled in the institute and made great spiritual progress. He willingly accepted assigned responsibilities, including assistance in outstation ministries. In his final year Art asked, "Henry, would you teach Navajo reading and Scripture to a couple in Hatch, Utah, every week?"

Henry Toledo and his wife

Week after week Henry faithfully drove to Hatch. His assignment from God, however, was much bigger than the one he had received from Art. When Art accompanied him to Hatch one week, he was surprised but elated to find Henry teaching not two, but twenty, people!

John Trujillo was another Navajo who became a dedicated preacher of God's Word. John became a Christian at Intermountain Indian School in Utah. He was greatly influenced in his Christian life by Jim Cook, a missionary assigned to

John and Nora Trujillo and family

Protestant missionary work at the school. As John studied Scripture, he became concerned for the spiritual condition of his people and wished he knew how to warn them of the consequences of not trusting Christ as Savior. He and his wife, Nora, also a Christian, returned to the reservation, where he began interpreting for the missionary at a church in Red Lake. Nora taught him to read the Navajo Bible, but he did not understand it. "God, I want to know what Your Word means. How can I learn it?" he prayed.

One day John told Nora, "I think God wants us to sell some of our things and go to Bible school." In faith the family moved to Navajo Bible Institute in 1972, and John began to find answers to his questions. His practical assignments included teaching released-time classes and preaching on the radio. "I'm not ashamed of the Gospel," he asserted. "I want to tell my people what I learned. I want them to go with Christ when He comes for us."

Years later John declared, "I never forgot what Mr. Norris taught us. He said, 'When you graduate, you'll go to dangerous places. Watch out for Satan's deceptions and stand strong. What you learn from the Bible is like your roots. Keep your nose in it; don't look anywhere else.'"

While pastoring a reservation church, John was the Navajo speaker for a "Deeper Life Studies" week at the Bible institute. Many students dedicated themselves to God for His service that week. "I believe that more was accomplished this week than at any previous conference," Art declared.

Some years later John, Jones Dehiya, and Art were asked to speak at the same camp meeting. "Mr. Norris wept when he got up to preach," John related. "He was so happy to preach with his former students. He asked everyone to pray for us. I'm so thankful for the way he taught us."

Men were not the only Bible school students who profited from the teaching and day-to-day influence of the Norrises and the NBI staff. Before her marriage to Woody Yazzie, Alice Naljahi came to the Bible institute in Cortez in the early 1960s. Raised in a Christian Navajo home, Alice was amazed that Art Norris knew more about her culture than she did. The morning he asked her to interpret for him in chapel, she thought, Why does he want an interpreter? He speaks good Navajo. When Art finished, he turned to her. "Now, Alice, interpret that into English."

"I thought he was a mean teacher," Alice said years later, "but he was really nice. He taught us verses and used illustrations how to witness. One day in class he said, 'We will witness to officers of our local government today.' He put chairs around the table in front of the room and called one student to be chapter secretary, one to be president, and one to be councilman. Then he asked different students to witness to them. He listened and told us how to do better. He used illustrations to teach us how to teach children, too, and to read Navajo and lead songs. We practiced on each other. 'You must be like headlights of a car, piercing the darkness and showing Christ's way,' he told us. 'And always be prepared to teach at camp meetings. If someone comes to accept Christ at a camp meeting, get up and talk to them. Don't just sit there and look at them.'

"When he took us to the Shiprock Fair, he told us, 'You don't go to the fair to see friends; you go to pass out tracts.' On the way home he told us what to do when people make fun and say they don't want that trash. He also took us to jail to witness. We just stood there and looked at everyone, but he helped us. I learned a lot from him."

Jones Dehiya was influenced as well by the Norrises at NBI. "The Navajos have things of this world but not the Lord Jesus Christ," Jones explained. "There was no one to tell them about God's Word in their own language. That's why I went to Bible school."

Grace Benally, who later became Mrs. Dehiya, also attended the Bible institute. "The Norrises called us their children," Grace recounted. "That showed they loved us. Art was like a father to us and Emalou like a mother. She really taught us girls how to take care of our home and how to live the Christian life. When we got discouraged, Art said, 'Keep going on. Keep working hard and trust the Lord.' Emalou said that too. That always encouraged us."

Jones and Grace Dehiya (right)

After Jones graduated, he and Grace began a difficult pastoral assignment at Mariano Lake, New Mexico. "When things are hard, we remember what Art said and it helps us keep going," Grace related. Little by little people responded to the Gospel. One day the Norrises visited the Dehiyas and found a vacation Bible school in progress. One hundred children were being taught by an all-Navajo staff!

In the 1980s the Dehiyas participated in the Dogrib ministries in the Northwest Territories (NWT). The paralyzing homesickness that plagued most Navajos did not affect them. "The Dogribs have a nice school, a good supermarket, a clinic, a hospital, nice houses, and lots of meat, but they don't know Jesus," Jones remarked. "Navajos were the same way, but now we have a lot of Christian Navajos and a better life because Jesus changed us. We must send a Navajo missionary to show Dogribs that God can change them too."

Clara Tohtsoni, George Tohtsoni's sister and another NBI student, was born in 1938 when the reservation was as it had been for centuries. Motorized vehicles were rare, dirt trails common. Her father was a medicine man, and the family lived in a traditional eight-sided home with a dirt floor. Shortly after Clara was born, a white missionary by the name of Clara Holcomb rode up to the Tohtsoni hogan on horseback and presented the Gospel in broken Navajo. The family did not fully understand, but they were interested. They even invited Miss Holcomb to name their newborn. Unable to pronounce "Clara," the suggested name, they wrote it on a piece of paper, hung it in a bag on the hogan wall, and called their baby Asdzą́ą́ Damóo, (Sunday Woman), the name by which they referred to Miss Holcomb.

As a child, Clara herded sheep and goats. During her teens her family lived with neighbors who took her, a brother, and her mother to a camp meeting at Mexican Water. For the first time the three of them understood the Gospel and believed. Eventually her father, nine brothers, and five sisters became Christians. Wanting to serve this God who had known and chosen her before she was born, Clara enrolled in NBI. The institute prepared her well, and she accepted Art's challenge to evangelize her own people. She interpreted for missionaries and assisted missionary Dorothy Hecker at Aneth with Sunday services and released-time classes. She taught ladies to read Navajo Scripture and sang, prayed, and memorized Scripture with them. She loved being a "Sunday Woman."

Over the years God has used this willing servant in numerous ways. She has taught Navajo literacy, helped to translate Scripture and other literature, visited Navajo homes, and taught Sunday school and after-school Bible clubs. At the mission school in Rock Point she teaches far more than Navajo reading, writing, and culture to the children. Using skills learned at NBI, she also tells them about Jesus.

David Gilliwood also faithfully serves God as a result of the ministry of Art and Emalou Norris. One day in the late 1950s Art remarked, "Emalou, you'd never guess who wants to come to Bible school."

"Who?"

"A fellow who attended our Sunday school at Rock Point and some of our Bible camps. The one that lay on the floor and didn't say a thing the whole time we visited his home ten or so years ago. Remember? I prayed for an opportunity to help him."

"Not David Gilliwood!"

"Yes, David Gilliwood!"

David arrived at the Bible school eager to learn. One day Art asked, "David, you remember that day my wife and I visited your family years ago? Why did you lie around and not say anything?"

"Well, there were a lot of things to do and a lot of kids to play with at the boarding school. At home there was nobody to play with, nothing to do. I was bored."

As an adult, David was anything but bored. He recognized that his people needed Christ, and he wanted to prepare for Christian service. After sitting under the teaching of Art Norris and the other NBI staff, he returned to Mexican Water to interpret for the Baptist missionaries. When the missionaries left the area, David and his wife assumed the work themselves.

When Vivian Shebala, an older student, entered the Bible institute, her great concern for the spiritually lost caught Art and Emalou's attention. Even at a young age Vivian's ultimate concern was God's will, and she chose not the easy way in a difficult decision, but the biblical way. That pattern continued into her adult life. Married to a Zuni man, she openly lived as a Christian in the Zuni culture in spite of slander and rejection. God sustained her as she reared her children, all six of them dedicated to

Him.

Vivian's command of Navajo, English, and Zuni was quite beneficial during her thirty-one years of service as a registered nurse with Public Health Service. Her life was full and satisfying, but she longed to know God's Word better. "I've spent my whole life serving my people's physical needs," she said after her husband died. "Now I want to serve their spiritual needs." She retired and entered NBI in the fall of 1981.

After completing the course of study, Vivian exclaimed at her graduation, "I thank God for the privilege of learning His Word and for teachers who taught me with love. I pray the Lord will show me His place of service."

Art followed up on that statement. "Vivian, you could become a missionary to the Dogribs in the Northwest Territories. They need the Lord," he challenged.

Vivian Shebala (center) with
Navajo team headed to Fort Rae

Stunned, Vivian wondered aloud, "Could that be why God has touched my life and made me want to learn His Word?"

In Fort Rae, NWT, with other Navajos in January of 1982, Vivian experienced Christ's love in a new dimension. She taught Dogrib children about Him and learned Dogrib ways. She stayed with a Dogrib family after the other Navajos returned home and took advantage of every opportunity to tell of God's love. Northern daylight hours were long, and the children went to her from early morning to late night for Bible stories. The village elders noted Vivian's exhaustion and cautioned the children, "Don't visit Mrs. Shebala after 10:00 p.m. She needs rest."

Vivian was a diabetic and could not maintain proper diet and rest while in the Northwest Territories. Her family begged her not to make a second trip, but she was certain of God's calling and willing to make any sacrifices necessary. In June the following year she returned to the Dogribs to share the Gospel. Both adults and children loved her and wanted her to stay, but her worsening diabetic condition mandated her return to the States.

Later, while Vivian was hospitalized for the amputation of both legs below her knees, Art and Emalou visited her. Vivian was quite weak, but her spirit remained strong. "After I'm healed, I'm going to go back north again in a wheelchair," she declared in a weak voice. The Norrises felt she would be an excellent long-term missionary to the Dogribs. God, however, had other plans and called her to Himself.

Another NBI graduate who served the Lord in spite of physical challenges was Cato Begay. When Cato came to the Bible school, he was the only Christian in his large family. Often his face wore a big smile when he returned from weekend visits with his family. "I led my sister to the Lord!" or "I led my brother to the Lord!" he would exclaim. By the time he graduated, only his father remained an unbeliever.

Cato learned to read Navajo and spent hours reading the Bible and preaching on the radio. Art Norris overheard him one day as he prepared a radio tape. "This one thing I live for," Cato had declared, "that my very own people might hear the Word of God and know Him."

Cato became an evangelist. Over the years he became blind, but he kept preaching to groups or one on one wherever an opportunity presented itself. One day Art drove to Shiprock, New Mexico. At the trading post he saw Cato. I bet I can fool him since he doesn't know I'm in the area, Art thought. He greeted Cato in Navajo. "Oh, Mr. Norris!" Cato exclaimed, "My father got saved!" Cato did not need to see his mentor to recognize him, nor did he need any prompting to share what was foremost in his mind.

In May 1987 Art drove to Red Valley, Arizona, to visit Cato at his home. They talked together for some time. When Art rose to leave, Cato accompanied him to the car. "Let's pray, Mr. Norris," he said. When Cato finished praying, Art looked up and saw a Navajo man walking toward them.

"Someone is coming, Cato. I wonder if he is a believer."

Cato turned to greet the man. Immediately he told him about Jesus and before Art left, the man was a brother in Christ. Art was moved to tears to see how God was using this single-minded servant to bring Navajo people to Himself.

Ryan Gorman was among the students whom Art taught and mentored. Reared in the home of a medicine man, Ryan had herded sheep until he started school at age twelve. All he had known about "salvation" was Mary, baptism, and communion, so every time he heard someone say "Jesus can save you," he was puzzled.

Ryan and Irene Gorman

As an adult, Ryan gradually became controlled by alcohol and spent most of his time alone. After his wife, Irene, and family left him and he was no longer able to keep a job, he contemplated suicide. One night after a car accident, he staggered into a camp meeting where an NBI graduate, Peter Burbank, was preaching. Irene, already a Christian, was at the meeting. What Peter said made sense, and Ryan confessed his sin and trusted Christ. The next day when he was sober, he knew that something significant had occurred. He was different. The change was obvious to others as well. Irene and the family returned to him, and the two of them went to Pastor Burbank for counsel. Pastor Burbank was able to answer their many questions, and he encouraged them to memorize Scripture.

In 1976 the Gormans enrolled in NBI. Sharing their testimonies in various Navajo homes was a frightening experience for them, but Art Norris helped them practice in the classroom. "Art always used role play and illustrations," Ryan recalled. "He really wanted us to move for the Lord. 'You can pray all you want,' he told us, 'but if you don't go, nothing happens.' He told us that God had other sheep up north, too, who needed to come to His corral and said we should go there and bring them back."

After Ryan graduated, Art called him into his office one day. "Here," he said, pointing to a map of the Northwest Territories. "This is where the Dogribs live. They really need the Lord. I'd like to see some of you take the Gospel to them." Ryan had heard about Northern Canada's First People. God seemed to be opening the door to these tribes, but Ryan knew that taking the Gospel to them might mean foregoing some of his own plans.

"Maybe we could tell about the needs up north at a camp meeting," Art suggested. Ryan agreed. He also began using his weekly radio broadcasts to encourage Navajo Christians to become involved.

Ryan was already involved in evangelism among the Navajos. As head of the Navajo Evangelistic Fund, he prepared tracts for the Shiprock and Window Rock fairs and took his children and others with him to the fairgrounds. They erected a stall, complete with loudspeaker, just outside the gate and distributed tracts and talked with people. The response was encouraging.

In 1982 Ryan and three other Navajo believers went with Art to visit the Dogribs, the first of many such trips. After introducing the Navajos, Art walked away and let them give their testimonies. Although few Dogribs responded, they were friendly and showered the group with moose, caribou, fish, and bannock.

Ryan faithfully tithed everything he earned at his secular job, believing that not doing so might give Satan an opportunity to pull him back into his old lifestyle. He also gave unstintingly of his time to help his and Irene's families, the Dogribs, and those suffering the effects of alcoholism. A living testimony of God's ability to free humans from anything that enslaved them, Ryan was greatly burdened for the salvation of his people. While unable to sleep one night, he pondered the Scripture that says if you don't provide for your own relatives, you are worse than an unbeliever. "I'm concerned about my parents and the other people living in Nazlini," he told Irene the next morning. "We don't have enough gas money to go there, but let's go anyway. God will provide."

At Christmastime they went again. Ryan's father had invited a number of people to his home for dinner. Afterwards he prepared to hand out gifts to all of them. As he did, Ryan interrupted, "Dad, I need to read the Bible first and tell what Christmas really is."

His father scowled and glanced at his mother. "Well, make it short," he snapped, and proceeded to sit with his eyes closed while Ryan spoke.

Later, Ryan's siblings reprimanded him. "Don't talk to Dad about this again!"

"How can I not talk with him about Christ? The Bible says that anyone who doesn't believe in Christ will go down forever."

Patiently Ryan waited for another opportunity. He was concerned about his mother as well, especially since she was not well. Thinking his dad was asleep during one visit, he urged, "Mom, I'd like you to come to Jesus."

"I want to," she replied.

At that Ryan's dad bolted from the chair. "Leave your mother alone! She's sick!" he yelled.

"I'll follow him," his mother said meekly, glancing at her husband.

"Maybe some other time, Mom," Ryan replied, but Death robbed her of that opportunity.

Not long after his mother's death, Ryan found his dad sitting on the couch crying. "I keep thinking about your mom," his dad said. "What will happen to me now?"

"Dad," Ryan pled, "let me read the Bible to you." His father nodded assent. As Ryan read, his dad's spiritual eyes were opened and he responded to God's gift of salvation through faith in Jesus Christ.

There was no church in Nazlini. The salvation of his father added to Ryan's eagerness to establish one. He looked to Art for advice and encouragement. "Would you go to Nazlini with me next Sunday?" he asked Art in 1997. "We've been meeting in a shade house, but my dad has released some of his land for a church and the people have agreed to let us build. A couple of other former NBI students are helping me. We have to get approval from the Game and Fish Department, the Road Department, and the Antiquities Department, and the land has to be surveyed and checked for suitability for a septic tank. There's a lot of red tape. We could use your help."

"I'd be happy to help any way I can," Art replied.

Before long the fledgling Nazlini fellowship asked the Norrises to teach Navajo reading so they could study their Bibles. Parking their motor home at the brush arbor church, Art taught the adults and Emalou the children. The people listened closely, grasping God's truths more quickly in Navajo than in English.

"Brother Art works with us and encourages us to keep going on," Ryan stated later. "I thank the Lord that he came to the reservation."

There were others who were grateful for the Norrises' presence and assistance. "Mr. Norris wanted us students to have a passion to witness,"

John Charley remarked. "When Lena and I were at Bible school, he told us, 'The Lord put you here for a reason. Go out and use what you learned.' His number one priority was for us to learn to read and write Navajo. He was like a father to me."

John had met Lena at NBI. Her pastor had assured her she would grow spiritually there. "At NBI we were expected to give our testimonies and sing in reservation churches. That's where I really grew," Lena declared. As students, she and John served at Montezuma Creek, Utah, on weekends. During the summers they helped at Aneth, John Ismay Trading Post, and Cortez.

John and Lena Charley
and family

"Art and Emalou were strict," Lena asserted. "When we did wrong, he told us to straighten up. So did Emalou. They both loved our people. Mr. Norris opened many doors for us and helped us not to be ashamed of God's Truth."

John's longing for the salvation of fellow Navajos took him to the Navajo Nation Fair in Window Rock in 1979. With another man he traversed the parade route in the hot sun and stood at the ticket gate distributing literature to hundreds who had never heard of Jesus. After his and Lena's graduation from NBI, Art asked them to pastor the Bluff church. It was a difficult assignment. Few people in the area were Christians. Many of those who were, lacked the biblical knowledge necessary for spiritual stability and maturity. Many people in the community were steeped in traditional religion. Some practiced Peyote and others promoted a social "gospel" tolerant of animistic worship. The Charleys found children's ministries to be the most promising, just as the Norrises had years earlier.

Experiencing financially lean years, the Charleys were grateful for the groceries and clothing which the Norrises gave them. "They helped in a lot of ways," Lena acknowledged. "Mr. Norris also helped us get started in the work. At first only two or three people came to church, but about a year later there were forty or more. Then Mr. Norris stepped back and let us carry on by ourselves. At first we felt like he didn't want us anymore, then we realized he had responsibilities many places and was encouraging others as he did us. Whenever we got discouraged, we prayed. Mr. Norris came in his camper sometimes and stayed several days to see how we were doing, so we knew he was still there for us. He prayed with us and told us to keep going on with the Lord no matter what."

The Charleys taught the believers, visited hundreds of homes, and spent hours comforting the elderly in nursing homes. They held services in their own home and drove thousands of reservation miles proclaiming the Good News at preschools, vacation Bible schools (VBS), and camp meetings. "Nowadays many people think you have a hidden reason for visiting them," Lena commented. "John is friendly and tells them up front he is a Christian and came to talk about the Lord. That's how Mr. Norris taught us."

In June 2001, on the second day of a VBS in the Charley home, Lena ran an errand to Cortez. On the way home she encountered a fierce wind, causing her to overcorrect and roll the pickup. She was soon in the presence of the Lord. "Shall we continue VBS?" a volunteer helper asked.

"Yes," came the answer. "That's what Lena would want."

Alone, John continued the work that God had entrusted to him and Lena. Week by week he visited nursing homes and senior citizen centers sharing Christ with those whose earthly lives were nearing an end.

God works in different ways with His chosen ones. He called Lena Charley into His presence, but He laid His miraculous hand on Kee Kohoe and strengthened him in a special way for His service.

Before Kee attended NBI in the early 1960s, he was one of the Navajo students bused by the U. S. Government to boarding schools miles from their homes. Kee was taken to a school in Oklahoma. Shortly after he arrived, doctors discovered he had tuberculosis and confined him to a sanitarium. His days were lonely. He knew little English and was too ill to participate in any activities. He asked for a transfer to Albuquerque, New Mexico, to be closer to his family. The Albuquerque doctors told him they needed to remove one of his lungs. Kee was scared. Then he remembered hearing that anyone who loved Jesus would go to heaven when he died; otherwise, he'd go to hell. "If You really are God, I want to know You," he prayed. "If I get well, I'll serve You my whole life."

After four days in the recovery room, Kee began to improve. There must be a God, he thought. He studied his tiny English Bible with the help of a dictionary and attended a Bible study led by a Navajo Bible school student. His love for Jesus grew. When the doctors discharged him from the sanitarium, they warned, "Never go out in cold weather. Pneumonia would be hard on you. Actually, it would be best if you would go to rehabilitation for a while."

From Kee's perspective, there was no time for rehabilitation. His heart was set on Bible school. At Bible school he met Art Norris. "Mr. Norris is a good man with one thing on his mind," Kee said later. "He wants students to know Jesus. He wants them to learn God's Word and go to their own people. He said that we teach our people better than he can 'cause we know our language. He thinks like a Navajo. He eats fry bread and mutton stew and sleeps anywhere just like a Navajo. He's that kind of man."

Despite frequent bouts with bronchitis, Kee served for a time after graduation as a full-time missionary. In 1982 he went to a clinic for relief from pain and coughing. The doctors cautioned him to keep himself warm. A week after his clinic visit, a friend asked, "Kee, could you go up to the Dogribs with us? One of our group had to cancel."

Up north? Kee thought. Where it's cold? The doctor said to keep warm . . . but I promised to serve God 'til I die. He is a miracle worker. I'll do what He says.

In spite of a fever, Kee boarded the plane to Denver with the team of Navajo Christians. While changing planes, he lost his ticket and ran back to the airplane to search for it. No ticket! "You lost your ticket because you're not supposed to go," the devil seemed to whisper. "Remember? All things work together for good to them that love God." Returning to the waiting room, Kee wondered if the Lord wanted him to stay home. Not knowing what else to do, he went to check in with the others. There on the counter lay his ticket!

In Edmonton that evening Kee still had a fever. He was breathing hard and coughing up blood. After the others went into town, he knelt by his bed. "Lord, if I'm making a mistake, let me know. The doctor told me not to go out in the cold. My life is Yours. I want to serve You 'til I die."

Kee fell asleep on the couch and did not awaken until the group returned. When he heard them upstairs laughing and talking, he sat up.

No pain! His chest was clear and he was breathing freely.

The next morning in Yellowknife, NWT, Kee stepped off the airplane in minus 40 degrees Celsius. For the two weeks he was in the NWT, he was free of health problems and preached to the Dogrib youth, several of whom professed faith in Christ. Arriving home, Kee made radio tapes for NGO's broadcasts to these northern Dene. He continues to serve among his own people. "Mr. Norris really helped and encouraged me," he said.

Although Betsy Newman, known in childhood as Bessie Denetsoni, did not attend the Bible institute, she was mentored by Art and Emalou Norris and encouraged to be a missionary both as a child and again in her adult years. As a thirteen-year-old in the mid-1940s, Betsy had assisted Art and Emalou at Rock Point. Years later she became the secretary for the manager of a coal mine in New Mexico. In the spring of 1983 Art telephoned her. "Hello, Betsy! Would you like to go with a group to the Dogribs in Fort Rae in a couple of weeks? They're distant relatives of the Navajos and they need Jesus."

Al and Betsy Newman

Betsy and six other Navajos accompanied Art. She recalled that trip some years later. "We traveled three days without our usual luxuries. Mr. Norris just kept driving way into the night, then we slept in the van. One night he dropped us off by twos and threes at different Christian homes. I was tired and achy and ready for rest. Another lady and I stayed at a house where there were a lot of children. After we visited with our hostess for a while, she told us she had no food for us. Her husband was an alcoholic, and she was caring for the children alone. I asked her where we were to sleep, and she pointed to a bedroom down the hall. There were no comforts and conveniences! I asked myself what in the world I was doing there, then I came to my senses and asked the Lord to forgive me for my attitude."

Betsy continued: "The reason no Navajo couple has been found to serve long term among the Dogribs is that they'd have to give up everything and really commit themselves–like Mr. and Mrs. Norris did. They left their homes, conveniences, and family. Navajos haven't been able to break away from what is so much a part of them. After that trip, I can relate to how missionaries must have felt when they came to Navajoland. All the hardships! I am forever thankful for Mr. and Mrs. Norris. They have had a large part in my being a missionary. Years ago

Navajo team ready to fly to Dogrib village

they took me to several missionary conferences, and it was always touching to hear them speak about their love for us. Once Mr. Norris told his home church that he had brought his 'brown jewels' to sing and testify. Later I told some people that if we are their 'brown jewels,' then they are our 'white diamonds.' Besides my parents, they started me on missionary work."

Jimmy Etcitty, another of the Navajo missionaries to the Dogribs, was influenced by Art Norris in Art's retirement years. Jimmy first met Art in 1984 in Yellowknife, NWT. "I never saw a man like him before," Jimmy stated. "Sometimes when he talks with people, he sheds tears. He never wants to take a rest; he just keeps going on."

Jimmy preached to the Dogribs and answered their questions. Seeing that he was bothered by noisy children, Art encouraged the children to listen. "Art never just sits around," Jimmy said. "If people stand far away, he brings them into the meeting. He really helps me witness to these people."

The Dogribs were captivated by Jimmy's testimony. "I was going to be the best medicine man on the Navajo Reservation," Jimmy began. "I even danced in fire and it did not burn me. I thought I was doing good, but I was unkind to my parents and hated white people. I even cussed out a missionary from Texas, but he kept visiting me. He always told me about God's love. I told him that God did not love me and that I didn't want the white man's religion.

"I worked in Portland on the railroad. Alcohol and peyote almost killed me. I thought I was a tough Indian, but something happened. About three in the morning I walked out of the bunk car and along the railroad track. I was about to die. I knelt down and prayed, 'Lord, if You are for me, help me.' I started weeping, and I noticed my attitude changed. My life was new! I was happy and smiling! I went home a different man. I didn't beat my wife or chase my kids away. My wife noticed I was different and asked what happened. She said she wanted what I had.

"I got a Bible and threw away my medicine man things. I thought I would just be a church member, but I learned that the Bible said 'Go.' That is why I go every place. I raised my family in the Gospel way. I thought my relatives would be happy I was a Christian, but they got mad at me and told me to go be with the white people. It was sad, but I got on my knees and wept for them. One by one they got saved. My grandmother was the first to get saved. Now there are three preachers in our family. Instead of a medicine man, God made me a preacher! That is a miracle! The Lord is powerful!

"I was guilty, going the wrong direction and dead in sin," Jimmy told the Dogribs. "You are like that too. You need Jesus."

After Jimmy spoke on the radio one day, Art said, "Jimmy, you could have as great an impact on these people through radio as you do on the Navajos." With his encouragement Jimmy made a month's worth of 15-minute tapes for the Canadian station.

Two more times Jimmy went north with Art. "One time," Jimmy recalled, "we saw some people having a drinking party. The young men were in bad shape. I told Art to take it easy, but he went in anyway. He didn't know that they were having a party. One man got mad and told him they didn't want a missionary there. Art apologized and started to leave. He told them that we just wanted to tell them about the Gospel and pray for them, and they said, 'Okay, just pray.' A man who knew Art went to the door with us and wept that Art was so concerned about his people.

"Things cost a lot up north, but Art said, 'Don't worry, God always supplies.' True! Two months before I was to retire from the railroad, the Lord wanted me to serve Him, but I knew that if I quit early, I would have no retirement. The missionary said not to worry. A lot of people thought was I crazy that I didn't wait to get retirement, but for the past six years I have served God and He has blessed me and my family. I want to preach salvation and to help my people grow in grace and become soul winners. The Lord takes care of our needs."

Jimmy recalled that, during his second trip to the North with Art, Art had to leave early because his brother was sick. "Art told me, 'Get home safe.' Then he pulled $200 out of his pocket and gave it to me. With tears he told me he loved me. When I got home, he called to make sure I had made it okay and said he was praying for me. He has God's love, not the world's love. He even cries when he touches the kids up north. His tears are real. I've never seen a missionary like that in all my life. Some missionaries come and go, but that man doesn't want to quit. I love missionaries. They come from a long ways and give up things so they can reach us for the Lord. They teach us how to make outlines for preaching and show us how God loves us even though we don't want to believe. I've lead about seven men to the Lord who are now preaching the Gospel. It's amazing how the Lord does it!"

Sitting in his humble home on the Navajo Reservation with simple equipment, Jimmy faithfully records half-hour messages in Navajo for the tribe's 5000-watt radio station in Window Rock, Arizona. Through the Holy Spirit's prompting, Art had encouraged him in his radio ministry, and through his messages a medicine man, a Peyote priest, and countless others known only to God have committed their lives to the Giver of eternal life!

The development of evangelistic indigenous churches was the impetus behind Bible camps, Navajo Bible Reading School, Navajo Bible Institute, radio broadcasts, reservation outstations, hogan visitation, literature distribution, and all of the other ministries of the Norrises. Thus every report of God's working in and through their spiritual children brought Art and Emalou intense pleasure and gratitude.

The Holy Spirit has accomplished much also in Northern Canada since Art Norris first entered the hamlet of Fort Rae, NWT, in October of 1981. During his first trip there, Art was keenly aware of satanic activity. The practices of shamans produced weird and sensational results, and ancestor visitation and fleshly manifestations of other inexplicable phenomena were common. But, as David Shed, the PBI graduate who became the missionary in that Dogrib area in 1994, declared, "The fruit of the Holy Spirit is also unexplainable and undeniable. No medicine man or false prophet ever imparted the supernatural love of God that causes a person to love his enemy." Just eight years after Mr. Shed and his family moved to Fort Rae, and fewer than twenty years since Art Norris' first visit, such activity of the Holy Spirit was recognizable in the lives of those who trusted Christ.

In the words of Mr. Shed, "The first thing noticed by all Dogrib converts has been the peace of God within them . . . the joy of the Lord. Smiling, one of the new believers entered her grandmother's home. 'You're drunk,' her grandmother accused. 'No, Grandmother,' the lady replied with lilting voice, 'I have just been visiting my Christian family.' [These] have endured the persecution of their friends and families and continue to walk with the Lord because they have found real life."

Since the early 1980s, new homes with oil heat and electricity have been built in Fort Rae, and trucks regularly deliver water to homes. Human waste is now disposed of in large underground tanks, then pumped out and hauled to a lagoon outside the village. Better schools have been developed, and Fort Rae now boasts a gymnasium and a large indoor skating rink. More noteworthy than any of the physical changes is the fact that, thanks to Wycliffe Bible Translators, the Dogribs now have several New Testament books and the *Jesus* video in their own language. The complete New Testament will soon be published.

Persecution and hardship of those committed to the Lord have driven them deeper into His love and love for fellow Christians. Sunday meals are often shared together. Christmas gradually became a time when believers enjoyed fellowship among themselves; however, at Christmastime of 2001 many of them found strength to return to their own families. They desired to take God's love to the very ones who, in many cases, were responsible for deep-rooted and painful memories. David and Glenda Shed "stood by and kept the coffee hot for those who returned to share their experiences or just get a hug."

Often thirty to forty people and sometimes as many as fifty crowd into the missionaries' 16- by 16-foot shed on Sunday afternoons for worship. The need for a church building for the Tli Cho (Dogrib) Christian Fellowship became great, a fact not unknown to God. He moved His people in a church on the Hobemma Reserve in Alberta to provide assistance. When

Mr. Shed read the letter from that church to the Fort Rae believers, tears flooded their eyes.

God has provided funds and land, and the fellowship has built its own house of worship. This blessing for the Dogrib believers has been accompanied by much persecution. Even so, there are signs of spiritual growth. The believers help each other and witness to those outside of Christ. Several of their group have attended or are attending Bible school. Although Satan still has his way in many Dogrib lives, hope and excitement characterize those who have been redeemed.

Jim and Mildred Taylor

And what of the outreach which the Norrises and Jim and Mildred Taylor began in the native communities of Northern Alberta in the early 1990s? There, too, the Holy Spirit has been active, and God has answered much prayer. In 1999 God directed Michael and Man Sandstrom of Northern Canada Evangelical Mission to that area. Settling in Fort Vermilion at the edge of several reserves, the Sandstroms serve the Little Red River Cree Nation and the Dene Tha reserves. The former is the largest reserve in the area, consisting of the communities of Jean D'or, Garden River, and Fox Lake; the latter includes the Slavey hamlets of Assumption, Meander River, and Bushe River.

Michael and Man Sandstrom and family with Art and Emalou

Many First Nations people have come to know Christ in Little Red. As many as sixty new believers plus children meet weekly for Bible study. "On September 22 [2001] the first ever Sunday service was held in a little plywood shed with tarp roofing," wrote Mr. Sandstrom. Expectant worshipers filled the building. They were not disappointed, for the Holy

Spirit initiated a time of forgiveness and reconciliation among them. These believers are reaching out to their own families and friends, as well as to Dene Tha people. They also are facing opposition and know that their faith might jeopardize their jobs and support systems. One native seeker has lost his job and has had his house vandalized.

A change in heart is occurring among the Slaveys of the Dene Tha reserves as well, although not yet to the extent observed in Little Red. The Ancient One is at work there, and the Sandstroms anticipate that more natives in those villages will turn to Him soon. In Assumption and Meander River more youth than adults have trusted Christ, due largely to the influence of summer ministries in recent years. It is encouraging to the Sandstroms to see increasing numbers of other ethnic groups reaching out to the First Nations people. Since 1999 many short-term workers from Chinese churches have become involved.

Such summer ministries in Northern Alberta have brought widespread blessing. The chief of one reserve offered the use of the local government building for Christian outreach. Tribal leaders on another reserve arranged the best housing available for a volunteer mission team and helped to bring youth to a daily vacation Bible school. Mr. Sandstrom asserts, "The doors to the reserves and the hearts of the people are wide open to the Good News of Jesus Christ." Eagle's Nest Bible Camp has contributed to that openness. From the small group of twenty campers at its first abbreviated session in 1994, it now accommodates as many as 550 campers in one summer. Youth from a number of reserves are learning who Jesus is and that He can make their lives victorious. While participating in a youth outreach with the Sandstroms in the Rockies, one young camper sensed God's calling to attend Bible school but lacked funds for tuition. Applying to Key Way Tin Bible Institute, that camper was accepted, and within a month the tuition fee was provided.

One other major concern of the Norrises and Taylors was that God would make Christian radio broadcasting available for natives of Northern Alberta 24 hours a day. Mr. Sandstrom shared that vision–obviously a God-inspired one–and labored to see it fulfilled. With the support of Industry Canada and Canadian Radio-Television and Telecommunication Commission (CRTC) and approval from CRTC, the project moved ahead. A radio station was built in Fort Vermilion, and God is providing needed personnel. On January 28, 2003, CIAM (Read See I AM) Radio went on the air with its first test broadcasting. The vision has become reality, and CIAM Radio, the first Christian community radio station in Canada, is now bringing Good News to Northern Alberta's people!

Such strides forward are not without sacrifice. As more native people have come to Christ, spiritual warfare has intensified. One battle involved Mr. Sandstrom's health. For a period of three weeks he experienced chest pain, breathing difficulties, and dizziness. The doctors were puzzled, unable to establish a diagnosis. Gradually the condition worsened. One Saturday as Mr. Sandstrom drove Gabriel and Lovisa, his children, to swimming lessons in High Level, he suddenly realized that he could not see clearly. "My head was spinning and I couldn't breathe," he wrote later. "I asked Gabriel and Lovisa to pray for me, and they did, fervently. The last thing I remember was calling out 'Jesus, help me!' Then everything went black. When I woke up, I was stumbling out of the truck into the hospital in High Level with Gabriel and Lovisa holding my hands. I could not remember anything from the moment of my blackout to my arrival at the hospital. Gabriel and Lovisa told me we had driven at a very high speed to and through the town, passing vehicles and not stopping for any stop signs. They told me I was constantly calling in a loud voice, 'Jesus, help me!'"

Miraculously, God had taken the three of them safely to the hospital, but again the doctors could find nothing wrong. The electrocardiogram and oxygen levels were normal even though Mr. Sandstrom was still breathing with difficulty. He felt as though he were being strangled, and his head continued to spin. The doctors referred him to another hospital which had specialized diagnostic equipment, but tests and examination revealed nothing. Two days after his bizarre experience, he began to breathe normally and lose the feeling of being strangled, although some dizziness remained for a time. He later learned that the medicine man had put a curse on him and on another leader, who had experienced similar symptoms.

The power of Christ and persistent, fervent prayer brought deliverance from satanic influence. Continued persistent, fervent prayer is essential for protection, provision, and boldness of missionaries and native believers alike as they grow in Christ and proclaim Him to First Nations people still in spiritual darkness.

As Isaiah wrote and Art and Emalou echoed, the hand of the Ancient One is not short. The Norrises themselves were transformed by His power and allowed Him to use them. He continues to transform lives from the Navajo Reservation to the Far North of Canada–and beyond. To Him be the glory; great things He has done!

Art and Emalou Norris (left) and Charles and Iris Girton (right)
with author

"Sing to the LORD a new song, for he has
done marvelous things; his right hand and
his holy arm have worked salvation for him.
The LORD has made his salvation known
and revealed his righteousness to the nations."
– Psalm 98:1-2

Appendix A
Navajo Gospel Crusade's Southern Work

(The Norrises desired that Charles and Iris Girton's work be included in their biography, since the Girtons played a vital role in the development of Navajo Gospel Crusade. The week I spent listening to these two dedicated couples and laughing and praying with them was pure joy. However, it became clear that including the Girtons' ministry in the Norris biography resulted in confusion to the reader. Thus, a brief overview of the Girtons' contribution to the outreach of Navajo Gospel Crusade follows.)

When Navajo Indian Gospel Crusade's (NIGC) leadership fell to Charles Girton and Art Norris in 1949, the Girtons took up residence at Pine Haven, about fifteen miles south of Gallup, New Mexico. While the Norrises were expanding the Bible training ministry and opening new outstations in the

Charles and Iris Girton

northern part of the Navajo Reservation, the Girtons pursued ministries in the southern part, including two ministries they inherited from George Moore, NIGC's founder.

Mr. Moore had been involved in an English radio broadcast with David Clark of Navajo Bible School and Mission in Window Rock, Arizona. Charles assumed that responsibility. Sometime later John D. Jess, board member of Navajo Gospel Crusade after the name change and speaker of the "Chapel of the Air" radio ministry, offered to pay for a Navajo broadcast. Thus began the fifteen-minute-a-day, five-days-a-week Navajo

Gospel Hour with native speakers such as Lorenzo Iashie, Kenneth Foster, Geronimo Martin, and Edward Thompson. Initially aired over KGAK in Gallup and offering a correspondence course, that broadcast gradually expanded to Aztec, New Mexico; Blanding, Utah; and Flagstaff, Arizona.

The second ministry to which Charles and Iris fell heir was the education of children. Mr. Moore had informed them, "I told the Navajos I'd start an elementary school in the Pine Haven area if they'd give me the abandoned chapter house. You need to follow through on that." With no teacher and no room for an elementary school, the Girtons began by boarding several Navajo children throughout the week in the early 1950s. Each school-day morning at 6:30 when the cowbell gonged, the children scurried to dress, clean their rooms for inspection, and gather at the long pine table for devotions and breakfast before catching the county's school bus to Gallup.

While the children were at school, Iris and Charles entertained Navajo visitors, visited hospital patients at Zuni, taught released-time classes in a government school, studied, and answered mail. Large segments of time were consumed in hauling water, cutting firewood, and going to Gallup for mail and supplies. Occasionally Charles served as deputy sheriff, though he initially refused the position. After school the boys carried in coal and wood and the girls set the table. With supper over and the house tidied, the children played until evening Bible reading and prayers. On weekends they were transported to their homes. Many of them professed Christ as Savior during those years. One even taught his parents his Bible memory verses; another interpreted Sunday messages.

Summer Bible camps were another fruitful ministry at Pine Haven. A number of campers became new believers in Christ; many grew spiritually.

Believing that reaching children was the most effective way to help the Navajos, Girtons longed for a mission school. Through his radio ministry, John D. Jess successfully raised sufficient funds for a forty-bed dormitory, and with the arrival of Wanita Sheagley in 1954, a mission school at Pine Haven became a reality.

Twenty pre-first through sixth graders kept Wanita busy that year. She was often forced to neglect the older students in order to help the beginners who did not understand or speak English. She did the best she could, even utilizing her portable sewing machine to add home economics to the curriculum. For ten years the boarding school ministry continued, providing many opportunities to teach by word and example.

In Bread Springs and Fort Wingate, New Mexico, weekday and Sunday classes at government boarding schools provided opportunities to touch the lives of as many as 250 other children during the school year. For a while during the summers, the Pine Haven staff drove to different locations in the surrounding area to get children for vacation Bible schools. "It would be more efficient to have vacation Bible schools nearer the children's homes instead of carting them here to Pine Haven," Charles declared one day. In 1966, assisted by students from Navajo Bible Institute in Cortez and volunteers from several states, the staff held vacation Bible schools in five different neighborhoods one day a week for five weeks.

The workers rejoiced in these opportunities to share the Good News, but they were less eager to share their blood with the swarms of black gnats which constantly plagued them at these locations. They tried to counteract the persistent pests by burning dried horse manure, but the "cure" was worse than the affliction!

The Girtons and Norrises prayed much about ways of reaching more Navajos for Christ. Charles and Art shared harmoniously in the leadership responsibilities of the mission. Distance and heavy workloads prevented them and their staffs from frequent or lengthy times together, but both the southern and northern staff members benefited greatly from mutual monthly prayer times.

Slowly a church began to emerge at Pine Haven. When the Girtons resigned in the early 1980s to care for Iris' aged parents, their son-in-law, Jim Christensen, and daughter, Estelle, assumed leadership. Nearly twenty years after the Girtons' departure, the church, which had come under United Indian Missions, sought and was granted independence. The Navajo leadership, like the Girtons, then turned their prayerful attention to the youth as the church's hope for the future.

Appendix B
Navajo Gospel Crusade Team Members

The Norrises were full of gratitude for the faithful servants who partnered with them in Navajo Gospel Crusade (NGC) over the years. Each gave valuable assistance. There were those who built, plumbed, painted, repaired roofs, cooked, canned, cleaned, taught, worked in the office, supervised student work assignments, oversaw the farm and garden work, and served in administrative positions. Some served briefly, some for years. For some, service among the Navajos was a prelude to service in South America, the Philippines, and Laos. Each one gave much and endured much. Listed below are many who served with the Norrises. For inadvertant omissions due to inadequate memories and records, I apologize. My only comfort is that the name of each is recorded in God's book.

NGC'S CORTEZ-BASED STAFF

Askey, Mary
Ball, Lillian
Bartholomew, Mr. and Mrs. Robert
Benally, Marie
Beverly, Eleanor
Brown, Martha
Charley, Mr. and Mrs. John
Chatlos, Esther, Lydia, Marie, and Ruth
Cook, Mr. and Mrs. Jim
Dehiya, Mr. and Mrs. Jones
Dennison, Mr. and Mrs. Tom
Felgate, Mr. and Mrs. Ed
Fleegal, Mr. and Mrs. Philip
Fletcher, George
Foote, Rosemary

Haak, Mr. and Mrs. Arnold
Hecker, Dorothy
Hellyer, Mr. and Mrs. Richard
Irving, Mr. and Mrs. Bill
Johannes, Mr. and Mrs. Everett
Kohoe, Kee
Lundquist, Ann
McAdams, Thurley
McIntosh, Pat
Mehesy, Mr. and Mrs. Joe
Natachez, Mr. and Mrs. James
Pearson, Mr. and Mrs. John
Sterns, Margaret
Stillhammer, Mr. and Mrs. Von
Stonehocker, Mr. and Mrs. Ray
Tohtsoni, Clara
Whistler, Dave

NGC'S PINE HAVEN-BASED STAFF

Burns, Mr. and Mrs. Howard
Chapman, Mabel
Christensen, Mr. and Mrs. Jim
Girton, Mr. and Mrs. Charles
Hecker, Dorothy
Iashie, Lorenzo
Johnson, Bernice
Johannes, Mr. and Mrs. Everett
Kirby, Molly
Paquette, Mr. and Mrs. Jerry
Peterson, Mr. and Mrs. Maurice
Sheagley, Wanita

LONG-TERM VOLUNTEERS

Calvin, Ross
Davis, Mr. and Mrs. Les
Emmet, George
Klassen, Mr. and Mrs. Pete
Ostergaard, Bill

BOARD MEMBERS

Balsley, Dave
Bartholomew, Robert
Benally, Ernest
Benson, Bob
Bergstrom, Carl
Coffey, Eldon
Coffman, Chris
Erickson, Erwin
Gabbel, Ed
Gardner, Gaylord
Hagg, Oscar
Harwood, Clarence
Harwood, Stan
Hayworth, Dave
Jess, John D.
Johannes, Everett
John, David
Keenan, Donald
Lamb, Fred
Lucer, Marco
Macaluso, Marshall
Matske, Dick
McAdams, Webb
Murphy, Pat
Natachez, James
Norris, Cyril
Posey, Jim
Sloan, Jerry
Thompson, Sam
Whitner, Andy

NOTES

Chapter 1
1. Hogans are traditional Navajo homes. Originally, they were small, rounded huts made of poles covered with mud. In more recent decades these structures, usually six- to eight-sided, have been made of rough-hewn logs plastered with mud and covered with a dirt or wooden roof. They face east because traditional Navajos believe that the rising sun brings blessing.
2. Animism is a worldview characterized by a belief in spirit activity of ancestors, animate beings, and inanimate objects.
3. A kiva is a ceremonial structure, usually round and partly underground.

Chapter 2
1. Www.white-star-line.ch/who.htm; www.home.gil.com.au/~dalgarry/sisters.html; www.powerscourt.com/liners/whitestar.htm.

Chapter 3
1. "Ebenezer" means "a stone of help," referring to the memorial stone which Samuel, the last of Israel's judges, placed as a reminder of the Lord's help in Israel's struggle against the Philistines.
2. L. E. Maxwell, *Quips and Quotes* (Three Hills, Alberta: Action International Ministries, 1992), 2.
3. L. E. Maxwell, *Crowded to Christ* (Grand Rapids, MI: Wm. B. Eerdmans Publishing Co.), 89, 136, 140, 147.

Chapter 4
1. Http://naid.sppar.ucla.edu/ny64fair/map-docs/sermonsscience.htm.

Chapter 7
1. A Navajo term meaning "Grandfathers of the Yé'ii," or "fearful one."
2. A quotation referring to I Corinthians 1:27-28.

Chapter 8
1. Alma B. Clark, *A Tribute to God's Faithfulness* (Window Rock, Arizona: Western Indian Ministries, 1993), 72.
2. *Developing Native Christian Leadership Among the Navajo Indians* (Window Rock, Arizona: Navajo Bible School and Mission, 1938)

Chapter 9

1. *Developing Native Christian Leadership Among the Navajo Indians* (Window Rock, Arizona: Navajo Bible School and Mission, 1938).

2. R. G. LeTourneau was a millionaire inventor and contractor in the earth-moving business who gave generously to the work of Christ and founded LeTourneau College in Texas.

Chapter 10

1. The Navajos refer to themselves as Diné, meaning "The People." They usually refer to non-Navajos by some other name–e.g. Béésh bich'ahnii, which means "Germans," literally "metal helmeted ones," or, generically, bíla'ashdla'ii, "five-fingered ones."

2. Http://emayzine.com/lectures/native20th.htm.

Chapter 12

1. Attributed to Dorothy A. Thrupp, "Savior, Like a Shepherd Lead Us."

Chapter 16

1. Joseph Hart, "How Good Is the God We Adore."

Chapter 18

1. Tom Dolaghan and David Scates, *The Navajos Are Coming to Jesus* (Pasadena: Wm. Carey Library, 1978), 3.

2. Tom Dolaghan and David Scates, *The Navajos Are Coming to Jesus* (Pasadena: Wm. Carey Library, 1978), 18, 21-23, 40-42, 44.

Chapter 19

1. Whereas the Navajos use Diné, the Dogribs call themselves Dene, which also means "The People."

Chapter 20

1. Douglas Todd, "Communion: A New Generation in Church," *The Vancouver Sun*, July 27, 1992.

Chapter 23

1. "When We See Christ," Esther Kerr Rusthoi, © 1941 Singspiration Music (ASCAP) (admin. by Brentwood-Benson Music Publishing, Inc.). All rights reserved. Used by permission.